The Emoji Revolution

Where have emoji come from? Why are they so popular? What do they tell us about the technology-enhanced state of modern society? Far from simply being an amusing set of colourful little symbols, emoji are in the front line of a revolution in the way we communicate. As a form of global, image-based communication, they're a perfect example of the ingenuity and creativity at the heart of human interaction. But they're also a parable for the way that consumerism now permeates all parts of our daily existence, taking a controlling interest even in the language we use, and for how technology is becoming ever more entangled in our everyday lives. So how will this split identity affect the way that online communication develops? Are emoji ushering in a bold new era of empathy and emotional engagement on the internet? Or are they a first sign that we're handing over the future of human interaction to the machines?

Philip Seargeant is the author of several books on topics ranging from language and social media to linguistic creativity to English around the world. His most recent work focuses on language, communication, and politics and the influence and impact on these of new technologies.

The Emoji Revolution

How Technology is Shaping the Future of
Communication

PHILIP SEARGEANT

CAMBRIDGE
UNIVERSITY PRESS

CAMBRIDGE
UNIVERSITY PRESS

University Printing House, Cambridge CB2 8BS, United Kingdom

One Liberty Plaza, 20th Floor, New York, NY 10006, USA

477 Williamstown Road, Port Melbourne, VIC 3207, Australia

314–321, 3rd Floor, Plot 3, Splendor Forum, Jasola District Centre,
New Delhi – 110025, India

79 Anson Road, #06–04/06, Singapore 079906

Cambridge University Press is part of the University of Cambridge.

It furthers the University's mission by disseminating knowledge in the pursuit of
education, learning, and research at the highest international levels of excellence.

www.cambridge.org
Information on this title: www.cambridge.org/9781108496643
DOI: 10.1017/9781108677387

First published 2019

Printed in the United Kingdom by TJ International Ltd. Padstow Cornwall

A catalogue record for this publication is available from the British Library.

Library of Congress Cataloging-in-Publication Data
Names: Seargeant, Philip, author.
Title: The emoji revolution : how technology is shaping the future of communication /
Philip Seargeant, Open University.
Description: Cambridge, United Kingdom ; New York, NY : Cambridge University
Press, 2019. | Includes bibliographical references and index.
Identifiers: LCCN 2019008399 | ISBN 9781108496643 (hardback : alk. paper)
Subjects: LCSH: Emojis. | Communication – Technological innovations. | Symbolism
in communication. | Interpersonal communication.
Classification: LCC P99.63 .S43 2019 | DDC 004.601/48–dc23
LC record available at https://lccn.loc.gov/2019008399

ISBN 978-1-108-49664-3 Hardback
ISBN 978-1-108-72179-0 Paperback

For
Luisa 🦔, Tiago 🎃 and Florence 🚜

Contents

Figures

Acknowledgements

Many thanks to Dan Berlinka, Korina Giaxoglou, Caroline Tagg, Bob Tsukada Bright, Frank Monaghan, Chris Corney, Tereza Spilioti, Jane Solomon, Gedeon Maheux, Jennifer 8. Lee, Barbara Mayor, Meta Klinar, Wipapan Ngampramuan, Selina Packard, Jon Pokroy and Kristina Hultgren. Earlier versions of a number of short sections from the book have been previously published in the following places: 'The dystopian smile behind *The Emoji Movie*', *The Huffington Post*, 1 August 2017; 'What can emoji teach us about human civilization?', *OpenLearn*, 17 July 2017; 'The whimsical world of emoji swearing', *Strong Language*, 14 March 2017; 'Five properties of creativity, and how they can help with the writing process', *Writers & Artists*, 9 March 2017; 'Can emojis play a part in debates about our national identity?', *The New European*, 3–9 March 2017, p. 41; 'How emoji are changing the shape of everyday English', *OpenLearn*, 8 March 2017.

Emojis used under a creative commons license, © Twitter. Full details:

Copyright 2019 Twitter, Inc and other contributors

Code licensed under the MIT License: http://opensource.org/licenses/MIT

Graphics licensed under CC-BY 4.0: https://creativecommons.org/licenses/by/4.0/

1 The What, the Why and the Where of Emoji

Thirty-Six Years into the Future 😄 *Tears of Joy* 😄 *What's in a Name?* 😄 *The Language of Language* 😄 *The Alien in the Machine* 😄 *Skeuomorphic Stickers* 😄 *Picture-writing and Idea-writing*

Thirty-Six Years into the Future

If you were writing a work of science fiction, how would you make the aliens speak? Would they use words and gestures, in much the same way we do? Or would you opt instead for some sort of inter-subjective telepathy? And how about the language of our distant descendants? Is human communication in this imaginary future going to resemble what we use today? Or will it have degenerated? Be changed beyond all recognition?

Then there's the technology. What part will this play in the way people of the future communicate? Will we be able to recognise the devices that dominate their lives? Be able to trace an evolutionary arc linking modern-day technology with what they'll be using then?

One of the most evocative ways a writer can bring an imaginary world into being is by describing its language. This can give substance to the speculative world you're creating – can add a veneer of verisimilitude. But on top of this, a language can be a vital part of character and plot. Language is such an essential element of our identity that we gain huge amounts of information about someone's background from how they speak. It can stand as a metaphor for an imaginary people's culture, for their personality. It can be an expression of the worldview to which they adhere. How does their language reflect the structure of their

1

society? Does it have hierarchies embedded in its grammar? Indexes of the caste system and the power relations that dominate their culture? Does the government use it to control the actions of its people?

If you were writing a work of science fiction back in the early 1980s, and setting it thirty-six years in the future (the same number of years that George Orwell was playing with when he wrote *Nineteen Eighty-four*), how would you have imagined the language of the end of the 2010s? Mobile phones and the internet were still almost two decades away from becoming mainstream back then. An English-speaking United States was already the dominant superpower but was rivalled in posturing, if not influence, by the USSR. In popular culture, the end of the 2010s was the imaginary world of Ridley Scott's *Blade Runner*; of Stephen King's *The Running Man*; of Katsuhiro Otomo's *Akira*. It was a vision of android–human conflict, of state-sponsored violence masquerading as reality TV, of the spectre of dystopia.

So how would you have imagined the language of the second decade of the third millennium? Would you have seen it as something which looked as if it were regressing back to the very earliest forms of human writing? But that at the same time could be communicated only via devices that were linked to a global computerised network which operated as the intellectual matrix for all of modern civilisation?

Would the language you foresaw be one designed not for the expression of rational thought but for sentiment? Invented to compensate for the growing emotional distance that characterised the way people were now relating to each other?

Would you have given this language a backstory that began with the hyper-cute handwriting of Japanese schoolgirls but ended with a highly regulated system that was policed by a small, unelected cohort of the world's biggest transnational corporations? Would you have written in the idea that this language specifically encoded Western liberal values through its design? But that at the same time it could be weaponised by white supremacists and used by radical Islamic terrorists as part of their recruitment drives?[1]

Would your language have been a perfect symbol of consumerist society, with an identity closely linked to the marketing strategies of those half-dozen corporations who also regulated it? Who'd also be able to track your mood, attitude and political beliefs via the messages you sent to family and friends? Would you then have imagined all this packaged in a set of smiling yellow faces, flamenco-dancing women and clinking champagne glasses?

Because if you had, you'd have inadvertently stumbled across the way that a seemingly innocuous form of online communication would become – at least for a fleeting historical moment – one of the defining features of life in the early part of the twenty-first century. And was something that would offer a compelling portrait of the many puzzles and paradoxes that characterise contemporary society. You'd have dreamt into being, in other words, the world of emoji.

Tears of Joy

By the time you read this book it will be out of date. Language always changes, of course. This is one of the few constants about it. But it's arguably changing at a faster rate now than at any previous moment in its history. And emoji – the set of picture characters that people use to punctuate their online correspondence – are at the vanguard of this frenzy for change.

Emoji are, in many ways, the perfect illustration of the adaptability of human communication. On one level they may seem little more than cute images used to decorate text messages. But on another, they're a cultural phenomenon which highlights the inventiveness at the core of communication and provides an early indication of the way that technology is revolutionising the way we relate to one another.

As a form of global communication, emoji only began their spread in 2011. Four years later it was estimated they were being used by over 90 per cent of the online population.[2] In excess of six billion were being sent every day.[3] Their prevalence in the culture was such that Oxford Dictionaries famously chose one as their 'word' of the year for 2015.

'Words of the Year' are those judged by organisations such as the major dictionaries to be reflective of the 'ethos, mood, or preoccupations of that particular year'.[4] As other recent winners illustrate, they tend to have a faddish quality about them. They're very much of their time. And often, once that time has passed, they fade from public consciousness almost as quickly as they arose. It's questionable, for example, whether 'omnishambles' or 'refudiate' will still mean much to most people in a few years' time. The first of these was chosen by Oxford Dictionaries in 2012 and refers to a situation of hopeless confusion and chaos. It derives from the BBC political satire *The Thick of It* and gained brief notoriety when Ed Miliband used it in a speech to parliament when he was leader of the Labour Party. But as politics and television move on, so do popular expressions. Already the word feels more of historical interest than a vital part of contemporary vocabulary.

Much the same applies to 'refudiate'. This was the winner in 2010, after Sarah Palin, former Republican candidate for US vice-president, used it in a tweet. Campaigning against the so-called Ground Zero Mosque (an Islamic community centre that was planned for lower Manhattan, two blocks up from the World Trade Center site), she urged 'Peaceful Muslims' to 'pls refudiate' the idea.[5] As is the way with social media, she was swiftly ridiculed for managing to mangle 'refute' and 'repudiate', thus accidentally creating a concoction all of her own.[6] Although, as she was quick to point out, 'English is a living language. Shakespeare liked to coin new words too.'[7] And for a few months, the word seemed to encapsulate perfectly the muddled antagonism of modern politics.

There's a good chance, then, that 2015's winner, the 'face with tears of joy' 😂, will seem equally dated in a few years. But the reasons *why* it will feel dated – and the implications this has for how we communicate – offer a fascinating insight into the way that society is evolving. These reasons are also, paradoxically, an intrinsic part of why emoji are revolutionising language and communication. The little yellow circle with dots for eyes acts as a surprisingly good prism through which to view the history of human communication. And to predict the trajectory of its future.

*

There are two main reasons why language changes. One is in line with society and the way that language mirrors the changes in how we relate to each other and organise our culture. As an expression of identity, it's adapted by different groups and different generations to reflect their own sense of self. It's also constantly assimilating the new concepts and phenomena that are evolving within society.

Words are being created for these reasons all the time. The *Oxford English Dictionary*, for example, is currently updated four times a year, with hundreds of new entries each time.[8] The last few years have seen additions such as *clicktivism* (activism via social media), *genericide* (the loss of a trademark's legal rights when it becomes the everyday term for a type of product), *non-apology* (a phrase which has the form of an apology but doesn't actually express any sense of regret) and *Brexit* (which probably doesn't need defining). All of these reflect aspects of modern life which didn't exist a few years ago or didn't have the same prevalence in the culture as they do now.

Yet despite being one of the world's largest dictionaries, the *Oxford English Dictionary* only scratches at the surface of the vast number of words that are coined and discarded each year by the hundreds of millions of English speakers around the globe. On this score at least, Sarah Palin was absolutely right. English is very much a living language. There's no refudiating that. And what's interesting about emoji in this regard is that they've added a whole new repertoire to this ever-expanding storehouse of symbols. At this point in our history, the gaps in our vocabulary are being filled not simply by new words but by a completely new system of expression.

The second major reason that language changes is down to technology – specifically, the ways in which the technologies we use have an effect on the process of communication itself. Both hardware and software influence what we're able to do, along with how and when we're able to do it. Because of this, new technologies result in us subtly changing the way we interact with each other and also altering the shape of the language we use. Take the invention of texting, for example. When this was launched in the 1990s, people were suddenly able to send written messages to anyone from anywhere. But because of the specific limitations of the technology at the time, coupled with the cost, these messages had to be very succinct. This led to the development of a whole new (albeit ephemeral) convention of spelling: txtspk.

Emoji are following closely in the footsteps of txtspk. They've evolved as a solution to the needs of mobile communication and have been made possible by advances in technology. In particular, they compensate for the way that computer-mediated messaging can sometimes tend towards the emotionally blunt. Whereas face-to-face, or even voice-to-voice, conversations can express emotional closeness though facial expression or tone of voice, this is easily lost when messages are rendered in a few short words on a small screen. Emoji are a means of restoring this emotional framing to an interaction – punctuating your missive with a smile.

But the symbiotic relationship emoji have with technology is also the main reason this book will start to look out of date by this time next year. Unlike almost any other type of language system, emoji have something akin to a built-in obsolescence. They're designed to be updated on a regular basis, in the same way the technology they're used with is. Just as smartphones and their operating systems have a frequent refresh rate, emoji also get routine enhancements. The look of the emoji you have on your phone now will undergo subtle redesigns over the course of time, and extra characters will be added. Because of this, their usefulness is artificially limited. It becomes functionally constrained, not to mention unfashionable, whenever new designs are released.

In the context of communication systems, this is something that's never previously been the case. In the past, people might have bought a new landline when they were tired of the design of their old phone or if they wanted to get one with whatever latest innovation was going around – an inbuilt answering machine, say. But they didn't have to upgrade the language they were using as well. Even when the fad for txtpsk was at its height, you didn't *have* to embrace it. Indeed, some people took great satisfaction in meticulously spelling out each complete word and properly punctuating each well-crafted sentence.

Emoji, on the other hand, are a case study in how technology and the human capacity for communication are working fully in tandem today – of how the onward march of technology exists at the intersection of consumerism, innovation and design. Moreover, the fact that they're at the front line of a relentless wave of technologically driven change in communications practices encourages – if not necessitates – a great amount of creativity and flexibility in the way they're used. With each new innovation, people need to evolve new practices of communication. Almost as soon as you've got used to one set of resources, another is pushed your way. It's for this reason, perhaps, that emoji are such a touchstone for creative expression.

Finally, there's the way they've become implicated in almost all aspects of modern society, from politics and pornography to marketing and mourning. Emoji are the subject of musicals and Hollywood films. They're the inspiration for fashion design, art and architecture. They're a staple in advertising and commerce. There are Frida Kahlo emoji,[9] Coca-Cola emoji and Catholic Church emoji (the latter including two popes as well as the patron saints of lost causes and the January blues).[10] Understanding why they've become so popular, and how they work, can not only explain something about the nature of language, therefore: it can also act as a prism for examining our relationship with technology, society and ourselves.

Emoji will undoubtedly continue to change their form, to expand in range and scope. At some stage they'll most likely be replaced by something completely different. But even if they're out of date by the time you read this, the issues they embody won't be. The communication revolution they're spearheading is set to continue, as technology becomes ever more choreographed with our everyday lives. So from one perspective, emoji are a simplified form of global communication which provide the perfect example of the ingenuity and creativity at the heart of human interaction. But they're also a parable for the way consumerism now permeates all parts of our daily existence. Exploring the ways in which they've been embraced by the world can thus explain everything from controversies over same-sex marriage and selfie culture to populism and post-truth politics.

Most of all, however, they illustrate the way that, despite humans having possessed language now for over a hundred thousand years, we're still striving to find a perfect way to communicate with each other. And in this sense, the story of emoji is anything but trivial. Yet before we get to the role they play in attempting to find a solution to this conundrum, it's worth first covering a few fundamentals, beginning with their name.

What's in a Name?

The Catholic Church has, over the years, assembled an eclectic list of patron saints. There's the Flemish Saint Drogo, for example, patron saint of those whom others find repulsive.[11] There's Saint Polycarp of Smyrna, whose patronages include earache and dysentery.[12] There's Bibiana, patron saint of insanity and hangovers. And not to forget Saint Fiacre, patron of gardeners, taxi drivers and those suffering from sexually transmitted diseases.

Given this roll call, the idea that there should be a patron saint of the internet isn't that remarkable. This office is held, at least in an unofficial capacity, by Isidore of Seville, the seventh-century scholar and author of the *Etymologiae*. Although not particularly well remembered today, the *Etymologiae* was a hugely influential book in its time, one whose popularity lasted for close on a thousand years. In essence it was an encyclopaedia, piecing together knowledge from a range of classical texts which covered everything from furniture-design to grammar and theology. As the title indicates, the approach was based around the belief that the etymology of a word (its origins and evolution) was an indication of its true meaning. Unfortunately for Isidore, a good half of his etymologies are highly fanciful, if not downright wrong. He asserts, for example, that the walking stick – 'baculus' in Latin – is thus named because it was invented by Bacchus, god of the grape harvest, in order 'that people affected by wine might be supported by it'.[13] A nice idea, but complete fantasy.

In classical and medieval times, folk etymologies of this sort – i.e. those which are based on coincidental similarities between different words – were often used as a means of finding some sort of divine order in the natural world. There was rarely any actual science to them. Instead they were acts of interpretative creativity that were used to illuminate the hidden symbolic meanings of concepts and the way language and the world fitted together into an intricate web of meaning.

All of which brings us, in a rather round about way, to the word 'emoji'. There's an assumption – a not-unreasonable one – that it's related in some way to the word 'emotion'. After all, one of the primary functions of emoji is to provide a message with emotive content. Add to this the fact that they're close cousins of 'emoticons' – a word which is a portmanteau of 'emotion' and 'icon' – and it seems perfectly natural to assume they derive from the same root.

In fact, the word is an import from Japanese and is composed of the kanji for 'picture' (e- 絵) and 'character' (-moji 文字). It's a loanword, where the form, rather than the meaning, has been imported into English. But it could just as easily have happened the other way round (what is known as calcquing) – we could have taken the meaning of the Japanese term and translated the constituent parts into English, resulting in us calling them 'picture-characters'.

This origin also explains why the plural of emoji is – or at least can be – emoji. Japanese doesn't mark a difference between single and plural nouns, so the same form of the word stands for both. Given that the word has been adopted into English, however, it also gets used with traditional English grammar, so some people do pluralise it by adding an -s.[14] At some stage one version may well win out over the other, and conventional practice will turn into a rule of style. But for the moment it's still a free choice.

To return briefly to Isidore of Seville: while he may have been woefully mistaken in many of his etymologies, he's not by any means the only one guilty of this sort of thing. In some cases, the way people see false parallels between words can actually shape the way language evolves. Take, for example, the words 'male' and 'female'. These derive from completely different roots, but the fact that their meanings mirror each other has led to their forms doing so as well. 'Male' comes from the Old French 'masle', which in turn comes from the classical Latin 'masculus'. 'Female', on the other hand, is originally from the Latin 'femella', which is a diminutive of 'femina'. It wasn't until the fourteenth century that the spelling of 'femella' was altered in mistaken imitation of 'male'.[15]

We can see something a little similar happening with 'emoji' as it's adopted into English. Although its origins have nothing to do with 'emotion', the way in which it's pronounced – at least with a general British or American accent – clearly shows the influence of the English word. The first two syllables of the words 'emoji', 'emotion' and 'emoticon' are all identical in English, whereas the Japanese would be more akin to the e- of 'etiquette' followed by the -mo of 'mosque'. In other words, the coincidence between similarities of form and meaning have transferred across to the way we pronounce it.

In many ways it's highly appropriate that this has happened, because both etymologies – the real and the imagined – encapsulate something fundamental about the identity of emoji. Research suggests that over 70 per cent of the emoji that people send are emotion-based (happy/sad faces, hearts and so on[16]) and that people tend to use them because they believe emoji can express feelings better than words alone can.[17] And of course, the way this emotional content is expressed is via the use of images. It's this, in fact, which marks emoji out from other modern writing systems – while at the same time being a throwback to the origins of the very first type of language technology.

The Language of Language

Another detail worth trying to pin down is what relationship emoji have to 'language'. Or, to put it another way, can emoji be said to be a language in their own right?

One of the qualities that makes human language such a powerful means of communication is its flexibility. The same word can be used to describe a specific entity in the world ('the apple I ate this morning'); a general category of things ('I'm particularly fond of apples'); or an abstract concept or emotion ('she's the apple of his eye'). But this flexibility can prove very frustrating in certain situations. In the early days of modern science, for example, the double-meanings and ambiguity that are inherent in English became increasingly infuriating for those who were trying to find a clear and accurate way to describe the workings of the natural world.

Take the word 'language' itself for instance. If we want to answer the question of whether emoji are a language, the initial, rather irritating response is that it all depends on what we mean by 'language'. Emoji are not, in and of themselves, the equivalent of a full natural language like English. Not by a long stretch. But then we use the word 'language' for other forms of communication which don't share the same properties as full, natural languages. We talk of 'body language', for example, or the 'language of music', or even the 'language of DNA'. In these cases, it could be argued that the word is being used metaphorically – that it simply indicates some general means of communication, which is similar to, but not the same as, actual language.

Yet even if we specify that we're using the word in a literal or technical sense, we still run into problems. From a technical point of view, the scientific study of language is linguistics. But different traditions of linguistics have different definitions of what language is. In fact, trying to define precisely what the word 'language' means is one of the main purposes of linguistics. Is it an innate instinct in humans, which has an underlying universal grammar? Or is it a set of social practices with which we're constantly improvising whenever we communicate with each other? Different schools within the same discipline have different views on this – and it's these differences which morph into the disputes and rivalries which drive scientific progress.

Then there's the fact that human communication is constantly changing. Take, for example, the plan that Mark Zuckerberg and his colleagues at Facebook have for us all to be typing with our brains in the near future. In early 2017 the company announced the development of a project which intends to decode 'neural activity devoted to speech', thus turning the 'words that you have already decided to send to the speech center of your brain' into text.[18] You'll no longer need to use a keyboard for writing messages. You'll simply be able to think the words, which will then be converted into text on a machine. If this comes to pass, it's going to fundamentally change much of our understanding of what qualifies as language. At its core, language will still be language. But the concepts of what counts as writing, what counts as speech, our understanding of the mechanics of what's involved in linguistic communication – all of these will have to shift or expand as we get used to new ways of conversing with each other.

So where does this leave the question of whether or not emoji are a language? There are two different approaches that can be taken to answering this. The first is to say that if, by language, we mean something equivalent to a full, symbolic communication system such as English, then no, emoji very definitely do not fall within this category. It would be better, instead, to refer to them in more convoluted terms, describing them, perhaps, as a 'visual-based communications system with emergent properties'. This isn't the most elegant way to proceed though.

The alternative is to take a more laissez-faire approach to the use of the word – in looking at how emoji work, to look also at how they relate to the rest of the process and paraphernalia that we use to communicate. How they combine with, substitute for, or extend the other linguistic resources we use. How they have certain similarities, but also distinct differences, with other writing systems. How the social and technological issues that influence our use of emoji are part of broader patterns in the way that language and communication are evolving. In other words, an examination of emoji can, in fact, help us understand what 'language' in the wider sense means today. Or, to put it another way, emoji, in and of themselves, are a noteworthy phenomenon; but it's in what they can show us about communication more generally, and how this is evolving, that the real interest lies.

The Alien in the Machine

So what exactly are emoji? In a fascinating article about millennial mating rituals, Nancy Jo Sales interviews a marketing executive from Brooklyn who explains how he's picked up women online without resorting to the use of words at all. 'I've gotten numbers on Tinder just by sending emojis', he tells her, holding up his phone to show how he'd managed this with a combination of beer and pizza characters.[19] Elsewhere in today's society, businesses are being urged to ensure they have an emoji strategy in place to make their 'brand or company more human . . . enhance your message . . . [and] make conversations with your customers, clients or followers better'.[20] Then there are charities, such as BRIS in Sweden, who used a specially designed set of emoji as a way of encouraging victims of child abuse to open up about their experience when other channels of communication weren't working.[21]

But while emoji have seeped into every aspect of our social lives, from the serious to the frivolous, for some they're still seen as a step backwards for civilisation. Writing in the *Guardian* newspaper a couple of years ago, the art critic Jonathan Jones argued that emoji are a sign of a devastating U-turn in cultural evolution. 'We're heading back to ancient Egyptian times', he lamented, 'next stop the stone age, with a big yellow smiley grin on our faces'.[22]

So what is it? Are we regressing to a form of communication which was rendered obsolete 1,600 years ago? Or are emoji really something that can simultaneously enhance your sex life, boost your business and fight social injustice? And how was it that this eclectic set of little pictures – which includes everything from a levitating businessman to a blowfish – came to be such cultural touchstones for our era?

To answer this question we can focus either on the technology or the semiotics. Semiotics, in this context, simply means the study of how we use signs to convey meaning. It covers everything from how complex sentences work to how we give directions by pointing a finger. In the case of emoji, it's not merely humans communicating with other humans, however. It's computers communicating with other computers. And for this reason, a brief overview of some of the technological basics makes for a good starting point.

A few months ago a friend received an email from a colleague which, when she opened it, read something like this: *Frst nryj o jp [r s;;d er;; eoyj upi.* The colleague who sent this can touch-type. He also, on occasions, has a rather abstract relationship with real life. In this instance he'd typed out what he wanted to say and pressed send without ever once looking at what was coming up on the screen. Unfortunately, he'd positioned his hands on the wrong place on the keyboard, so everything he typed was one letter off.

There was a time, only a couple of decades ago, when text sent from a computer in one country to one in another would have ended up looking much the same as this. While the information would have been nicely coherent when rendered on the original computer, once it had traversed the globe and was converted back into text by the receiving computer it would become unreadable. The Japanese have a term for this: *mojibake* (文字化け), or garbled characters that result from text being encoded and decoded using incompatible systems.

Around the turn of the millennium, as the practice of everyday global communication became ever more ubiquitous, the world-wide computing industry decided on a standard system of encoding which would prevent this sort of thing from happening. Unicode, as it's known, can today handle texts written in the vast majority of the world's writing systems. It supports over 110,000 characters, from 130 different scripts, covering almost anything you could wish to write in any language. And, crucially, it allows computers the world over to accurately decode and display this vast array of characters. The Unicode Consortium, which oversees the system, explains its aim as being to 'enable everybody, speaking every language on the Earth, to be able to use their language on computers and smartphones'.[23] The only scripts that aren't supported at the moment are historical and liturgical ones, plus a few invented or fictional ones (so no Klingon, for example).

Emoji, when they first started out, suffered from the same compatibility issues as international scripts in the 1990s. They were originally created by the Japanese telephone company NTT DoCoMo, as part of i-mode, the world's first widespread mobile internet platform. Their popularity was such that soon other mobile carriers in Japan began creating their own versions. But each company used a different encoding standard, so the characters would only display properly if you were writing to someone on the same network. If your boyfriend was signed up with a different phone company you couldn't send him a row of hearts at bedtime – all he'd receive would be garbled, incoherent nonsense.

It wasn't until the end of 2010 that emoji were incorporated into Unicode, following a lobbying campaign from companies like Google and Apple, who were keen to incorporate them into their own software. The following year Apple included emoji in its operating system for the iPhone. And it was this that kick-started their unstoppable global spread.[24]

The initial set of emoji, created by Shigetaka Kurita for DoCoMo, consisted of just 176 characters. When Unicode began standardising them there were 722. There are now well over two thousand, with sixty or so new ones being added each year. And although there are strict guidelines about the sorts of thing that can and can't be added, the current crop is nothing if not eclectic, ranging across everything from a unicorn to a set of painted nails to a cat seemingly imitating Edvard Munch's 'The Scream'.

The yearly additions don't simply expand the range of subjects covered, however. As well as adding new categories such as zombies, dinosaurs and fortune cookies, they also evolve in terms of the image of modern society that's on offer. This can be seen most clearly in the way gender and racial diversity has been incrementally addressed with each update. In 2012 Apple first included same-sex couples; in 2014 they added more black characters; in 2015 this was expanded to give the option of different skin tones for different characters; in 2016 they began showing more gender diversity among the professions and occupations; and in 2017 they offered gender-non-specific people for the first time. All of these features are now written into the official Unicode templates.

Standardisation via Unicode is only part of the process, however. The encoding consists of a number (U+1F602, for example, for the 'face with tears of joy') plus a basic picture symbol (in black-and-white), which indicates what the character should look like. This is a bit like a Platonic ideal for each character. But for emoji to actually be rendered onto phones or computers, the software that the device is using also needs to support them. They're universal, in other words, as long as you have the correct and up-to-date equipment to support them. If not, you're in much the same situation as when all the networks had different encoding standards. In 2015, for example, after one of Apple's periodic software updates, iPhone users were bewildered to suddenly find

the symbol of an alien in a box showing up all over their messages
👾.[25] It turned out that this was inserted as a substitute for any
character that their phone's software didn't support. It simply
meant that part of the message they'd been sent remained stuck in
interplanetary limbo.

The other aspect of the system that's not standardised is the
actual look of the characters as they appear on your phone. Again,
it's the operating system that your phone uses that designs this,
drawing on the template given by Unicode. The individual platforms choose the colour and look of the emoji, usually working to a
particular house style. This is why emoji have a slightly (or occasionally very) different look depending on which platform you're
using.[26] The ghost, for example, may be smiling and sticking his
tongue out on an iPhone but grimacing on Android, while the
aliens and robots come in all shapes, colours and sizes, from purple
space invaders to Area 51–style skulls.[27] As we'll see, this issue –
sometimes referred to as emoji fragmentation[28] – can have notable
implications for how they work as a form of communication.

What's been described so far are those characters encoded in the
Unicode standard which can be exchanged between pretty much
any messaging app on any modern device, providing the necessary
software is in place. When talking of emoji as a new writing system,
or even a new language, these are what people are generally referring
to: the Unicode standard emoji. The fact that everyone has access to
them means that conventions can develop in how they're used and
interpreted. They become a shared means of expression, a code onto
which we can impress our cultural values in the same way we do
with other forms of language. But there's more to the world of emoji
than just the Unicode standard. There's an entire other species out
there which also needs to be taken into consideration.

Skeuomorphic Stickers

The Catholic Church emoji, along with rival Pope emoji,[29] aren't
strictly orthodox. The same goes for the sets of vagina emoji, or

the Hieroglyphics emoji (Hieroglyphics the Californian hip-hop collective, that is, not the Egyptian writing system).[30] Or those based around Hatsune Miku, the Japanese holographic pop idol.[31]

While emoji depicting all these subjects exist, none of them are supported by Unicode. Instead they're either created by companies which offer them as separate apps for you to buy and download or produced independently by the different messaging services. And rather than being limited to a few hundred characters in total, there are thousands of sets of these, themed around specific subjects. If, when writing to a friend, you'd like to register your impatience in the form of a picture of Snoopy tapping his foot, you can. If you feel your current state of mind is better conveyed by a symbol of Donald Trump hiding behind a wall, or by Hatsune Miku (the Japanese holographic idol) sulking on the floor, those options are also available to you.[32]

Although these are sometimes still referred to as emoji – especially when it comes to their branding (Popemojis,[33] Emojews,[34] Berniemojis,[35] etc.) – they're more properly known as 'stickers'. The name is a nod towards the fact that they're less a writing system and more a means of online decoration. They're akin to the sort of picture slogan you'd stick on your exercise book at school or paste across your guitar case.

Taking the name of something that already exists and transferring it over to a brand-new technology is a common way of coining new terms. It's a type of linguistic skeuomorphism. This is the design approach where features that were intrinsic in the original structure of a product are maintained in the new version despite no longer serving any actual purpose: brass rivets on jeans, for example, or digital cameras which still make the sound of a shutter click. Although there's no practical need for these features any more, they offer a sense of familiarity to the user and so help with the transition from old to new.

Words can provide a similar bridge between technologies. The vehicles we drive around in haven't (for the most part) been powered by actual horses in over a hundred years. Similarly we're still CC-ing colleagues into emails (either purposefully, accidentally or passive-aggressively), although the concept of a actual carbon copy is something that a lot of people today will never have experienced or even recognise. So calling these little images 'stickers' (or, as the Japanese do, 'stamps' スタンプ) ties them to a tradition of real-world technology and the practices that go along with this. They're something ephemeral that can be exchanged. And, crucially, they can be commercialised. The production of stickers, despite their seemingly slight and frivolous nature, is huge business. Well over a billion are sent every day.[36] And although some are given away free, for the most part they're either sold at a dollar or so per pack or used as a form of brand promotion.[37] Such is the market for them that a company like the Japanese messaging app Line can generate over $270 million a year in revenue this way.[38]

There's a fundamental difference, then, between stickers and the standardised, Unicode-supported emoji. In effect, stickers are little image files which get cut and pasted into your messages. When you send a Unicode emoji from one platform to another, it's encoded as part of the actual text of the message, whereas with the sticker you're sending the image itself. The fact that they're created by third-party applications and aren't regulated by a standard also allows them to be much more diverse and to be created and circulated very quickly. This means they're often more event-oriented than standard emoji, while also being able to represent real people, organisations and companies – all subjects which are prohibited for Unicode emoji.

But the fact they're not standardised also means they don't build up conventions of use. They're more likely to be sent as single, self-contained snatches of communication rather than being integrated into a verbal sentence or strung together to form a more complex thought. And to understand the implications of this difference (the standard versus the custom-made), we need to turn from the technology to the semiotics and see how emoji work from a basic communicative point of view.

Picture-writing and Idea-writing

When the alien in a box character started appearing in people's messages, it caused confusion because its meaning wasn't intuitive. There was nothing to link the image with what it was supposed to represent. Maybe, once you knew it meant that something was wrong with the encoding you could interpret it as representing a malevolent presence in the machine and see it as a slightly oblique visual metaphor. But this requires quite a leap of imagination. In the case of most emoji, however, their meaning is precisely what they look like. The standard alien face, for example (this fellow 👽), is just an alien face.

Although of course it's not quite as simple as this. Emoji may be a lot more intuitive than alphabetic writing systems, which you have almost no chance of interpreting if you can't read them. But they're still semiotically fairly complicated. And their meaning often isn't *that* transparent. Yes, 👽 can mean 'alien'. But there are other contexts where it can mean Vladimir Putin (as we'll see in Chapter 6). While a character like 💮 will be comprehensible to someone with a knowledge of Japanese culture but confusing to pretty much anyone else. To understand why all of this is the case, we need to take a brief detour via the seventeenth-century Bishop of Rochester.

In the 1630s this office was held by one Thomas Sprat. In addition to his career as a churchman (which culminated in the bishopric of Rochester) and at one stage being falsely implicated in a bizarre plot to restore the deposed King James II to the British throne, Sprat was one of the founders of the Royal Society. In fact, he wrote a history of it.

Among the many preoccupations of the Royal Society in those early days was the reformation of language. As was alluded to already, for the purposes of science there was constant frustration that natural languages – Latin, English, etc. – were full of ambiguities and idiosyncrasies and were therefore a very shoddy tool for the clear and accurate representation of the world. In the introduction to his history, Sprat wrote that one of the Society's key aims was to 'return back to primitive purity, and shortness, when men deliver'd so many things, almost in an equal number of words'.[39] The idea was that language was to be reshaped so that it would operate as a systematic and straightforward mirror of nature. It would be transformed into a reliable catalogue of the world as it actually is, so that there would be no vagueness and confusion in the way people interpreted each other. And this was to be achieved by the design of artificially created 'philosophical languages', such as that devised by the secretary of the Royal Society, John Wilkins.

The philosophical language that Wilkins created never really took off, unfortunately, and this episode in intellectual history wouldn't be much remembered beyond specialist circles if it weren't for the fact that it was satirised by Jonathan Swift in *Gulliver's Travels*. In Book 3 of the novel, Gulliver runs across the ingenious linguistics professors of the Academy of Lagado, who've decided to abolish words altogether. Since 'Words are only Names for *Things*',[40] they reason, communication would be much more accurate and direct if everyone carried about them the set of things they needed to talk about. When you met someone you wished to speak to, you'd simply remove the relevant objects from the sack on your back and show them to your interlocutor. The only downside to this scheme was that the professors were forever sinking under the weight of the collection of objects they had to haul around with them everywhere.

Emoji aren't quite a modern-day version of the Lagado sack of objects, simply shrunk to the size of a smartphone and carried around in your pocket. But there's an aspect of words-standing-for-things in the way they work. From a semiotic point of view, emoji are picture characters which represent objects, actions and ideas. In other words, they're a mixture of pictograms and ideograms.

Pictograms are symbols which represent an object, an activity or a place by means of an illustration of that thing. An alien face

represents an alien. A picture of a sailboat represents a sailboat.
It's as simple as that. Ideograms, on the other hand, are pictures
which represent ideas. When Shigetaka Kurita was devising the
first set of emoji he was inspired by the popularity of the two
image characters that were available on pagers (this was in the
days immediately before the mobile phone). If you had a pager
you could send an image of either a phone or a heart to anyone
else with a pager. The phone meant 'call me back', while the heart
was a sign of affection. In both cases these are ideas rather than
concrete things, so the symbols are ideograms rather than
pictograms.

Most of the standardised Unicode emoji fall into one of these
two categories. The 'camera' and the 'hot beverage', for example,
are pictograms which represent exactly what they show. The 'face
with tears of joy', on the other hand, expresses an emotion – you
send it when you want to convey the idea of being uncontrollably
happy. Likewise with the group image of two women and a girl 👩‍👩‍👧.
The significance in this grouping is that they represent a family
with same-sex parents – a cultural idea which is indicated by, but
not explicitly represented in, the picture.

Some emoji have both types of signs combined in the one
character. The 'No Mobile Phones' sign 📵, for instance, has an
illustration of a smartphone (a pictogram) as well as a red circle
with diagonal bar representing the idea of 'forbidden' (an ideo-
gram). We conventionally understand a red circle with a diagonal
bar as meaning 'forbidden', but it doesn't represent anything in
nature which embodies that meaning.

It's often the case, in fact, that most pictograms have meanings
which can extend beyond the specific to the general and so also
work as ideograms. 📷 can stand simply for a camera, but it can
also convey the activity of photography. ☕ can stand for a
straight-up cup of coffee but also for the idea of taking a break
from work.

Ideograms and pictograms are still in use throughout society –
they can be seen in public toilets, road signs, train stations and so
on. Mostly they crop up in places where there are likely to be

visitors from various different linguistic backgrounds, and so some form of simple, universal code is needed. Significantly they also provide the very early foundations for the writing systems of almost all the languages around the world. But over the years, each and every one of these has evolved into something rather different.

Take, for example, character-based writing systems like Chinese or Japanese kanji. Despite their pictographic roots still being clearly apparent, these are now what's known as logographic systems. Logograms are written characters which represent words rather than meanings: that's to say, they're specific to a particular language, and each character has a pronunciation directly associated with it. So 女 represents *onna* in Japanese, which in turn means 'woman' in English; whereas 👩 represents a woman, whichever language it's used in. In alphabetic systems, such as the one used for English, the characters again represent sounds rather than concepts. But in this case they need to be combined together before they produce words. W-O-M-A-N is five separate characters, each with its individual pronunciation, and only in combination do they create the sound which then creates the word.

While English uses a predominantly alphabetic writing system, it does include some logograms, such as the symbols @ and &. Conversely, although emoji are mostly a mix of either pictograms or ideograms, the standard set also includes a few which have elements from both logographic and alphabetic systems. In certain cases this is simply for decorative purposes. For example, the white flower symbol 💮 (*hanamaru* はなまる), which is used as a stamp by Japanese teachers to reward good work, has, on the iPhone version at least, a phrase in Japanese written inside it. 大変 よくできました (*taihen yoku dekimashita*), it says, which translates as 'Very well done'. This isn't strictly necessary for the meaning of the emoji – and versions on different operating systems omit the phrase. But it adds a bit of verisimilitude to the detail of the image.

There are other emoji, however, where characters from a verbal language are a central element of the meaning. Several signs have a single kanji or Chinese character on them, indicating some sort of guidance about behaviour. 禁, meaning 'prohibited' or 'restricted' in Japanese, is one such, where the meaning of the overall symbol is a combination of the kanji and the red background – red being a conventional signal for a warning.

A few characters also have English words in them – the arrows with 'top', 'back' and 'up' written next to them, for example. There's even one which has an example of Japanese-English. This is the NG sign – NG being an acronym for the English words 'no good', used for anything that doesn't quite work.

Then there are the non-verbal sign systems which also make up a key element of the emoji lexicon. In many ways all the smiley ideograms could be seen as representations of a sort of non-verbal communication – and this is something we'll look at in more detail later. But facial expressions aren't culturally created systems of meaning in the way that, say, the thumbs-up sign is. Alongside facial expression, emoji include a large range of very specific cultural gestures, from various different contexts. There's the 'person bowing deeply', for example 🙇. Known as *dogeza* (土下座) in Japanese, this is a traditional element of Japanese etiquette, which involves bowing low enough for the head to touch the floor as a sign of sincere apology.

Given the origins of emoji, Japanese culture is well represented in the range of gestures available: there's also the 'OK gesture', the 'No Good gesture', and the 'Information desk person' gesture 🙆🙅💁. But the universal ambitions of emoji are such that even non-terrestrial communication is represented, in the form of the Vulcan Salute from *Star Trek* 🖖. (As a side note, the inclusion of this means that while Klingon may not be supported in Unicode, Vulcan, inadvertently, is.)

Then there's the ILY sign which was introduced in 2017 🤟. This originated with hearing-impaired children using American Sign Language to create a composite symbol from the letters I, L and Y, standing for 'I Love You', but has since moved into the mainstream. It's also the gesture used by Spider-Man when firing his webs.

As we can see, then, emoji are far more than a simple set of pictures-representing-objects. To understand the full range of even the standard Unicode ones, you need to have some familiarity with the cultural conventions of various aspects of contemporary society, along with an eclectic range of knowledge from Eastern and Western written and gestural languages, sign languages and even fictional communication systems. But for all this, their essence is still in communication via pictures. And in this respect they hark back to the very beginnings of human writing.

2 Emoji and the History of Human Communication

The Prehistory of Emoji ❤ *The Aleph* ❤ *Enabling Technologies* ❤
Yes, That's the Joke ❤ *Point d'amour* ❤ *Ecks-dee*

The Prehistory of Emoji

Language hasn't always been wedded tightly to technology, but, since the moment it first was, the relationship between the two has been of huge significance for the evolution of our species. Today, a vast proportion of all the language we encounter is mediated by some form of human-designed communication tool. From the lyrics on the radio and the words on the back of the cereal packet through the road signs on the way to work, the texts we type up on the computer and the dramas we watch on TV at night – a huge amount of our interaction, our information and our entertainment is facilitated in one way or another by technology.

Language is one of the most powerful and important tools that humans possess. Without language there would be no civilisation. Language allows us both to refer to the world around us and to express abstract concepts such as friendship, envy and faith. It lets us articulate complex ideas and construct the social systems by which we organise our communities. And, of course, it operates as a means of establishing and maintaining interpersonal relationships with each other. Its status is such that for many people it's a marker of what it means to be human. It's what sets us apart from all other animals. In the words of the philosopher René Descartes, 'there is no other animal however perfect and fortunately situated it may be that can … put words together in a manner to convey their thoughts'.[1] *Homo sapiens*, the rational animal, is also *Homo loquens*, the speaking animal.

Language evolved in *Homo sapiens* around one hundred thousand years ago (give or take thirty or forty thousand years either side – it's difficult to be too precise when one gets that far back in history). And between that time and the end of the fourth century BC, it had one specific but significant limitation: it could only be used for communication between people who were physically in the same space. If you wanted to pass information from one place to another, you had to move across to that place yourself (or send a messenger). A speech could only be heard by those who were able to congregate within earshot of it. And for information to be passed from generation to generation, it had to be committed to memory and recited down through the years. Transmission and repetition of messages relied entirely on the cognitive abilities of the human mind.

Around five-and-a-half thousand years ago, in the Sumerian region of Mesopotamia (present-day Iraq), this began to change. Pictures and symbols had been used from time to time prior to this as a way of expressing messages. But they'd never operated as a systematic means of recording events and ideas. In need of a way to keep track of their goods, the Sumerians began engraving symbols on fired clay tablets. At much the same time, in Egypt, a similar scheme of symbols, scratched onto bone, was also being used for the same purpose: to record the nature and number of people's commodities. By the end of the fourth millennium BC, this innovation – which began life as a simple accountancy tool – had developed into flexible and complex systems for recording the Sumerian and Egyptian languages. Writing had been born, and with it a whole new chapter in human civilisation.

The invention of writing changed both the way we use language and the benefits we get from it. It made it far easier to accumulate knowledge, to develop science and to record history. And it did this by extending the capabilities of language by giving it an external and permanent existence. Writing was, in other words, the first major communications technology. Messages which are written down (as opposed to simply being spoken) can be passed from person to person and from age to age with ease. They can be consulted and accurately copied. And the same message can be read by an almost unlimited number of people. Writing allows language to travel effortlessly through time and space. What was once an ephemeral utterance, which lightly brushed the airwaves and was then gone, could now be transported from place to place, from community to community and from generation to generation. All subsequent innovations in language technology, from printing to the internet to mobile phones, further extend this reach – and further loosen the impediments set on human communication by distance and time.

The centrality of technology can be seen in the names we use for both these original writing systems. Mesopotamian writing became known as 'cuneiform', from the Latin word 'cuneus' meaning 'wedge'. This was because the implements used to write it were made from reeds which were then imprinted into clay tablets, creating wedge-like shapes. Similarly, the word 'hieroglyphics' comes from the Greek 'hieros' meaning 'sacred' (the symbols were originally used predominantly for memorials to gods and royalty) and 'glyphein' meaning 'to carve'. Indeed, the English word 'write', along with those used in nearly all Indo-European languages, derives originally from a word meaning to 'carve', 'scratch' or 'cut' – underscoring the importance of the simple mechanical process behind our entire literate culture.

Writing as we know it today was not a single technology stemming from a single invention, however. It's a combination of various innovations which took place over a long period, with differing effects in different parts of the world. But the stages of evolution it went through are very similar in all these different places. The earliest incarnations of all these writing systems were pictographic. They consisted of simplified drawings acting as stylised representations of concrete entities: a house, a river, a drawing of the head of a cow to represent a cow. As their use spread, so they began to accrue broader meanings based on the context of this use and to be combined together to create ideograms. Bird + egg, for example, represented fertility. But the most significant stage in their development was when they began to be used to represent not simply ideas but also sounds. Once this happened, writing could emulate spoken language rather than operating as a separate, parallel system of communication. It was this transition which led to the fully flexible systems we have today.[2]

A key invention in the evolution of writing was the alphabet. This originated somewhere in the vicinity of Egypt or Palestine around 2000 BC and produced a writing system which was easy to learn, was quick to write and avoided the ambiguities of many earlier scripts. Speakers of English, for example, only need to know about 52 alphabetic signs (the lower- and upper-case letters) along with numerals, punctuation marks and a few logograms in order to be able to read and write the language. A reader of hieroglyphics had to have a working knowledge of about six hundred characters to understand complex texts. The way the alphabet provided such a compact and flexible system was by severing completely the relationship between the look of a sign and its meaning. In other words, the shapes of the letters we use today no longer physically resemble the concepts to which they're referring in any meaningful sense – even if traces of their pictographic origins still exist.

The Aleph

It's just about possible to trace the Vulcan salute all the way back to the earliest forms of writing. In his autobiography, Leonard Nimoy, who played the part of Spock in *Star Trek*, writes of how he based the gesture on a blessing used by Jewish priests. The blessing involves the hands imitating the Hebrew letter Shin ש, which in this context stands for El Shaddai, the Almighty. The letter ש in turn can be traced back through earlier writing systems, particularly Phoenician, all the way to the pictogram for 'tooth'. (Through a slightly different genealogy, this pictogram also evolved into the Greek letter Sigma Σ, which gave rise to the Latin S.)

This same type of trajectory is thought to be the case for nearly all the letters of the Roman alphabet (🐖🏠), which we now use to write English. We may not realise this when we use them – and the conceptual meaning of the modern-day symbols is entirely unrelated to the objects they once depicted – but there's an evolutionary chain which stretches back to the very origins of writing, and thus to pictorial representation, even today.

Our letter A, for example, comes from the Phoenician letter 'aleph', which has its roots in the Egyptian hieroglyph that depicted an ox's head. The rough outline of an ox's head can still be seen in the shape of a capital A, although it's been rotated through 180 degrees so the horns now point downwards. The character was originally used in the Phoenician language for the sound of a glottal stop (the swallowed 't' sound in 'gotta' as pronounced with an Estuary English accent, for example). It was rotated to the side at this stage (as Jorge Luis Borges writes, its shape 'that of a man pointing to the sky and the earth, to indicate that the lower world is the map and mirror of the higher'[3]). In the eighth century BC the Greeks developed their own alphabet based on the Phoenician's, and, as they didn't need a glottal stop, they used the aleph for the vowel 'a' instead, renaming it 'alpha' and turning it upright. The Romans then adopted the Greek alphabet via the Etruscans, keeping both the sound and shape, resulting in the letter we use today (see Figure 2.1).

Likewise the Greek 'beta' derives from the Phoenician letter 'beth', which comes, ultimately, from the hieroglyphic for 'house' – the shape of the capital B still vaguely resembles a two-storey building.[4] The Hebrew ב 'beth' also traces back to the same root, which is apparent in place names such as Bethlehem, 'house of bread'. For a few of the letters, early pictographic origins are even clearer. M, for

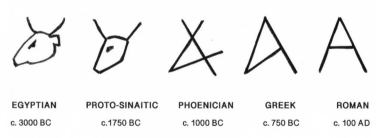

EGYPTIAN	PROTO-SINAITIC	PHOENICIAN	GREEK	ROMAN
c. 3000 BC	c.1750 BC	c. 1000 BC	c. 750 BC	c. 100 AD

Figure 2.1 Evolution of the letter A

example, with its wave-like shape, derives ultimately from the hieroglyphic for water; while the distant ancestor of the letter O was a hieroglyph of an eye.

In the earliest days of their existence, when they were being used to list tomb goods in the mausoleums of kings, hieroglyphics didn't represent sounds – they were straightforward pictograms and ideograms, the meanings of which weren't reliant on any specific spoken language. And for several centuries after they'd died out, when knowledge of how they'd once worked had been forgotten, the belief was that they'd remained fundamentally an ideographic system throughout their existence. All through the Renaissance and right up until the early nineteenth century, this was the popular view of them: a system of stylised pictures which stood for what they depicted. In actual fact, the majority of hieroglyphics represent sounds and can thus be used to spell out spoken language. But it wasn't until the deciphering of the Rosetta Stone that this was fully understood.

The Rosetta Stone was 'discovered' in 1799 by French soldiers close to the city of Rosetta (modern-day Rashid). From then it somehow ended up in the hands of the British and now resides in the British Museum. The importance it has for our understanding of the development of writing is due to the way it's inscribed, with three versions of the same royal decree, each written in a different script. Two of these are in Ancient Egyptian – one using hieroglyphics, the other what's known as Demotic (a writing system used originally for administrative and legal purposes) – while the third is in Ancient Greek.

The hieroglyphic portion was finally deciphered by the French Egyptologist Jean-François Champollion in 1822. His key insight was realising that the names of people in the text were written by means of what's known as the rebus principle. A rebus, in Dr Johnson's definition, is 'a word represented by a picture; a kind of riddle'. It's a way of spelling things out by using pictures of objects which are pronounced in a similar way to elements of a word. So, for instance, 👁🐝🍃 approximates to 'I believe' (eye-bee-leaf). Or, rather more impressionistically (and perhaps a little less intuitively), you could spell out 🌾🗻⚫🍃✕ (hi-row-GU [Guam]-leaf-x).

In looking at both the Rosetta Stone and similar inscriptions from the same period, Champollion worked out that, for example, the first character in what he'd identified as a person's name was a sun, which in a late form of Egyptian was pronounced 'ra'. Knowing that the last two symbols in the same cluster both represented 's' he was able to guess that the full word would thus be pronounced Ramesses, a name very common among the pharaohs.[5] (Were we to try spelling this out in an emoji rebus, it might look something like this 🌞🐝©©.) Applying the same principle to other names, it became clear that hieroglyphics did in fact have a strong phonetic element – they represented the sounds of a spoken language, and that language was Egyptian. This was the key to understanding not only how hieroglyphics worked but ultimately how all full writing systems work, because this same principle – using symbols to represent the sounds of the spoken language – is a fundamental component of every writing system around the world. It's what underpins alphabets and what underpins scripts such as Chinese and Japanese. Importantly, however, all these writing systems use both sounds-symbols *and* logograms. English s-p-e-l-l-s words out & uses symbols which represent whole words. The only thing that differs between the different writing systems is the relative proportion of phonetic signs to logograms.

As we've seen, however, emoji are neither predominantly phonetic nor logographic. And in this way they differ fundamentally from the complex writing systems of all the pre-existing languages in the world, including hieroglyphics – which prompts the question why, after five-and-a-half thousand years of evolution, are we seeing this resurrection of picture-based writing.

Enabling Technologies

Before we look at why emoji should differ so much from other writing systems, it's worth briefly running through the rest of the history of human communication to note how evolving technologies have continually influenced the way we interact with each other. There were countless other important inventions which complemented the conceptual technologies of writing. There was paper, for example, initially invented in China early in the second century BC, which travelled via the Arab world to reach Europe in the eleventh century, allowing books to become cheaper and more portable. Then there was the idea of inserting spaces between words. Early Greek and Latin inscriptions are in what's known as *scriptio continua* (continuous script), which means that the words all run together in one long block. Whichmadethetextverydifficulttoreadunlessyoualreadyknewthecontent. By introducing spaces, 'sight reading' became much simpler. (*Scriptio continua* is still used for some languages, such as Japanese. It's also a feature of web addressees, such as www .damnyouautocorrect.com, where use of the space character is not, as yet, permitted.) Then there's punctuation, which again gave structure to a written text and helped organise meaning in clearer and more comprehensible ways. All these various enhancements made the basic technology of writing more flexible, convenient and effective.

The next truly revolutionary innovation, though, was printing – and specifically the use of movable type. The invention of the printing press by Johannes Gutenberg in the 1430s allowed for the fast, cheap, mass production of texts. Gutenberg's first published book, the Bible, had a print run of 180 copies. For a scriptorium of monks hand-writing the text, it would have taken years to produce this same volume of output. The printing press thus pushed writing out into the general populace, leading to greater access to literacy.

Printing also had an effect on language itself. When people such as Gutenberg in Germany, and William Caxton in England, began to print books for distribution across the country, they had to make decisions about which dialect of their language to use and which spelling conventions to adopt. Prior to this there was huge linguistic variety from region to region, with different communities using different words for the same concept. (This is still the case, of course, but not to anywhere near the same degree.) Spellings would depend on how the word was pronounced, which also varied from district to district. The introduction of printing thus had a standardising effect on languages, which was further consolidated with the compilation of dictionaries and grammar books. Our ideas of what counts as 'correct' and 'incorrect' usage stem directly from this process.

Printing was followed by a variety of other inventions which further extended the reach of language. During the nineteenth century, two-way communication was revolutionised first by the telegraph, which allowed for text-based interaction over long distances, and then by the telephone, which made possible real-time conversations at a distance. Technologies for producing other forms of recorded media were also developed: photography in the 1830s, sound recording in the 1850s and the moving image in the 1890s. At the turn of the twentieth century it became possible to send sound and images through the air via electromagnetic waves, which led to the invention of radio in the 1890s and television in the 1920s.

With each extension of the reach of language came a change in the way people were able to relate to each other, which in turn produced changes in the way they organised themselves into communities. This is referred to as the 'co-evolution' of technology and society. As technology changes, society adapts by exploring and exploiting these changes. Politics, the law, science, religion, literature – all of these were dramatically affected by the inventions first of writing and then of printing. The written word mediates our relationship with the past, with the state and with society. For those who believe, it mediates the relationship with God. Writing therefore created the circumstances which structure the nature of these relationships. Print had the effect of democratising many of these relationships – of spreading access to the knowledge that regulates our social structures. These two inventions were thus fundamental in creating what we understand today as society.

Then, in the last quarter of the twentieth century, a shift began to take place from analogue to digital technology. Today, practically all electronic devices are digital: from cameras and televisions to computers and phones. The speed at which these changes have altered the communications landscape has been much faster than for any of the previous technological revolutions. In 1969 the internet came into existence with the founding of the ARPANET (Advanced Research Projects Agency Network), a computer network funded by the US Department of Defense. The 1970s saw the invention of the personal computer, which gained in popularity throughout the 1980s and had become practically ubiquitous (in developed countries) by the end of the 1990s. From the 1990s onwards, the process of change became even more rapid. It took twenty-one years between the printing of the first book in Europe (1455) and the establishment of the first printing press in England (1476). In our own era, the last two decades produced huge changes. Twenty years ago, mobile phones were still mostly the preserve of the rich, the World Wide Web was in its infancy, and Google had only just been founded. Until the middle of the first decade of the millennium, there was no Facebook, no Twitter, no Skype. Today these technologies are an integral part of the fabric of everyday life.

Emoji, as has been mentioned, are a form of communication which have developed directly from our relationship with digital technology. They're the product of the marriage between human communicative need and technological possibility. Yet they also, on the face it of it, resemble one of the very earliest forms of linguistic technology in their use of pictograms. So why, if all previous writing systems which began in this way have evolved into something else, are we now seeing a revival of this millennia-old approach to the expression of meaning?

The simple answer is that, rather than being a return to first principles, emoji can, in fact, be seen as the end point in the evolution of one particular aspect of writing. Although on the surface emoji share various properties and characteristics with other systems, they're actually adding something quite new to the resources we use to express ourselves. To understand what this is, we need to look at the system of marks and symbols used to organise how a written text is presented and understood. We need to look at the properties and functions of punctuation.

Yes, That's the Joke

In his essay 'The Analytical Language Of John Wilkins', the Argentine author Jorge Luis Borges writes of his subject that he had a range of different interests including 'theology, cryptography, music, the building of transparent beehives, the orbit of an invisible planet, the possibility of a trip to the moon [and] the possibility and principles of a universal language'.[6] He could have added the invention of flying chariots and submarines, as well as speculation that the moon – were we to be able to take that trip there – was already populated: 'tis probable there may be inhabitants in this other World,' Wilkins wrote, 'but of what kinde they are is uncertaine'.[7]

This is the same John Wilkins who was an associate of Thomas Sprat in the early days of the Royal Society. Amongst these eclectic interests, it's his universal language which was perhaps the most developed and which, as we've seen, was satirised by Jonathan Swift in *Gulliver's Travels*. In 'An Essay towards a Real Character, and a Philosophical Language', published in 1668, Wilkins set out his blueprint for this language, which was intended to improve on English by creating a more logical and exact system of communication. One of the many innovations he included was the idea of a specific punctuation mark to indicate irony.[8] The symbol he proposed for this was an inverted exclamation mark '¡'.

Wilkins was arguing for an 'irony marker' three hundred years before the internet was invented. His contention was that ironic intent can often be misunderstood in writing. And although this is true of any form of writing, it's something which has become more salient – and probably more frequent – since the advent of computer-mediated communication.

An emblematic example of the treacherous nature of online irony is the way that people on social media often feel the need to explain jokes back to those who first posted them. They take at face value what was meant to be humorous – and, in their desire to correct factual blunders wherever they find them, clarify the various ways in which the original poster's logic has inadvertently let them down. The Twitter account 'Yes, That's the Joke' has a string of good examples.[9]

> As if The Bible wasn't farfetched enough they've had Jesus being born on Christmas Day of all days. It's a stretch too far for me I'm afraid.
> *Jesus was the reason Christmas happened. Do your research.*

> Another embarrassing u-turn for climate 'scientists'. First they said May was the hottest month ever recorded. Now they're saying it's June.
> *You do realise that June comes after May, right? SO it could have gotten progressively hotter and thus broken the record?*

Comedy works on misdirection, of course. It works because you're anticipating one thing and are instead confronted with another. Yet mostly when we encounter a joke we're already primed to be expecting it. It doesn't come completely out of the blue. This priming can take a variety of different forms. It can be explicit: 'Here's a good joke … '. It can be the result of some general knowledge of, or experience about, the world: knowing that the person we're talking to always tends towards the flippant, for example. Or it can be related to the context: going to watch a comedy gig, for instance. In all these scenarios we've already been tipped off about the sort of reaction that's expected of us, so we're on the lookout for things not being quite what they seem.

This isn't always the case, however. There are contexts where this framing can be far less clear. And social media is one of these. As you're scrolling through your Twitter feed, the first post you read could be a political diatribe, the second someone mourning a national tragedy, the third an act of self-promotion and the fourth some off-the-cuff satirical comment. Social media can flatten out different types of stories. This means you're often confronted with wildly different 'genres' of message all lined up next to each other. And the only things indicating how they're meant to be interpreted are the words themselves.

While we can sneer at the idea that people misread irony, one of the basic dynamics underpinning all human communication is the fact that the default setting in conversation is for people to believe what you say. This is known, fairly straightforwardly, as the co-operative principle. It was proposed by the philosopher Paul Grice, who contended that there are a set of unconscious assumptions we all abide by whenever we take part in a conversation. These shared assumptions are what allow us to coordinate the conversation and productively communicate meaning to one another.[10] One of these expectations is that we believe that what our participant is saying is truthful. If this weren't our default setting, then the power of words would become so debilitated that conversation would be all but impossible. There could be no such things as promises, declarations or agreements: nothing to securely tie what someone is saying to the world around them.

Of course, it's not quite as simple as this. There's clearly not an unproblematic dividing line between being truthful and not truthful. There are infinite shades of meaning in between. There's understatement and overstatement, metaphor and analogy, vagueness and allusion. And irony. Irony exists as part of almost all human interaction, from flirting and teasing to bullying and criticising to comedy. And although irony is a form of saying what you don't mean, it doesn't necessarily involve being untruthful. When you know that something is meant as ironic, you interpret it accordingly, and this allows for co-operative conversation to continue. It's when the ironic intent is missed – when irony is taken for earnestness – that communication can stumble.

A good writer can often make it clear that irony is being used simply through the manipulation of the words he or she uses. But in contexts where the audience is varied, and at a distance, and where there are no priming mechanisms to help with the interpretation, any subtlety of tone can easily get lost – even for an experienced writer. As Wilkins's proposal for the ¡ shows, this has been an issue for at least 350 years. And it's something to which internet-based communication is particularly susceptible.

This susceptibility is highlighted by what's known as 'Poe's law': the adage that, unless you clearly indicate that you're being ironic, it's impossible to write a parody of an extremist view on the internet, however absurdly exaggerated, that someone won't take at face value. The maxim is named after Nathan Poe, who made a comment to this effect when discussing religious fundamentalism online.[11] You could write something that you thought was so patently over-the-top, so utterly preposterous, he said, and yet still someone, somewhere, would believe that you were being sincere.

A key reason for why this happens is the social element of social media. As the computer scientist Scott Fahlman explains, in a previous era if a hundred thousand copies of book were printed and 1 per cent of its readers misread the irony and so failed to get the joke, this wouldn't spoil the experience for the other 99 per cent. But if this 1 per cent somehow had the means to 'write a lengthy counterargument and to flood these into the same distribution channels as the original work', suddenly everyone's enjoyment becomes compromised.[12] Welcome to the interactive world of Web 2.0.

The democratisation of publishing that the internet makes possible has thus given rise to an epidemic of people publicly missing the point. And the only way to avoid this, Poe suggests, is to include some mark or symbol to show that you're being humorous. In other words, you need an irony marker, of the sort that John Wilkins was proposing back in 1668.

Point d'amour

It was a dispute over punctuation that, in a way, kicked off the Russian Revolution. In 1905, typesetters at a print-works in Moscow went on strike, demanding a higher rate of pay for each 1,000 letters they set and insisting that punctuation marks should be included in this calculation. This was the first upsurge of political and social unrest that was to spread across the Russian Empire, eventually turning into the 1905 revolution. As Leon Trotsky wrote in his treatise on the period, 'This small event set off nothing more nor less than the all-Russian political strike – the strike which started over punctuation marks and ended by felling absolutism'.[13]

The relationship between punctuation and politics in this instance was circumstantial rather than substantial. Yet punctuation is a topic which can and does provoke a great amount of agitation for reasons directly related to its status and purpose in society. There was, for example, a small but impassioned media outburst in the UK in April 2017 when it was claimed by some that the design for the new £5 note included what was described by certain newspapers as a 'major grammar blunder'.[14] The 'mistake' people were complaining about was the omission of quotation marks from the Winston Churchill quotation that was printed on the front of the note. Despite being positioned away from any other text, and thus clearly a quotation, the omission of the quote marks was evidence, apparently, that we're living in a 'post-punctuation world'. It was the type of incident that should have us all despairing at the way a once-proud institution like the Bank of England – one of the cornerstones of our society – is now happy to ignore the correct use of English with gleeful impunity.

It's the relationship between punctuation and grammar that leads some people to get so upset about it. Missing apostrophes, incorrectly positioned commas, semi-colons substituting for colons – all of these are, for those who get incensed by them, liable to subvert the meaning of an utterance and turn sense into nonsense. They're thus damning evidence of a decline in traditional standards of education (and, by extension, the first sign of decay in the social infrastructure of a nation).

Yet the origins of punctuation are nothing to do with grammar. Punctuation began as a means for helping with the interpretation of texts, particularly when they were being read aloud. It was a way of indicating when to pause between phrases so as to make a piece of writing as rhetorically persuasive as possible. Back in the third century BC, when the basics of our punctuation system were first invented, most texts were still written in *scriptura continua*. To help with the practice of public speaking, a scholar named Aristophanes of Byzantium introduced a system of dots to mark out different phrases in a speech. The position of the dot indicated the length of pause needed when reading it aloud. A short passage · known as a *komma* · was marked with a dot in the middle of the line. A slightly longer passage had the dot at the bottom of the line . and this was known as a *kolon*. And for long pauses – *periodos* or sentences – it was placed near the top ˙

Over time the names of these units of speech were transferred to the symbols themselves, which in turn gradually morphed into different shapes. But not only do we retain these basic terms (comma, colon and period); we also still use punctuation for similar means, helping us break up a paragraph in order to make it easier to parse. And while punctuation has also evolved as a key element of organising the meaning of a sentence – marking the relationships between phrases, indicating contractions between words, signalling shifts of speaker and so forth – its original purpose for helping to indicate the rhythm and tone of expression still co-exists alongside its grammatical function. A comma, for example, can be used to indicate a non-defining relative clause or when listing a set of concepts. But it can also be used to break up the rhythm of a sentence, to add cadence and shape to the way it flows.

Punctuation that's explicitly designed to help with expression, however, is rather limited. In effect there are only two symbols available for adding the same sort of meaning that intonation does in speech: the question mark and the exclamation mark. The question mark dates back to the eighth century BC, when, or so the story goes, the English scholar Alcuin of York became frustrated with the limitations of the rather rudimentary system of dots-on-different-levels and created the *punctus interrogativus* or interrogation point. He did this by adding a sign resembling a tilde (~) above a dot, creating something which was supposed to represent the rising tone of voice one uses when querying something. It wasn't until the seventeenth century AD, however, that the symbol took on the precise form it has today (the tilde bending down into a hook above the dot) and started to accrue the rules of use it now has.[15]

The uses of the quotation mark are fairly simple. It has one main purpose, and for the most part it carries this out with a straight-forward efficiency. The exclamation mark, on the other hand, is both more flexible and more ambiguous. And because of this, its uses can be far more contentious.

In an early short story called, simply, the 'The Exclamation Mark', the Russian writer Anton Chekhov narrates the adventures of a middle-aged civil servant, Perekladin, who realises, after forty years of writing out official documents, that he has no idea of how to use exclamation marks. He's perfectly confident in his use of all other types of punctuation. But when it comes to the exclamation mark he's at a loss. And the more he thinks about this, the more it turns into a bizarre existential quandary. His wife explains to him that you should use an exclamation mark whenever you wish to express exultation, indignation, joy or anger. But not once in his forty-year career, he realises, has he ever had to express a single one of these emotions. As he muses over this realisation, so he begins to see exclamation marks following him around wherever he goes, taunting him over whatever he does, until finally he gets so worked up that, when signing a card for his boss, he puts three successive exclamation marks after his name. And in that one moment he feels a wave of exultation, indignation, joy and burning rage flowing through him.

Fittingly, given its ambiguous nature, the origins of the exclamation mark are more obscure than those of the question mark. It's believed to have evolved in the Middle Ages, with one theory being that medieval copyists would conventionally write the Latin word 'io', meaning 'joy', at the end of sentences when they wanted to stress the meaning in some way. In writing this the 'i' was placed above the 'o', and over time this mutated into '!'.[16] Its uptake, though, was slow and patchy. Throughout its history it's had its fair share of detractors. Its critics may not have been pursued around the streets by an exclamation mark made flesh in the way that Perekladin was, but ambivalence to the symbol runs very deep. For F. Scott Fitzgerald, for example, to use one was like laughing at your own joke.[17]

But nowadays it seems that the exclamation mark has fully come into its own. It has become such a mainstay of online orthography that *not* using them in an email or other forms of online communication can often make it appear as if you're being purposefully curt. And the range of uses it has is extensive. There are Perekladin's exultation, indignation, joy and anger but also, as the linguist David Crystal notes, surprise, commands, expletives and emphatic agreement.[18]

> I cannot believe it! 😮
> What the @#$%&! 😡
> Don't you dare! 😠
> Absolutely! 👍

And, of course, it can be used to signal irony.

> Yeah, right! 😏

The problem, however, is that this promiscuousness of possible meanings prevents it from acting as an unequivocal marker of ironic event. In the age of the internet, the duties of the exclamation mark are being overstretched and its effectiveness is becoming blunted. There's still a gap in the market for a dedicated irony marker.

Keith Houston, in his book *Shady Characters*, writes of how appropriate John Wilkins's choice of the ¡ was for this purpose. The exclamation mark already changes the tone of a statement, and turning it upside-down to form 'an i-like character both hints at the implied irony and simultaneously suggests the inversion of its meaning'.[19] But for some reason, the idea never caught on. Neither have any of the other countless attempts to modify the existing set of punctuation in order to refine its expressive range.

A century before Wilkins upended the exclamation mark, Henry Denham, a sixteenth-century printer, was reversing the question mark (؟) and creating what he called a 'percontation point', which was to be used to mark rhetorical questions. Two hundred years after Wilkins, an advertising executive named Martin K. Speckter then tried combining the two existing expressive marks – overlaying a question mark with an exclamation mark – to create the 'interrobang'. The name for his new punctuation mark derives from the Latin *interrogation*, meaning 'question', and the printers' slang for an exclamation mark: 'bang'. Its purpose was to indicate questions which expressed a sense of excitement or disbelief: 'You did what‽'; 'You're how old‽' Again, though, the idea never really took root, despite a few models of typewriter being produced with a dedicated key for it.[20] One problem was perhaps that much the same effect can simply be achieved by printing one mark after another!?

Then there was the French novelist Hervé Bazin, who proposed *five* new punctuation marks, to cover a range of different situations. One of these was irony, for which he suggested the use of the Greek letter ψ with a dot underneath it. But there was also the 'doubt point', for when you wanted to add a note of scepticism to a sentence; the 'certitude point', for when you wanted to say something with utter conviction; the 'acclamation point', for when you wanted to demonstrate a sense of goodwill towards your addressee; and the 'authority point', to indicate your expertise or moral clout in making an assertion. And finally there was the 'love point' or 'point d'amour'. This was to be made of two question marks facing each other but sharing the same point, thus resembling the shape of a heart (see Figure 2.2).

Yet all these innovations now exist simply as anecdotes illustrating the way that the purposeful engineering of language so often has little, if any, effect on how things actually evolve. Instead of any of these, what ended up happening was that people began using existing punctuation marks to create something which harked back to the pictorial origins of the earliest writing :-)

Figure 2.2 Le point d'amour

Ecks-dee

The history of emoticons conventionally begins with the computer scientist Scott Fahlman who, in 1982, combined a colon, a hyphen and a round bracket as a way of indicating that a given statement was meant as a joke.[21] The idea came to him when he was chatting with colleagues on a bulletin board about the limits of online humour. They'd been quipping back and forth about an imaginary mercury spill in the elevators (as you do) and started to worry about what would happen if people misinterpreted their humour. Like Wilkins before him, Fahlman was concerned that ironic intent could easily be overlooked in writing. As a solution he proposed:[22]

> the following character sequence for joke markers:
> :-)
> Read it sideways. Actually, it is probably more economical to mark things that are NOT jokes, given current trends. For this, use
> :-(

The idea of playing with punctuation like this had, in fact, been suggested before. All the way back in 1881, *Puck* magazine included a short inset about 'typographical art', offering up four different combinations of basic symbols which could represent joy, melancholy, indifference and astonishment (see Figure 2.3). There's a difference though between this and what Fahlman instigated, because there's no evidence that people ever used the *Puck* faces to modify their writing. So while they may resemble emoticons in form, they don't in function.

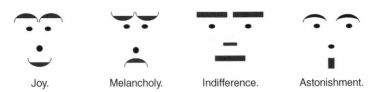

Joy.   Melancholy.   Indifference.   Astonishment.

Figure 2.3 *Puck* magazine's 'typographical art'

For some, the hunt for the first emoticon leads even further back, with candidates including a 1648 poem by Robert Herrick and an 1862 *New York Times* article reporting on a speech by Abraham Lincoln. In both cases, a round bracket was used in a context which could, seemingly, be interpreted as a smile. But again, neither of these appear to have been purposefully meant in the modern sense. It's more likely, in fact, that they were both just simple typesetting errors.

More obviously intentional was the suggestion from the satirist Ambrose Bierce, author of the *Devil's Dictionary*, who wrote an essay in 1887 on the reformation of language. Among his various proposals was the need for what he called a 'snigger point': a single bracket rotated horizontally so that it resembled a smile, which could be added 'to every jocular or ironical sentence'.[23] Then there was Vladimir Nabokov, who made a similar suggestion in an interview in 1969. 'I often think,' he said, that 'there should exist a special typographical sign for a smile – some sort of concave mark, a supine round bracket'.[24] Both of these prefigure the rough shape of the emoticon. And both were proposed to fulfil the same general purpose as the emoticon. The difference between them and Fahlman's suggestion, however, was that neither was ever actually picked up and used as a punctuation mark.

Once Fahlman had kicked off the modern incarnation of the idea, it spread both quickly and widely. It also diversified. From the original happy/sad dyad were born hundreds of different facial expressions. In his 1997 book *Smileys*, David Sanderson includes over 650 different designs, ranging across categories such as 'emotions, attitudes, persons and personalities, animals, hair styles [and] special interests'.[25] (As a side note, Sanderson's book is also notable for the way the cover image shows a selection of emoticons embossed onto yellow badges, thus pre-empting the aesthetic of the emoji.)

By the early 2000s, James Marshall was listing over two thousand designs in his online emoticon dictionary.[26] These covered a variety of basic facial emotions, similar to those now found in emoji, such as:

- The winking face, which uses a semicolon instead of a colon ;-)
- The surprised face, which uses an 'o' instead of a bracket :-o
- The combination XD, which is sometimes referred to with the phonetic transcription *ecks dee* and is used as the equivalent of the 'face with tears of joy' or as a graphic interpretation of the acronym LOL.[27]

They also included several which weren't intended for conventional communicative purposes but were instead simply creative ways of representing elements of popular culture:

Homer Simpson	(:o (|)
Abraham Lincoln	=):-)=
Frankenstein	[:-|I
Schrödinger's emoticon	(:(or):)

As with the Scott Fahlman originals, most Western emoticons involve tilting one's head to the left to view them properly. There are one or two which involve tilting in the opposite direction:

Heart	<3

And a few which don't involve any tilting at all:

Cat	=^.^=
John Lennon	//oo\\
The 'I love you' sign	\Iii/

In Japan, on the other hand, it's the un-tilted format which is the default. Arising in the mid-1980s, this alternative tradition is known as *kaomoji* (顔 *kao* = face, 文字 *moji* = character) and results in designs such as (^_^) for 'happy', and (>_<) for 'angry'.

It also makes use of some of the lesser-used characters on the keyboard, as well as the occasional symbol from the *katakana* syllabary. This allows for more complex designs, such as the table flip (╯°□°）╯ ︵ ┻━┻, for when a sense of uncontrollable rage overwhelms you,[28] or the shrug ¯_(ツ)_/¯, for when basic apathy seems the most appropriate response to a situation.

Despite their use of slightly more obscure characters, both of these emoticon-expressions have attained international popularity. The shrug, for example, came to prominence in English when the rap group Travis Porter tweeted it in response to the way that Kanye West reacted after his bizarre intervention against Taylor Swift at the 2010 Video Music Awards. But the sentiment it represents has been a mainstay of popular culture for a couple of decades (the closest verbal equivalent is something like 'meh'). And despite Unicode unveiling a dedicated shrug emoji in 2016, for many people the original *kaomoji* manages a more precise expressiveness and so continues to be used today. In March 2018 the *New York Times* even ran a headline with a shrug in the title: 'A Second Winter Storm Is Coming. How Much Snow? ¯_(ツ)_/¯'.[29]

It's not just Japanese scripts that get pulled into service to extend the traditional set of punctuation marks. There are symbols from a host of other writing systems which lend themselves well to representing facial or gestural emotions.[30] For example, ٩(͡๏̯͡๏)۶ (throwing your hands up in exasperation) uses the 9 and 6 from the Persian alphabet for its outstretched arms. While ง'̀-'́)ง (a boxing stance) uses the letter *ngor-ngu* from the Thai alphabet as a way of representing the raised fists. And in China, the character 囧 (meaning 'patterned window') is often used all on its own as an emoticon because of the way it resembles a person with their mouth wide open, thus expressing shock or embarrassment.[31]

There are more prosaic ways of expressing your mood as well, of course. On Reddit, users tend to write /s after any sentence they want to flag up for its sarcasm or irony.[32] And there's the equally literal j/k ('just kidding') that was a staple for tongue-in-cheek comments written in friends' high school yearbooks.

So why was it that the emoticon somehow succeeded where the percontation mark, the snigger mark, the point d'amour and Wilkins's upended exclamation mark had all tried and failed? The answer is that it both fulfilled a particular contemporary need and was intuitive to use. With the advent of mass online communication, what had previously been a desired innovation now became a pressing concern. Written communication via social media is conversational in style but also retains all the limitations for expressing voice and tone that all writing has. :-) is easily written on a keyboard, and its meaning is relatively transparent. Based, however crudely, on the human face, it doesn't need to be learnt in the way that a newly invented symbol would. Instead, it simply mimics the type of non-verbal expression that's already taking place in face-to-face conversations. In this way it prepared the ground perfectly for the advent of the emoji.

So if the search that John Wilkins began back in the seventeenth century with his upside-down exclamation mark – that passes through Bierce's snigger point, through Fahlman's emoticons and through the outstretched arms of the *kaomoji* – finally finds a successful conclusion with emoji, does this mean we've now cracked the conundrum of how to flag up ironic intention in writing? Do emoji add that all-important emotional framing that writing traditionally lacks and which can so easily cause people to miss the note of sarcasm in what someone's saying?

Well, yes and no. Certainly you can use emoji to qualify the spirit in which a message is meant. A little yellow face beaming at the end of a sentence is a good way of indicating you're not being entirely serious. And if the face is upside-down, so much the better 🙃.

Yet research is inconclusive as to quite *how* useful symbols of this sort are in this respect. A number of studies have looked at whether emoji and emoticons really do help people pick up on a layer of sarcasm which might otherwise have been overlooked. The evidence is rather mixed.[33] One of the first studies along these lines, by Walther and Addario, concluded, for example, that emoticons can complement what the verbal message is saying, but they won't contradict or enhance its meaning.[34] Then there's the fact that emoji themselves can also be used ironically. They're not set apart from the rules of normal communication. They're not some sort of pure, inviolate form of meaning-making which is immune from the complexities that characterise all human relationships. So putting an emoji at the end of a sentence as a counterpoint to the literal meaning of the words won't necessarily remove all the ambiguities from what you're saying. It could, in fact, simply amplify them – and provide yet a further level of irony to the message.

– Okay, well, good talking to you 😵

3 Making Faces

The Porphyrian Tree 🌳 *Poker Face* 🌳 *The Duchenne Smile* 🌳
Astro Boy 🌳 *Into the Void*

The Porphyrian Tree

The aim behind John Wilkins's universal language was to be both
a means of international communication for travellers and diplo-
mats and also an accurate and logical way of recording the
advancements of science. Throughout the seventeenth century
there was a belief that natural languages were holding back scientific progress. They were seen as being too full of inconsistencies.
Their structures were arbitrary. They were often vague and
unspecific. And there was very little regularity to them. If it
were possible to build a language which mirrored precisely the
way the human mind ordered our understanding of the natural
world, the task of analysing that world would be much easier. As
the French philosopher René Descartes wrote, if we were able to

> explain correctly what are the simple ideas in the human imagi-
> nation out of which all human thoughts are compounded ... I
> would dare to hope for a universal language very easy to learn, to
> speak and to write. The greatest advantage of such a language
> would be the assistance it would give to men's judgement, repre-
> senting matters so clearly that it would be almost impossible to go
> wrong.[1]

So effective would this language be, Descartes believed, that
peasants would become better judges of the truth than philoso-
phers currently were. But although he was fully convinced that
such a language was theoretically possible, in practical terms he

thought it was unlikely ever to come about. Not that this stopped people like Wilkins from dedicating half their lives to the ambition.

The idea behind Wilkins's language was to analyse the entirety of the natural world and break it down into its elementary particles. He did this by means of what's known as a Porphyrian tree: a structuring device for the analysis of knowledge, named after the third-century Greek philosopher Porphyry. This draws up a list of distinctions between the essential properties that different things have, moving from the general to the specific. It's usually represented in a diagram which divides things into successive branches of a tree. Figure 3.1, for example, is a map of the distinctions which make up Wilkins's definition of a monkey.[2]

In other words, a monkey is a 'beast', which is 'viviparous' (it gives birth to living young rather than laying eggs), is 'clawed', is 'not rapacious', is 'man-like' (in having a human-like face and ears) and is smaller rather than larger in size (and so has a long tail and is nimble). If you were to take a different fork at any branch of the tree, you'd end up with a different type of animal. If you'd taken the 'cloven footed' branch instead of the 'clawed', for

Figure 3.1 John Wilkins's definition of 'monkey'

example, and then chosen 'horned but not ruminant' (rather than 'ruminant but not horned'), you'd be describing a rhinoceros.

Using a mixture of this simple structuring device and a huge amount of intellectual work, Wilkins managed to plot his way through everything he knew about the world. To convert this into a language, he then gave all the elementary particles a symbol. In order to create the word you wanted you simply combined the relevant symbols together. Words thus fitted the logic of nature, rather than the other way round. Or at least, that was the intention.

The only snag with the whole endeavour is that, as Jorge Luis Borges pointed out, however expansive your map of the natural world might be, the organisation of the different categories is always going to be somewhat subjective. 'It is clear that there is no classification of the Universe [that will not be] arbitrary and full of conjectures', writes Borges in his essay about Wilkins. And the 'reason for this is very simple: we do not know what thing the universe is'.[3] Nature isn't, unfortunately, a set of elements organised like an encyclopaedia. And the way that humankind experiences and understands nature certainly isn't by means of a tidy mathematical formula.

Borges illustrated this by famously comparing Wilkins's ordering of the world to an imaginary Chinese encyclopaedia, the 'Celestial Empire of benevolent Knowledge', which, in its wisdom, categorised animals using the following sub-headings:

> (a) belonging to the emperor, (b) embalmed, (c) tame, (d) sucking pigs, (e) sirens, (f) fabulous, (g) stray dogs, (h) included in the present classification, (i) frenzied, (j) innumerable, (k) drawn with a very fine camelhair brush, (l) et cetera, (m) having just broken the water pitcher, (n) that from a long way off look like flies.

There's something remarkably similar to this fantastical Chinese encyclopaedia about emoji. Emoji themselves are a woefully incomplete, often highly random, mix of symbols. For 'suckling pigs', 'stray dogs' and 'animals which have just broken the water pitcher', there are water buffalo, nine different types of train and minidisks. It's a symbolic representation of elements of the world – but one which is more whimsical than logical.

There is, in fact, a very rudimentary system of categorisation for emoji. On keyboards they're grouped according to basic types: Smileys and People; Animals and Nature; Food and Drink; Activity; Travel and Places; Objects; Symbols; and Flags. It's not quite the exhaustive cataloguing of the entire natural and mental worlds that Wilkins was aiming for. To find 🐿 at the moment, all you have to do is scroll across to Animals and Nature, and there it is between 🐨 and 🐾. But even with the few hundred currently available, searching for the right character in amongst these categories can be time-consuming. As the range expands, it's perfectly possible that software developers might decide to further subdivide the categories, creating more Porphyrian-like branches.

At the moment, however, it's a very truncated vocabulary. The full emoji lexicon is currently a little over two thousand symbols. Compare this with the number of words in the *Oxford English Dictionary*, which today stands at 171,476.[4] Fluent speakers of English don't have a working knowledge of all of these, of course. But they're likely to know around fifty thousand; perhaps seventy-five thousand if they're well educated.[5] Not that you need anywhere near this many to communicate sufficiently. Dr Seuss's book *Green Eggs and Ham*, for example, was written with just fifty different words. Still, in comparison with a natural language like English, emoji are highly diminished. So, if they don't match the typical properties of a natural or artificial language, what exactly do they do?

Poker Face

Throughout the history of human culture, there's been a long-running battle about the relative merits of speech versus writing. The French Enlightenment thinker Jean-Jacques Rousseau, for example, believed that speech was clearly the purer form of language. For him, 'feelings are [better] expressed in speaking, ideas in writing'.[6] It's our feelings, he believed, which are at the heart of what it means to be human (he is the father of Romanticism, after all). Writing, on the other hand, substitutes 'exactitude for expressiveness'. It allows us to order our thoughts in a rational way. But it does this at the expense of a more basic, passion-based eloquence.

As we saw in the previous chapter, writing developed much later than spoken language. Even today, of the approximately seven thousand languages spoken around the world, only about half (3,866) have a full writing system.[7] One of the consequences of a written language is that it allows for permanence and mobility. It makes possible a stable notion of history and a complex society at a completely different scale-level than oral-only cultures can. It is, arguably, the foundational technology upon which human culture as we now experience it is built. But it's not simply the fact that writing has permanence and that it enables communication across space and time that distinguishes it from speaking. The two also display very different characteristics. And it was this that led Rousseau to portray the one as a vessel for thought, the other for passion.

Conventionally, writing and speaking have been seen as distinct forms of language because they're used in different ways, for different purposes, and involve a different range of technologies. The type of language we produce varies depending on whether we're using a computer, a pen or just our own voice. This influence isn't simply a matter of the obvious superficial differences – that one involves modulations of sound in the atmosphere, while the other consists of arranging symbols across a page or screen. It's also a matter of the way that the message itself is structured. Speech is likely to be more immediate, more dependent on the context in which it occurs and the human capabilities of the speakers. It has to rely on what we can retain in our memories as we process what we want to say. It's composed and edited on the go. The result is a pattern of short phrases, simple vocabulary, filler words such as 'er' and 'you see', and a succession of false starts and self-corrections.

Writing, on the other hand, allows for more deliberation. We can choose our words with care, ensuring that the grammatical elements of the sentence all cohere and that the meaning flows in a smooth and comprehensible fashion. We can deliberately edit and re-edit how we phrase things. This results in more complicated sentence structures, with clauses nesting inside one another to allow a level of precision in the meaning. It results in the use of a broader range of vocabulary and an altogether more artfully designed discourse. When scribbling down notes we may not worry too much about the coherence or elegance of the text, but in other traditional forms of writing – in essays, letters, books – the structure of the language is markedly different from the structure of casual, everyday speech.

Writing in computer-mediated communication complicates this clear division, however. It's often seen as an intermediary form: a sort of informal chat conducted via writing. Online writing replicates the patterns – and sometimes the pronunciations – of spoken language in order to convey an intimacy or friendliness. Because it's usually more rushed and ephemeral than most offline writing, there's less concern about correct spelling or punctuation – less concern about the way it looks. This isn't to say that *all* online writing is like this. But as digital and mobile technologies have led to an increase in everyday written communication – with people today often preferring to message their friends than phone them – so the style of written language is expanding to mirror patterns of speech.

Another obvious but important difference is that with writing the addressee usually isn't physically present when you're composing your message. And this also has implications for the structure. When writing a letter, for example, you need to take into account the fact that the person you're writing to won't read it for a day or two. Any references you make to time and place will need to be spelt out explicitly. 'This afternoon' will become 'last Wednesday' once the letter has navigated the postal service. As your addressee isn't physically on hand to ask clarification questions, you need to make sure you're as overt as possible about your meaning. And while in online messaging the distance and delay may be lessened, these general principles still hold. The words alone are forced to carry more responsibility.

Then there's the part the body plays in face-to-face communication. There's an old adage in the game of poker that you should play the person, not the odds. As a contest of human interaction, success isn't so much about strategy and good fortune as about predicting your opponent's behaviour and pre-empting their actions. In the absence of being able to see the hand they've been dealt, you try to pick up on clues from the way they're acting – examine their physical demeanour, the subtle shifts in their body language. An online guide to how to do this lists a long roll call of tells – the physical signs that people make as an unconscious expression of their attitude. These range from whether your opponent is smiling, blinking, staring or looking compulsively at the chips to whether their blood pressure is making them red in the face, whether they're breathing heavily, or whether they're sitting up attentively in their seat.[8] All of these can inadvertently indicate a player's attitude to the state of the game and undermine the inscrutability they think they're projecting.

Tells in poker are a subtle form of non-verbal communication. Whenever we interact with people, a huge proportion of the information we express comes via body language. This meaning can substitute for words: a disapproving stare can cut short an argument. Or it can act as an accompaniment to speech: tone of voice can indicate sarcasm or jocularity. There are a host of ways in which non-verbal communication occurs. There's the pitch, speed and volume of the voice. There are hand gestures and facial expressions. There's posture, stance and the distance at which you stand relative to the listener. There's eye contact. Even how you dress can be a form of non-verbal communication in the way it acts as a type of self-expression.

In written communication, all this is stripped from the equation. 'In writing,' as Rousseau said, 'one is forced to use all the words according to their conventional meaning. But in speaking, one varies the meanings by varying one's tone of voice, determining them as one pleases.'[9] One varies the meaning through the myriad of ways that the body reacts when conversing with a fellow human being. And a focal point for this, in the most literal sense, is the face.

The Duchenne Smile

Duchenne de Boulogne was a nineteenth-century French neurologist who hypothesised that the range of facial expressions that people make can be interpreted as a God-given language of signs. In order to investigate this hypothesis, he wired his patients up with electrical probes which triggered contractions of the facial muscles. In this way he was able to produce a compendium of grotesque expressions, which he then recorded using the newly invented technology of photography.

The work Duchenne did in this field, while not quite in line with modern-day ethical considerations, has been highly influential – so much so that one of the smiles he identified is now named after him. The 'Duchenne smile', formed with both the mouth and the eyes, is one which conveys an authentic expression of happiness. The muscles at the corners of the lips pull up, raising the cheeks and pinching the area around the eyes. This is in contrast to a smile where only the corners of the lips are raised and the eyes remain unmoved – the sort of smile which indicates politeness rather than real joy. As Duchenne remarked, the absence of movement around the eyes 'unmasks the false friend'. There's a plastic quality to it. These days it's known as a Botox smile.

One of Duchenne's beliefs was that people the world over share the same reactions to the same range of facial expressions.

> Once this language of facial expression was created, it sufficed for [God] to give all human beings the instinctive faculty of always expressing their sentiments by contracting the same muscles. This rendered the language universal and immutable.

This belief in the universality of facial expression was also held by Charles Darwin, who saw it as a product of evolution. But for most of the nineteenth and twentieth centuries, the idea was disputed. Anthropologists such as Margaret Mead and Gregory Bateson believed that smiling, as with so much else in human behaviour, was a product of the culture in which one was raised. It wasn't until the 1960s that the psychologist Paul Ekman pioneered the detailed study of the relationship between emotions and facial expressions and in doing so proved the validity of Duchenne's universal and immutable 'language'.

In order to distinguish between cultural influence and innate predisposition, Eckman began his research with a remote community in the highlands of Papua New Guinea who'd previously had no contact with Western culture. It was a cannibalistic tribe – they ate the dead of their own community – but, despite these obvious noticeable cultural differences when compared to the Californian academic circles that Eckman came from, he found that the people of the tribe all expressed happiness, sadness and fear in exactly the same way that he himself did. Cultural differences exist for what *motivates* the display of emotions. They also exist in terms of the rules people have for hiding or celebrating their emotions (a stiff upper lip versus wearing your heart on your sleeve, for example). But the underlying facial expressions we all make are innate and are shared across the whole species.

Based on this and subsequent research, Eckman drew up a categorisation system for all the various human facial expressions, known as the Facial Action Coding System (FACS). Like Duchenne before him, he put needles through the skin to electrically stimulate particular muscles – but he carried this out on himself rather than on his patients. He then mapped out the combination of muscles movements which produced the thousands of different expressions that the face makes, and he plotted these against the sentiments that caused them.

One of the consequences of this was identifying the signs that betray people when they're lying. He called these 'micro expressions', the very brief facial movements that reveal the emotions people try to conceal. As he writes in his book *Emotions Revealed*, this work brought him into contact with 'spies, assassins, embezzlers, murderers [and] foreign national leaders', all of whose facial expressions he was able to study and document.[10] Beyond law enforcement and security scenarios, the work also found applications in health care and therapy, where it's now used for a range of contexts: from doctor–patient interaction to assisting people with autism to identify emotional expressions in their everyday life.

In 2013, as part of the 'Emoji Art Show' in New York, the performance artist Genevieve Belleveau drew on Ekman's research for a piece called Emoji Autism Facial Recognition Therapy.[11] This involved visitors to the gallery positioning different emoji on an 'Emoji Recognition Chart', which categorised the emotional meaning of the different characters according to their official Unicode names (e.g. 'relieved face', 'persevering face').[12] The chart mimicked Ekman's categorisation system and was used to examine the varying interpretations that people make of the different emoji expressions.

As Malcolm Gladwell writes in an article on Eckman's work, the face is 'an extraordinarily efficient instrument of communication'.[13] And as we saw with the emergence of emoticons, even the most basic representations of facial expressions can enhance online written communication. Emoji have built on this, adding an image-based means of bringing some of the framing of non-verbal communication to conversational written language.

It's a very rudimentary system, of course, compared to the use of our actual faces. According to Eckman, a face can make more than ten thousand expressions. He identified eighteen different types of archetypal smile, each conveying a different emotion. There are smiles of misery, of embarrassment, of disdain. There's the 'angry-enjoyment' or Schadenfreude smile. There's Mona Lisa's classic 'flirtatious smile'. In the current set of emoji, however, there are only around fifty expressions.

But are these emoji expressions universally understood in the same way that actual smiles and frowns are? As an art project, Belleveau's work had no real scientific pretentions, but what it did highlight was the difference between the official definitions of emoji and the various interpretations people actually have of them. It showed, that with a new and evolving communicative system, everybody has slightly different interpretations of what a sign means. The 'relieved face' 😌 may look relieved to some people but smug or self-satisfied to others. Far from being a universal language, in other words, emoji are one which, at the moment, is in the process of being culturally constructed through use and the development of convention.

This highlights two important points about emoji. While they add an element of the emotional framing that comes from non-verbal communication, they're obviously only *representations* of facial expressions. What's more, they're very stylised representations. This is reflected in the approach to their design. As Gedeon Maheux, co-founder of the Iconfactory – which worked on the design of both the Twitter and Facebook Messenger emoji – notes, the look of the smiley faces is usually purposefully exaggerated for emotional or comedic effect.[14] In this way, while they may be based on real facial expressions, they're tailored to suit the way they're commonly used. If you want to tell a friend you're feeling sick, for example, a picture of a face the colour of rank spinach which is struggling to stifle the urge to vomit is better than one looking ever-so-slightly queasy. Likewise, just as we exaggerate in verbal language with phrases such as ROFL, so the emoji of a face laughing so loud it's crying has a much stronger pragmatic effect than one simply pursing its lips in a faintly amused smile.

But there's also another important element to the way in which emoji symbolise different emotions. This also is based less on how the face actually registers emotions and more on a specific created 'visual language' – one which has its origins in Japanese comic book culture.

Astro Boy

The website *Comic Book Resources* runs a feature called 'Comic Book Urban Legends Revealed', and number 110 in their series explores the rumour that a 'comic character was made an actual citizen in Japan'.[15] As the site confirms, this particular legend happens to be true. In 2003 the city of Niiza in western Japan awarded citizenship to a young boy named Tetsuwan Atomu.[16] Known in English as Astro Boy, Tetsuwan Atomu (鉄腕アトム) is a fictional robot, created in the 1950s by Osamu Tezuka, one of the founding figures of Japanese manga.

Manga are an important influence on the way that emoji convey meaning. Over the years they've developed a particular 'visual language' – a grammar of different visual symbols representing ideas or emotions – and many of the standard tropes of this language derive from the pioneering work of Osamu Tezuka.[17] The distinctive look of manga characters comes from their large eyes, big hair and diminutive mouths. The way these features dominate the face is so conventional that it's often difficult to distinguish one character from another, and artists have to resort to more superficial differences such as hair colour to indicate individual identities. Manga characters, in other words, are highly stylised versions of real people. Yet in Japan, at least, they exist as a hugely important and emotionally engaging form of cultural expression.

It's the prominence of the eyes that's the most notable influence on emoji. But the way emotions are expressed through conventionalised tropes is also a direct carry-over. The iconography that's developed to represent these expressions is known as *manpu*. This consists of expressions which aren't real – they're not a direct copy of the catalogue of expressions that Eckman identified – but are instead a symbolic way of expressing various situations, reactions and emotions. For example, embarrassment or nervousness for a manga character is represented by sweat drops. A bloody nose indicates lust. If the eyes are glowing it means she's glaring. If there are bubbles coming from his nose it means he's on the brink of sleep. And if the eyes are all blacked out this indicates that the character is consumed by anger.

Many of these conventions have been incorporated directly into emoji. There's the sleep-induced nose bubble 😪. The cold sweat of anxiety 😰. And the two different types of crying: a tear in the corner of the eye 😢, or the vertical lines streaming down the cheeks 😭. Even the pose which looks like Edvard Munch's 'The Scream' is, in fact, a staple in manga for representing shock 😱.

Not that all standard manga tropes have been picked up by emoji. The way that characters in a comic can suddenly sprout wolf ears and a tail when they're leering hasn't yet made its way into the emoji lexicon – perhaps because there's already the less-metaphoric drooling emoji 🤤.

This doesn't mean, of course, that everyone necessarily uses these emoji to express these emotions. *Manpu* is a learned system of meanings, which may feel intuitive to those brought up on manga but for others needs to be acquired in the same way that any other code is. For those who regularly read comics, these conventions will be internalised as a form of visual language, and readers will transfer them across to the meanings of emoji. For others, the ways in which the pictograms resemble actual facial expressions is more likely to influence their interpretation. So 😪, for example, might convey crying rather than dozing, based solely on the way it looks.

As part of their Unicode template, all emoji are given official names. In the case of the faces, these is an unsystematic mixture of descriptions of the literal look of the picture and descriptions of the emotional state being represented. 😮, for example, is called 'Face with open mouth', while 😥 is called 'Disappointed but relieved'. But these are more a technical nomenclature than a reflection of actual patterns of usage (as the response to Belleveau's art piece demonstrated). For the moment, at least, there's no authoritative dictionary listing what the different characters are supposed to mean, and thus people improvise the meanings as and when they use them.

The way people use emoji clearly isn't exactly the same way they use actual facial expressions, then. Yet there is a link between the two. Likewise, the conventional iconography that's borrowed from manga doesn't always have a direct impact on the way people use emoji. But again, there are clear links. Instead, the use of emoji draws on a middle ground. It draws on people's intuitive sense of the types of emotions that the representations of facial expressions resemble; and also on conventional meanings that have developed (and are continuing to develop) around the way they're used.

For some people, the closed set of emoji are in fact a more reliable way of expressing emotion than the 'living canvas' of our actual face. Jonathan Nolan, writing in the *New Yorker*, worries that his real face is too blunt an instrument. 'The human face is a mess', he writes, 'roiling with divergent emotions, as if your id had signed up for Twitter'. Emoji, on the other hand, allow him an 'almost virtuosic mastery of my emotions as presented to others'.[18] In other words, you have a level of control over the type of face you want to present via social media. You're able to purposefully choose how to express your emotions, without your body, and its complex in-built scheme of non-verbal tells, inadvertently betraying anything as inconvenient as your real feelings.

Into the Void

In his top ten tips for writers, Friedrich Nietzsche underlined the importance of paying attention to your projected reader. 'Style', he wrote, 'should be suited to the specific person with whom you wish to communicate'.[19] What he's noting here is the fact that communication is always a collaboration between two parties. There's always a speaker and an audience, always a writer and a reader. Even in situations where the person you're communicating with isn't physically present, you're engaged in a dialogue with someone.

One of the consequences of this is that we tailor what we say to the expectations of the person with whom we're communicating. We alter our style of communication – how formal or informal we are, what type of vocabulary we use – based on what we think is most appropriate for the relationship we have with our inter-locutor, what we're trying to achieve in the encounter and how the other party is reacting to what we say.

This is true of any type of communication in any context. When we're addressing someone we know, and talking to them face-to-face, we can make decisions about how we do this based on the way they're responding. Or, to take another example, a good stand-up comedian will play off the reaction of the audience, modulating his or her performance in response to the laugher it's prompting.

In essence, this is what we all do when we're in conversation with someone. We respond to minute cues from the person we're speaking to – the 'uh-huhs', 'I sees' and nods of the head – none of which add anything much to the meaning of the discussion but which are important for keeping things jogging along. This is known as backchannelling, and it's a way of letting the other person know you're listening and that you're following what they're saying. If you've ever had a conversation over a phone line which completely cuts the incoming channel whenever you're speaking, you'll know how disconcerting it is not being able to hear these little prompts.

It's an obvious point in many ways – that talking is a two-person activity – but it's a vital part of the dynamic of communication. And in terms of the non-verbal cues we've been discussing, it means that it's not just the facial expressions or body language of the speaker which shape the meaning of what's being said. The listener's body language is equally important. The flow of conversation will proceed very differently if you're talking to someone who's smiling attentively rather than someone struggling to hide their boredom. Or someone who's clearly picked up on the irony in your voice versus someone who seems to be taking everything at face value.

When we're communicating online, this aspect of the interaction becomes a little more complicated. We can't judge the mood of the person we're talking to so easily because we can't see their reaction. Technology has therefore developed new ways of fulfilling this function. Facebook's 'Like' button, for example, is a way of replicating some sort of backchannelling process for social media. It lets you show your interlocutor that they're not communicating into the void – that there's someone out there listening and, occasionally, agreeing with what they have to say.

It's a minimal response, of course. And even since Facebook introduced the palette of additional reactions in early 2016, giving six different options – symbols they call *love, haha, wow, sad* and *angry*, as well as the traditional *like* – it's still little more than a gesture towards the fact that your post is part of a dialogue.

The Unicode emoji offer a much broader palette of responses. And research shows that this has always been an important element of the way they're used. For example, a study of Japanese university students that was carried out by Kazuko Miyake back in 2004 – i.e. long before they'd become a global phenomenon – showed how emoji were often being used at the end of a sentence or message as a way of marking the completion of a thought or topic.[20] As Miyake noted, backchannelling is particularly frequent in Japanese culture. This was transferred across to online conversation in the form of emoji, which were used by both speaker and listener as a way of orchestrating the rhythms of the dialogue.

Then there's the way they can be used to politely bow out of a conversation when you want to wrap things up. As Katy Waldman writes in *Slate* magazine, one of the consequences of the way that online interaction isn't limited by time, distance or location is it can simply run and run.[21] There's no real equivalent of the 'Yours sincerely' or 'All the best' that concludes a letter, no picking up from someone's stance or the way their gaze is starting to wander that they're ready to move on. For those times when there's nothing more to add to a conversation but you don't just want to sever the connection without some sort of acknowledgement, an emoji is perfect. As Waldman says, they 'feel inviting and social even when you are putting a pin in a conversation – they shut it down without "shutting it down"'. An impressionistic emoji is far better than an unconvincing 'Okay, must dash' or 'I'd better get back to work'. And it doesn't necessarily even really matter which one you use. A positive valediction obviously works well 🐱👋. But so also does something completely abstract.

4   Metaphors and Moral Panics

Euphemistically Speaking ✎ *It's Only a Metaphor* ✎ *The Knife and the Rod* ✎ *The Eggplant Emoji* ✎ *The Dutiful Computer* ✎ *Are Emoji Ruining English?*

Euphemistically Speaking

So the face-based emoji, along with many of the hand or body gestures, approximate to some of the non-verbal communication that's a fundamental part of how we talk to each other. We use them to indicate emotion, to acknowledge that we're part of a conversation, to modify or temper the bluntness of words. But how about the other symbols? How do we meaningfully make use of the strange selection of trains, speedboats and avocados to enhance our online conversation? After all, as Jonathan Swift's Lagardian academicians show, if you're only able to talk about the objects you have immediately to hand, your conversation will be extremely limited. And even with several hundred objects represented in the full emoji lexicon, this doesn't scratch the surface of the infinite variety of nature.

An article by Nimrod Kamer back in 2013, only a couple of years after emoji had begun their global conquest, suggested a number of ways in which they could usefully be employed in society.[1] Among Kamer's ideas were ordering food and using them to replace PIN codes at ATMs. Within two years, most of his suggestions had come to pass. Restaurants such as the Little Yellow Door in London were allowing customers to send in emoji-based orders via WhatsApp.[2] Cocktail bars such as the Coconut Watering Hole in Shoreditch were doing the same via

Instagram.[3] And British start-up Intelligent Environments suggested that replacing numerical passcodes with emoji-based ones (PIEs rather than PINs?) would increase their security by a factor of five hundred.[4]

One of the things that Kamer's article didn't predict, however, was using emoji to order pornography. But given that they're an internet-based communications system, it was never going to be very long before porn got involved.

In the standard set of Unicode emoji there are no explicitly sex-related characters. This isn't the case in the unregulated outlands of the stickers and non-standard emoji, of course. The gay social network app Grindr, for example, released a set of gaymoji in 2017.[5] And the website Flirtmoji, who produce what they describe as a 'visual language designed to empower people of all sexualities to communicate their desires, concerns, and flirtations',[6] have a number of adult-themed sticker sets, including one dedicated exclusively to the vagina. Although, when this was released, it almost immediately ran into controversy when it turned out that some of the designs they were using had been plagiarised from someone else's vagina art.[7]

But Pornhub, the internet's largest porn site, wanted to capitalise on the universal nature of the standardised set of emoji. They wanted to offer a service whereby people could order porn over the internet in just the same way they were now ordering cocktails or food. And without literal symbols for some of the scenarios they had on offer, they turned to metaphor. After all, metaphor and euphemism are a fundamental part of the way we talk about sex in verbal language. So why not in emoji as well? They thus picked a selection of the standard emoji – 🍑, 🍆, 🐌, 👅 – and had these symbolise categories from their website.

In this case it's the context that creates the meaning. Context is a vital part of any process of communication. Whenever we interpret a message, we're supplying contextual information which helps make it meaningful to us. For example, I recently went to a friend's Halloween party. Despite having been to his address once or twice before, I didn't remember the house number, and in the dark all the houses looked much the same. About halfway up the street there was one house covered with police 'do not enter' tape. This was stuck across the door and windows, wrapped around the front gate. Ordinarily I'd have taken the directive on the tape at face value. But given the context, in this particular instance the message it conveyed was the precise opposite of what the words actually said.

It was this sort of contextual meaning that Pornhub used when they invited customers to text them an emoji, in response to which they'd send a 'free, specially curated video from the category corresponding to that emoji'.[8] If you end up on Pornhub, after all, the chances are you're expecting that whatever you find there is going to be porn-related. Their categories were all fairly straightforward metaphors which, for the most part, already exist in English. So, for example, ♈ stood for 'Lesbian', ♐ for 'Solo Male', ♜ for 'Hentai', ▤ for 'Amateur'. Most of these symbols wouldn't stand for these concepts as a general rule in everyday use, but in this context their meaning becomes relatively clear.

A couple of years later, the website YouPorn made a similar foray into the world of emoji by introducing a 'search by emoji' function for its videos. This allowed visitors to their site to input any of over seventy-five different emoji, each of which had been matched to a search term in its catalogue.[9] The YouPorn emoji lexicon isn't always quite as intuitive as Pornhub's, however. For instance, while the 'robot face' 🤖 represents 'virtual reality'–themed videos, the 'exploding head' 🤯 supposedly brings up 'face sitting' videos.

A footnote to this is that it's not simply what the symbols represent that creates their metaphorical meaning – it's also how they look. As a general rule of thumb, the less specific they are as images, the more flexible they can be as communicative symbols. This was notably highlighted when Apple changed the design of the peach emoji a couple of years ago.

A peach has been part of Unicode since late 2010. It wasn't long after this debut that it began to be used metaphorically, due a certain visual similarity between its design and the shape of the human backside. In the absence of a 'butt emoji', Apple's peach was seen as a perfect stand-in. In October 2016, however, as part of one of their periodic updates, the company decided to redesign their version of the fruit in order to make it look more peach-like. Overnight it suddenly acquired a photo-realist quality. But, in being thus transformed, it lost some of its euphemistic possibilities. Over the next few days there was an outcry from users, with media outlets then picking up on the story and spreading the dissent.[10] As the tech journalist Jay Hathaway put it, the 'scandalous de-assifying of the peach caused a . . . backlash', so to speak, until Apple were finally forced 'to restore it to its former anatomical glory'.[11]

It's Only a Metaphor

In the guidelines that Twitter gives out about how people should use its logo, there's a stipulation that the symbol shouldn't be used metaphorically to suggest a bird. 'It's not a bird', the rules explain: 'it's a symbol of Twitter'.[12] This seems rather counterintuitive, especially as the logo was originally named 'Larry the Bird', is now called 'Twitter Bird' and is supposedly based on a mountain bluebird. Plus, of course, the name of the company is a word meaning 'chirps from a bird', which, according to its co-founder Jack Dorsey, perfectly represents what the product does.[13]

Visual metaphors such as Twitter's bird-which-isn't-a-bird are a common device in branding and advertising copy. Take, for example, one of the classic Volkswagen ads from the early 1960s, which shows a Beetle with a large wind-up key protruding from its back. The metaphor works by representing an object or concept by means of or in association with a visual image of something else, thus highlighting some quality that both are meant to share – in the case of the VW, the idea that the car runs like clockwork.

As we saw with Pornhub's suggestive menu, visual metaphors are a key way in which emoji are used to manufacture meaning.

The limited vocabulary of the current set of emoji can be extended by having them substitute for something which they resemble or which echoes a pre-existing verbal metaphor. One common way in which emoji are used is mimicking and extending verbal slang. Within days of Apple releasing their 2018 emoji update, for example, people had begun adopting some of them as shorthand for various slang expressions, playing specifically on the metaphorical potential of the images. The bald emoji, for instance, was being used to represent 'wig snatched' – a phrase that has its roots in African American slang and expresses an overwhelming sense of awe over someone's performance or achievements (you're so bowled over in admiration that your wig flies off). Then there was the receipt emoji, which offered a perfect visual complement for the phrase 'show/bring the receipts', meaning to provide counter evidence (a screenshot of an incriminating post, a video clip, etc.) for an incident that someone is falsely trying to assert about you.[14]

But not only can emoji be used metaphorically: many of them also incorporate visual metaphors into their design. There's the 'money-mouth face' 🤑, for example, which has dollar signs for eyes and a banknote in place of a tongue. Or the face with a closed zipper for a mouth 🤐, the emoji equivalent of the phrase 'zip it'. Then there's the use of personification, whereby human characteristics are attributed to an abstract concept, as in the Mother Nature emoji exhaling the wind 🌬.

There are also a few emoji which exist in a no-man's land between the literal and the figurative: the levitating businessman 🕴, for instance, who can presumably be used to denote an actual businessman but is more often exploited for his fuzzy metaphoric potential. Of all the current emoji, he has one of the most esoteric backstories. Designed by Vincent Connare, the man responsible for the endlessly divisive **Comic Sans font**, he's based on the logo for the 2 Tone record label, home to The Specials and Madness.[15] The logo itself – known as Walt Jabsco – was in turn based on another cultural artefact, a photo of the musician Peter Tosh from the cover of the 1965 album *The Wailing Wailers*.[16] It's the sort of etymology that would have traumatised

John Wilkins and his friends at the Royal Society but reflects precisely the haphazard way that languages actually develop.

Such is the obscure appearance of the levitating businessman that he almost invites people to project their own biographical narratives onto him. Dan Piepenbring of the *Paris Review*, for example, sees in him 'a rich kid who's just aced his LSATs – a simpering, dubiously pompadoured fella in polarised glasses and a natty suit ... He's a superhuman exclamation point. He's the floating face of capitalism.'[17] But it's not just the more esoteric symbols onto which people project their own narratives and interpretations. The same thing happens for many of the more straightforward characters. A survey by researchers at the University of Minnesota found that the meanings people ascribe to emoji can vary significantly and that any form of stable consensus is unusual. And although this can happen when different people are shown exactly the same design (this fellow 😝 looking relieved to some people, smug and self-satisfied to others),[18] the major reason for varying interpretations is the fact that each platform has its own design for each and every emoji.

As people are becoming ever more aware of this as a technical limitation, so it's spawned a range of reflective memes. One of these is the genre of 'emoji reviews', which lists the multiple designs of an emoji, giving them each a brief critique plus a score out of 10.[19] The trend began in earnest in early 2017, with a review of eleven different designs for the horse emoji.[20] This included appraisals such as the following for the Samsung horse, which has a broad, toothy and slightly demented smile:

> woah there! this dudes makin eye contact AND smiling. he has a lil heart for the top of his mane. this dude clearly has the chompers needed for eating some primo hay
> *5/10 because he looks like a cow at first glance*

Such examples showcase some of the many ways in which metaphor is used to generate meaning from emoji. In all these cases, though, we've been looking at individual symbols. Communication would be very limited if all we were able to do was indicate discrete concepts one at a time. Language, however you conceptualise it, isn't simply a list of words. It's also how you combine those words – and the grammatical rules you use to do this.

The Knife and the Rod

In the early Middle Ages, grammar, along with the other liberal arts, was often personified as an allegorical female figure.[21] One of the most common images was of an old woman carrying a box full of medical implements which she'd use to correct the failings of children. As the twelfth-century English scholar John of Salisbury explains:

> [Grammar] uses the knife to prune away grammatical errors, and to cleanse the tongues of infants as she instructs them ... [She] employs her rod to punish offenders; while with the ointment of the propriety and utility which derive from her services, she mitigates the sufferings of her patients.[22]

In other tableaux she has a book and a whip, symbolising her commitment to helping the studious and reforming the indolent. A famous sculpture at Chartres shows her with two students, one bent studiously over his work, the other letting his book slip from his knees, with Grammar standing over him about to wield the whip.

The view of grammar as a strict set of rules which needs to be nurtured is still very prevalent today. The predominant discourse amongst the general public is that grammar is about the 'correct' use of language. But in linguistic terms, it's more properly understood as the way in which words are combined to make complex meaning. And it's one of the essential elements of anything that qualifies as a full language.

For emoji to be considered a language in their own right, they'd need to have an established set of grammatical rules. Infographics such as road signs – the other form of pictographic communication system that's most common in modern-day society – can't be combined together to create sentences, other than in the most rudimentary way. You can juxtapose a swimming sign and an arrow in order to indicate that the swimming pool is over there. But this isn't the same as being able to articulate an abstract idea like 'I've had a deep-seated fear of swimming ever since I was stung by a jellyfish in Lanzarote'.

So how about emoji? Are they stuck towards the infographics end of the spectrum? Or are they capable of more extensive, elastic expression? Unicode are very explicit about the fact that 'Emoji aren't really a "language"; they don't have the grammar or vocabulary to substitute for written language'.[23] Certainly, there's no codified grammar primer for how they're to be used. At present, people are still very much experimenting. That said, there are some simple, frequently repeated patterns emerging, which suggests the early evolutionary steps towards a basic grammar.

Grammar consists of the internalised rules for how a particular community of speakers arranges words to make meaning. It governs the composition of individual words (morphology), as well as phrases (word order, or syntax), which link ideas together to create more complex ideas. Different languages do this in different ways. Modern English, for example, primarily uses word order to organise the grammar. Other languages rely more on adding suffixes to the ends of words to indicate the relations between concepts.

As we've seen, the possible meanings of emoji can be extended by using them metaphorically. In terms of 'word' formation, they can also be extended by combining symbols to create composite concepts, which are often direct translations (or calques) from English words. For example, 'bombshell' can be conveyed by 💣💥.

Metaphor is again often part of this process, whereby the figurative senses of the two characters combine to make a new concept. You can write 🍑📞 for 'booty call' for instance. Or 📺❄️ if, for some reason, you wanted to emojify 'Netflix and chill'. In both these cases the emoji are actually being used in a mixture of metaphoric and metonymic ways. Metonymy is a similar trope to metaphor but one in which a concept is used to represent something with which it's directly related – the 'silver screen', for example, to mean the cinema. Or in this instance, popcorn (which is traditionally associated with watching a movie) to symbolise Netflix.

There are, then, a few simple ways in which the vocabulary of emoji can be extended. But how about grammar more generally? A study by the linguist and data scientist Tyler Schnoebelen examined a number of ways in which grammatical patterns are beginning to evolve for emoji.[24] He found that for the most part they're being used in combination with written text, creating a mixed form of communication. When used in this way, emoji function as a form of punctuation, placed at the end of sentences and acting as a counterpoint to the words – as with the irony marker discussed in earlier chapters.

When emoji are combined with each other they appear to be evolving a grammar in much the way that a pidgin does. A pidgin is a simplified means of communication which develops between people who don't have a shared language but are regularly interacting with each other for purposes such as trade. Over time they create a hybrid language, usually building it around a simple form of the grammar of the native language of one party or another. Emoji communication does much the same in the way that it copies some of the basic rules of English grammar, such as the subject-verb-object structure. 'Sentences' in emoji tend to have a linear structure, with the agent or actor coming first, followed by the action. This often means that a phrase will start with a face displaying an emotion then follow this with an explanation for that emotion. The linear nature of the way they're combined also tends to represent the chronology in which events take place: things on the left first, followed by things towards the right. In this micro-narrative, for example, the linear pattern structures the development of the meaning: 😀🛏🕷🔫.

There are, however, some specific considerations for emoji which determine how they're combined. Chief among these is the direction in which objects are facing in the designs of the symbols. In different parts of the world, not only are alphabets and writing systems different but so is the direction in which they're written. Modern European languages run left-to-right, languages such as Arabic and Hebrew right-to-left, and character-based languages, like Japanese and Chinese, can go from the top of the page to the bottom. Another alternative, though not one in common use today, is what's known as boustrophedon, from the Ancient Greek meaning 'ox-turning', which involves each line of the text being read in a different direction.

> So you read from left to right for the first line, then right to left for the next, and so on. And when the writing is going from right to left the letters themselves also point in that direction.

The reason this is significant is that the direction in which we're used to reading things has implications for how we interpret visual meaning. Take, for example, the Japanese artist Hokusai's famous print of the wave (which happens to have its own emoji 🌊). As English speakers accustomed to writing from left to right, the direction we 'read' this image is with the flow of the wave. Both the curl of the spray and the trajectory of our eyesight are moving in the same direction. If we were used to reading in the opposite direction, as is the case in Japan, we'd see it as looming up directly towards us, making its meaning that much more menacing.[25] Precisely the same image, then, can have a slightly different complexion of meaning due to different cultural conditionings.

In emoji there are a number of symbols where the direction in which they are pointing has an influence on how they are used. The gun is the most notable of these. It has the barrel pointing towards the left, so that if you want to suggest it's aiming at someone, you need to place that person *before* it. As the lexicographer Jane Solomon writes, '[to] put it simply, order very much matters when we're talking about who is being shot and who is pulling the trigger'.[26] But this, of course, is in conflict with what we've said about subject-verb-object word order, where it's normally the agent (i.e. the person executing the action) who would be on the left. In cases such as this, then, the specifics of the design overrule the conventions imported from verbal languages.

A similar issue exists for many of the animals. On an iPhone, for some reason, the snail is the only creature pointing towards the right, while all the other animals face left. Were he to be juxtaposed with the gun, therefore, the snail would look as if he was facing down the threat ![] ; while the turtle would be doing his best to flee ![]. Again though, this is something that varied from platform to platform. A Samsung snail, an HTC snail and a Facebook snail used to all be heading in the opposite direction from the Apple snail, so they too would be doing their best to escape if they happened to get caught in this situation. At time of writing there are plans for reversible emoji to be included in a future Unicode update, so at some stage this constraint may no longer be an issue.

The examples we've looked at so far are all quite basic grammatical constructs, and they hardly constitute complex sentences. The difficulty in terms of conveying anything more complicated is that, at the moment, several fundamental word classes simply don't exist in emoji. There are no pronouns, no conjunctions. People can improvise these, using a mixture of the rebus principle or metaphor and metonymy, such as the following:

![] (or ![]) = I
![] = but
![] = and

But none of these have become conventionalised yet. For the moment, it's always a matter of deciphering rather than simply reading their meaning.

Although emoji are listed as an optional written 'language' on your smartphone – sandwiched in between Dutch and Estonian – they're significantly different in many ways from all the other languages you can choose from there. Thinking of them along the lines of natural languages, or even of invented ones such as Esperanto, misses the point that for the most part they're used in combination with, rather than as a replacement for, a verbal language. They're most commonly used interspersed with verbal phrases, either as a type of punctuation or in the way that a multilingual speaker might switch between two languages. For now, at least, when emoji are used in any sustained, self-contained way, it's not as a straightforward attempt at everyday communication but for creative or playful purposes.

The Eggplant Emoji

When Kim Jong Nan, the half-brother of the North Korean leader, was murdered in Kuala Lumpur Airport in February 2017, many of the headlines in the world's press picked up on the macabre detail that one of the alleged killers was wearing a T-shirt with 'LOL' printed across it.[27] There was something chillingly incongruous about the word in this context – both because of its literal meaning and because of its associations with informal modern culture.

'LOL' is an initialism – an abbreviation made from the first letters of an expression or name – which developed in texting and online messaging but has now entered the mainstream English lexicon. In 2011 it was included in the *Oxford English Dictionary*, along with other initialisms such as 'OMG'. (The term 'acronym' can also be used for these, although it's usually reserved for abbreviations where the initial letters of a phrase are run together to spell out a new word: so *radar* is an acronym, while *CIA* is an initialism.)

In fact, both of these had been around long before the digital era:[28] 'OMG' recently celebrated its centenary,[29] while examples of 'LOL' crop up from the 1960s onwards, although in those days it was used to refer to a 'little old lady'.[30] But it was txtspk which led to a spike in their popularity. And although they started as written shorthand, they've since crossed over into everyday language and, in the case of LOL, can now be used as both noun and verb: 'doing it for the lols'; 'she lol'd'.

Since emoji have replaced txtspk as the current focus for linguistic innovation (not to mention media obsessions about the way they might be ruining English, as we'll see later in the chapter), the question is whether a similar process of influence is likely to happen with them as well? Are emoji now such an integral part of everyday life that they're leaving their stamp on English beyond the realm of social media?

The big difference between txtspk and emoji, of course, is that the former is verbal while the latter are pictorial. For an emoji to influence spoken language, it would have to cross modes. There are precedents for this happening. A number of punctuation marks have moved from page to speech, often as a way of empha-sising a point. A notable example was then–White House Press Secretary Sean Spicer's infamous assertion in early 2017 that Donald Trump had 'the largest audience to ever witness an inauguration, *period*'.[31]

Then there are uses such as the name of the 'slash fiction' genre, which comes from the punctuation symbol used to juxtapose the two characters being written about in a romantic liaison in fan fiction.[32] Or the way that 'hashtag' has migrated from Twitter to spoken language, where it's used as a means of retrospectively framing the meaning of an utterance.[33] And beyond punctuation there are examples such as the facepalm gesture, indicating frus-trated or exasperated disbelief, which has become so ubiquitous that 'facepalm' itself is starting to be used as a form of reflexive interjection in writing.[34]

So how about emoji? Is anything similar likely to happen with them? At the moment the evidence is slight. But there are one or two instances in which similar patterns of transference are taking place.

One of the inadvertent consequences of the metaphoric use of emoji discussed earlier in the chapter is that it can trigger the sort of moral panic in the popular press over the 'hidden' meanings that people (mainly children and teenagers) are supposedly encoding in their messages. An exposé in the *Daily Mail*, for example, pruriently claimed to reveal to its readers that 'the snapping camera can be used by someone looking for sexting to be taken to the next level' or that the 'innocuous mailbox emoji' can be used to mean sex.[35] In fact, examples such as these are just a straightforward form of slang – and not even an especially covert one.

One of the most established slang terms amongst emoji is the use of the eggplant to represent male genitalia.[36] According to one short history of the symbol, it's 'precisely because Americans had no cultural association with eggplants prior to the emoji revolution that it was the perfect euphemism'.[37] In other words, it wasn't getting used for its literal meaning (as it may do in a culture where eggplant-based cuisine is widespread) and was thus an empty sign looking for a meaning. And the penis was the meaning which seemed to fit best. (Although as a postscript it should be noted that some men occasionally, as the journalist John-Michael Bond puts it, 'use the shrimp in the interest of accuracy'.[38])

Referring to this as a euphemism isn't entirely accurate. After all, the eggplant emoji is not being used as a less explicit alternative for something else. As with other sex-related terms, there's no literal icon for 'penis' in emoji. But the eggplant has now become so conventionalised for this meaning that in certain contexts it's being adopted back into verbal language.[39]

A notable example is the hashtag #EggplantFriday, which was begun by hip-hop artist B.o.B., and subsequently led to a trend for men posting below-the-belt selfies on Instagram at the end of the working week. When Instagram then blocked this as a search term, worried it was flouting their standards of moral decency, the term gained even more notoriety – and the practice migrated to other, more broad-minded sites such as Tumblr.[40]

The term was also used in print when naked photos of the singer Chris Brown found their way online, and one gossip website reported the news with the headline 'Chris Brown's EGGPLANT PICS Leaked'.[41] Then there's the Ben Stiller-produced Netflix comedy announced in 2017 under the title *The Eggplant Emoji* (although ultimately released as *The Package*), which tells the story of a teenager who accidentally emasculates himself while on a camping trip and then runs around trying to save the severed member before it's too late.[42]

In fact, the term has become so established that the metaphor is transferring out into the real world in a variety of both abstract and concrete ways. First there was Durex announcing the introduction of an eggplant-flavoured prophylactic as part of a spoof publicity stunt in reaction to the Unicode Consortium turning down their proposal for a condom emoji.[43] Then there's the company Eggplant Mail,[44] which will anonymously send an actual aubergine, inscribed with a message of your choice, through the post to anyone you think might appreciate one. The purpose of this? For people to use 'the phallic fruit to make up, break up and celebrate life', apparently.

And to add to the cultural penetration, a company in Philadelphia now sells a vibrator made in the shape of an eggplant – the so-called emojibator.[45] Although, as *Cosmopolitan* notes, 'at 4.84 inches by 1.22 inches, it's smaller than your average grocery story eggplant'.[46]

Although for the moment the eggplant has a certain momentum behind it, whether this meaning will endure in the long term is difficult to tell. Slang is notoriously ephemeral. On the other hand, the general process that's happening with this emoji is precisely how language evolves. After all, the word 'penis' itself began as a metaphor, deriving originally from the classical Latin for 'tail'. But over time it became so firmly rooted in the language that these metaphorical beginnings are now long forgotten.

The Dutiful Computer

So emoji are clearly having a significant impact on culture in general and communication in particular. And, to an extent, they're affecting the way people use language – even, in one or two notable ways, leaving their mark on the shape of English. Should this be a cause for concern, then? Are emoji having an adverse effect on the language? Harming the way that people, especially the young, are writing? Generally contributing to the dumbing-down of culture?

As we discussed in Chapter 1, language changes. It's in a constantly dynamic state, altering with the shifts and swells that take place in society more generally. If we take the word 'computer', for example, today this refers to 'an electronic device used for storing and processing data'. Electronic devices used for storing and processing data have been around for about sixty years. The word, on the other hand, has been around for four hundred. It was first recorded in English in the early 1600s. That's three hundred and thirty years before Alan Turing and John von Neumann, early pioneers of computer science. It's three hundred and sixty years before the Apple II or the IBM PC, two of the earliest popular personal computers. In fact, the word 'computer' predates the word 'electricity' by thirty years. In the initial stages of its life, then, it clearly didn't mean what it means today.

We can see what it did refer to by looking at an example of its use from before the digital era, in an extract from a book about the scientific institutions of London in the mid-nineteenth century:

> [T]he computer laboriously makes his way through line after line of his work till he arrives at the bottom of his pages, when his work is complete, and he passes it on to another person for examination. But his duty is never-ending; a new set of computations, involving the same monotonous labour, is awaiting him, and new observations are continually supplying the places of those which have been reduced.[47]

The laboriously employed computer in this scenario is a person rather than a machine – someone whose job it is to make calculations and computations. This was the word's primary meaning until well into the twentieth century. But just as the social world has changed since the days when this profession existed, so the language has also changed. In this case the word has undergone a process of semantic shift. Its form has stayed the same, but its meaning (semantics) has altered to accommodate the new inventions and practices that have entered everyday life.

All languages have a history, which itself is a product of the histories of the people who speak them. The history of English, for example, begins about sixteen hundred years ago when a group of Germanic tribes – the Anglo-Saxons – invaded the island of Great Britain. Given that the human faculty of language first evolved in the species around a hundred thousand years ago, the entire history of English – and all the culture and literature that's been produced in it – is comparatively very short. It occupies little more than 1 per cent of the history of human language. But even in this short space of time it's changed dramatically. Old English – the form of the language spoken between the Anglo-Saxon invasions in 449 AD and the Norman Conquest in 1066 – is almost indecipherable to a modern-day speaker. Here's a line from the *Anglo-Saxon Chronicles*, a history of the British Isles originally compiled around 890:

> Her gregorius papa sende to brytene augustinum mid wel mane-gum munucum þe godes word engla þeoda godspellodon.

Translated into modern English this reads: 'In this year Pope Gregory sent Augustine to Britain with very many monks, who preached God's word to the English nation.'[48] You can probably see a similarity between some of the Old English words and their modern equivalents: *brytene* is Britain; *munucum* is monks; *papa* is pope; *engla* is (of the) Angles (i.e. the English). But there are only two words (*to* and *word*) which are identical in both versions. All the others have changed to some degree, as has the grammatical structure of the sentence. Old English even has letters of the alphabet that we no longer use, such as þ, or 'thorn', which is used for the sound *th* in a word such as *thistle*.

The reason for the constantly changing nature of a language is the constantly changing nature of society. A language changes as populations shift, as societies alter. It changes under the influence of the technologies used to transmit it. Invasions by the Vikings and Normans, the introduction of Christianity, innovations in technology – especially the printing press – all had an impact on English. They introduced new vocabulary from other languages, altered grammatical patterns, standardised spelling and punctuation conventions. This process of language evolution is inexorable and inevitable. And the times we live in are no different in this respect.

It's often argued that the digital revolution is having an outsized effect compared to previous eras of social change on language. For example, this article from back in 2001 contends:

> Not since man uttered his first word and clumsily held a primitive pencil nearly 10,000 years ago has there been such a revolution in language. From tapping abbreviated words into a mobile phone to emailing people on the other side of the Atlantic, today's technology is changing the way in which we communicate at an alarming rate.[49]

As with much mainstream media discussion of the topic, this quote tends towards exaggeration. For a start, it extends the history of writing by five thousand–odd years. But putting aside the hyperbole, is it correct in its general assessment of the situation? Is the digital revolution having profound and deep-rooted effects on language itself? And how do emoji fit within this cycle of change?

One of the most obvious linguistic effects of the digital revolution are the scores of new words flooding into the language in response to new technologies. When someone invents an electronic device for storing and processing data, for example, we need a word to refer to it. There are many different ways in which new words are coined. In the case of 'computer', a process of semantic loaning has taken place: the meaning of a pre-existing word has been extended to include a new sense. This is a common strategy. The same process has happened for words like *mouse* and *tweet* and for countless others: *desktop, spam, web, avatar, troll* and so on.

Another way of forming new words is through blending, as in the examples of *emoticon* or *sexting*. This is how, for example, the Icelandic word for computer was created. When, in 1964, the University of Iceland received its first computer, there was no native word for it in the language. So the writer Sigurður Nordal created one by blending the words for number (*tala*) and prophetess (*völva*) to produce *tölva*, which thus has the etymological meaning of 'prophetess of numbers'.[50]

Or you can add prefixes or suffixes to existing words. This is known as agglutination – new words are created by gluing together parts of other words. In this way we get *retweet* and *unfriend*. In the case of *unfriend*, a process of conversion has also taken place. A new word has been formed by changing the word class of an existing one: the noun *friend* becomes the verb *to friend*. In the same way – although moving in the opposite direction – the verb *like* has changed to a noun.

These types of additions to the lexicon are entirely natural. People might occasionally moan – especially when a pre-existing word has its meaning co-opted or begins to get used as a verb instead of a noun – but in the scheme of things these are all rather superficial changes. The more profound way in which technology has an effect on language is in terms of what it does and doesn't allow people to do. That is to say, people adapt their language practices to the constraints imposed by the technology. And over time, these practices develop into linguistic conventions.

An example of this is the way that English became the dominant online language in the early days of the internet. There were two reasons for this: one of them geographical, the other technological. The first was that much of the early development of the internet took place in English-speaking countries (particularly the United States), so early adopters were mostly English speakers. The second was that the internet's infrastructure largely operated through English. Early character-encoding systems such as ASCII favoured the English alphabet (i.e. the Roman script, but with only those letters of the alphabet used in English and none of the diacritics – such as á, ç, è, ñ, ö, û – that are used in various other alphabetic languages). This meant that, in the early years of the internet, online writing could only use these 26 characters. If you wanted to write in French or Japanese, for example, you had to make do with a modified spelling system which dispensed with all the accents (*vous aviez a ecrire tout sans accents*), or to transliterate everything into the English alphabet (*subete no moji o romaji ni shinakereba naranakatta*). Alternatively, you just wrote in English.

The situation has changed dramatically since then, with much of the internet now being able to cope with a great range of alphabetic and non-alphabetic different scripts, as well as both left-to-right and right-to-left languages – thanks mainly to Unicode. In fact, the internet is now proving to be an excellent tool for helping with the survival of endangered languages.[51] But for the first years of its existence, the capabilities of the technology dictated certain important aspects of people's language practices. The machines in effect enforced a restrictive language policy on anyone who used them.

Another notable example of the architecture of technology influencing the way people use language was texting. SMS (short message service), or texting, was developed in the mid-1980s as one of many initiatives that were introduced as a by-product of the standardising of cellular networks. Initially it was seen as something that would allow telephone engineers to send messages to each another. The idea that it might become one of the defining modes of communication for the first decade of the twenty-first century would have been inconceivable to its developers. It worked by employing unused parts of the telephone system to send written messages. But in order to fit with the signalling formats that the telephone companies were using, the length of the messages was limited to 160 seven-bit characters each. (Which is precisely the length of the previous sentence – minus the full stop.)

This restricted space into which all messages had to be squeezed led to txtspk and the use of a number of common patterns of abbreviation:

> Hope ur feeling a lot better 2day. Sorry so little contact yest. I'm starting 2 hate Tues – nightmare when everyones mind on 5 things @once! M

> Hey philip, how r u? what r yr plans 4 the summer? i m in Slo-intensive lang.course, then paris, then SLO again, then i don't know :). have u finished The Book? p

The majority of abbreviations here make use of logograms, of the sort discussed in Chapter 1. For example, because *2* is pronounced *to*, it can be combined with *day* to form *today* (*2day*). There are also some simple 'shortenings': *yest.* for *yesterday*; and *slo* (in both lower and upper case) for *Slovene*/*Slovenia*. Then there's the omission of vowels (what's sometimes called 'disemvoweling') – e.g. *yr* for *your* – and the use of initials standing in for whole words. Here we've got *M* standing for the texter's name, Martha; while the *p* at the end of the second text is a multilingual example – it stands either for the Slovene *pozdrav* (*greetings*) or *poljubček* (*kisses*) and acts as a farewell.

It's not only vocabulary that gets abbreviated in txtspk – grammar does as well. For example, the sentence *Sorry so little contact yest.* is a condensed form of the more standard *I'm sorry we had so little contact yesterday*. There are also shortcuts taken with capitalisations and punctuation – particularly in the lack of capitals for sentence-beginning words, proper names and the first-person singular pronoun, all of which is a result of the relative complexity of shifting between lower- and upper-case letters on a rudimentary alphanumeric keyboard. Sticking to lower-case letters, or missing out the odd apostrophe (e.g. *everyones*), saved several keystrokes in the pre-smartphone era.

Many of the linguistic innovations found in texting – the features that make it look distinctive and have led to it being described as a new 'dialect' of English – are ways of making the most of what the technology allows. If space weren't restricted, and if keying in letters hadn't been so time-consuming, these abbreviations wouldn't have been so commonplace. Nor are they unique to texting. Many of them were being used in earlier online contexts such as chat rooms, where both speed of typing and brevity were important. When you're rattling out responses on a keyboard in a real-time conversation, speed becomes more important than traditional spelling conventions. And of course, the abbreviation of words generally is not unique to this age or medium. It happened in medieval manuscripts; it happened in the early years of the printing press; and long before textese there was telegraphese.

The heyday of txtspk existed when texting meant using an alphanumeric keypad and when it was the only way to send short messages from mobile devices. Since then, smartphones have brought mobility to other forms of messaging, while predictive texting and touchscreen keyboards have removed the motivation for many of these abbreviations. Much of the linguistic usage outlined has thus already drifted off to become part of the history of the language.

Some of the features of txtspk have spread to other platforms, and the informality of dialogue on social media means that writing conventions are still very relaxed. But even when new technologies impose similar restrictions, this doesn't necessarily mean that the same linguistic forms are used. Twitter, for example, had very similar limitations to texting in terms of message length for the first eleven years of its life yet generally used less abbreviation of this sort. This is probably because it's a much more public form of broadcasting, so people want others to clearly understand what they write (and standard English, as the term implies, suits this purpose much better).

Yet for the decade or so in which txtspk flourished, the effect it was having on language and literacy caused consternation and fear in the more easily excitable portions of the media – much of which has now been passed on to emoji.

Are Emoji Ruining English?

The response to the rise of texting in the 2000s often seemed to take a wholly pessimistic view of the subject. One of the most cited examples of this is the British broadcaster John Humphrys's infamous assertion that 'the texters, the SMS vandals ... are doing to our language what Genghis Khan did to his neighbours eight hundred years ago. They are destroying it: pillaging our punctuation; savaging our sentences; raping our vocabulary.'[52] Even allowing for the fact that the rhetoric has been ratcheted up in the spirit of arresting journalism (the linguist David Crystal calls this some of the most apocalyptic language he's ever encountered on the topic[53]), this is an uncompromising opinion. John Humphrys didn't like texting, at all. And he wasn't the only one.

Since txtspk has disappeared in the rear-view mirror, moral panics of this sort have mostly shifted their focus to emoji – complete with the same 'back to the dark ages' analogies. The marshalling of historical detail is often rather sketchy, but the message is consistent. Kyle Smith in the *New York Post*, for example, grumbles that '[t]ens of thousands of years ago, humans communicated in pictures. The thoughts they sought to convey weren't complicated. That's why we call them cavemen.'[54] Or there's Ben Smithurst, cited in the *Huffington Post*, complaining that 'after 5,000 years of technological progress, we've returned to eking approximate meaning from pictograms'.[55] Then there's Jonathan Jones again, in *The Guardian*, who's convinced that 'the simplest and most common-sense historical and anthropological evidence tells us that Emoji is not "progress" by any definition. It is plainly a step back.'[56] In fact, according to Seema Mody at *CNBC*, the fear is that what we're seeing with emoji is basically 'the death of written language'. And what's particularly concerning is that it's damaging children's ability to communicate effectively. 'If [school] classes need to incorporate the language and symbols used in the mobile/digital world, aren't we just regressing back to the age of hieroglyphs?'[57]

So why is it that new forms of communication – first texting, now emoji – generate such bad press? What is it that provokes such disapproval? And is there any truth to the claims made in attacks like these? There are two points worth making here. The first is that articles which voice this sort of opinion are often based on little, if any, evidence. Empirical studies that have explored the influence of new technologies on language often in fact strongly contradict these sorts of claims. The second point is that these stories are often veiled critiques of a variety of other aspects of contemporary society. It's not just language and literacy they're railing against: it's the way that society is changing in general.

The sociolinguist Crispin Thurlow surveyed a large number of newspaper articles all addressing this topic in relation to texting and found a few distinct patterns in the coverage.[58] In particular he found a tendency for articles to frame their discussions as critiques of the communicative inadequacies of the young. Time and again, direct links were made between a perceived 'decline in standards' and the habits and practices of the younger generation. The articles also tended to negatively contrast modern usages with what they saw as 'correct' or 'proper' English, as this is represented in the works of canonical authors such as Shakespeare and Jane Austen, in order to give the impression that txtspk was uneducated, lazy and inelegant. But the evidence they drew on was inevitably either non-existent or fabricated. In other words, most of the scare stories about the detrimental effects of texting were based on gross exaggeration or pure myth. Thurlow's overall conclusion was that not only is computer-mediated language being badly misrepresented in the media, it's also being used as a scapegoat for general anxieties about the rapid pace of change in society and the perceived threat this poses to the status quo.

As noted earlier, the evidence that does exist indicates that practices such as texting can in fact be an aid to literacy. A study carried out at Coventry University in the UK in 2008, for example, found that – far from having a detrimental effect on children's reading and writing skills – texting was associated with high literacy levels.[59] The researchers showed how txtspk requires an awareness of the relationship between sounds and written English, so when children substitute letters according to the way they're pronounced, such as using *l8r* for *later*, they need an understanding of what the original word should be. Being able to handle linguistic abbreviations thus relies on an underlying knowledge of the conventional spelling system of English. And, more generally, due to texting and other mobile communication systems, children today are simply more engaged with written language than children of even a generation ago.[60] In other words, literacy is becoming ever more central to everyday life as a direct result of these new technologies.

There's similar evidence that emoji can be very beneficial in educational contexts. Their visual appeal, and the intuitive way they work as a communication system, has made them especially useful as a learning resource for younger or more vulnerable children, as well as those struggling with language disorders.[61] In Australia, for example, emoji-based projects assist with the Child Protection Curriculum and are used as a way of supporting pupils at the very beginning of their school careers when they may feel particularly vulnerable or anxious.[62] Then there are apps such as Wemogee, a collaboration between speech therapist Francesca Polini and Samsung, which translates verbal phrases into emoji as an aid for people with aphasia.[63]

Beyond these specialised uses, emoji can also serve a more heuristic educational purpose. The fact that they've evolved from similar basic practices as all other forms of writing means they can be an excellent prism for understanding human communication in general. They're especially insightful as an exemplar of the increased role that technology is playing in our lives – and how this is forcing us to come up with solutions which are both completely modern while also harking back to the very earliest forms of literate culture.

In many ways it seems strange that people should get so upset about innovations in the shape of language. The linguistic forms that provoke so much complaint when used online are likely to be easily tolerated, if not celebrated, in other contexts. The demise of punctuation conventions in online communication may worry some, but then the final chapter of James Joyce's *Ulysses* is entirely punctuation-free (except for one full stop at the very end). There may be a rise of colloquialisms and non-standard spelling creeping into online language use, but then writers from Emily Brontë through George Bernard Shaw to Irvine Welsh have all exploited the use of regional and social dialects in their work. And, as we'll see in Chapter 8, the creative potential that emoji provide is one of the main drivers behind their popularity. As a species we've always adapted language to the contexts and purposes for which we use it; and colloquialisms, abbreviations – and now emoji – are perfectly suited to the casual, personal communication that takes place via social media. The overriding point to make, then, is that the way the language looks at any one stage of its evolution does not impact in any fundamental way on how we live our lives. Of far greater importance than fluctuations in linguistic style and form are the types of communication that digital technologies facilitate and what these mean for people's interpersonal relationships. And it's here where more of a critical approach to emoji *is* probably justified. Yet oddly, this has been almost completely absent from the media discourse.

5   The Shaping Force of Digital Technology

*3.5 Degrees of Separation 💾 Upgrade Culture 💾 A Proposal
for Correcting, Improving and Ascertaining Emoji 💾
Malevolent Literary Devices 💾 The Robot's Handwriting 💾
Prêt-à-parler*

3.5 Degrees of Separation

Jonathan Swift wrote of four different journeys that Gulliver
undertook. It was during the third of these that he was shown
around the city of Lagado, where he met the academicians who
spoke with objects instead of words. By the end of his fourth
journey, he'd returned to England. But by this time he could no
longer abide living in human society, so he became a recluse,
spending most of his days talking to his horses.

Two hundred years later, the Hungarian writer Frigyes
Karinthy resurrected Gulliver for two further adventures. In the
first of these, *Voyage to Faremido*, Gulliver crashes on a planet
populated by robot-like beings who speak a language made
entirely of musical sounds. In the second, *Capillaria*, Gulliver
travels to an undersea world ruled exclusively by women. The
male inhabitants of this world are all of diminutive stature and are
fed upon by the hedonistic women – thus setting up a scenario in
which Gulliver can muse on the differences between the sexes,
both here and back on planet Earth.[1]

Frigyes Karinthy is probably more famous today for his short
story 'Chain-links', in which he introduces the idea that everyone
in the world is connected to each other through six degrees of
separation. In the late 1990s, this idea was taken as the name for

the first recognisable social media site, SixDegrees.com. Six links in the chain was always a speculative number – Karinthy simply made it up – and these days people estimate that modern social media means you're only ever an average of 3.57 links away from anyone else in the world.[2] In other words, there's a good chance that one of my friends will have a friend who will be friends with someone you know.

The site SixDegrees.com didn't last long – the technology to sustain it wasn't sufficiently developed at the time – but the concept it kicked off was adopted and taken forward by others: first Friendster, then MySpace and then, most successfully, Facebook. The rise of social media changed the internet from being a place where people consumed information and content to one built around participation and interaction. The online experience became more dynamic, no longer primarily about reading or watching but also about writing and creating. More and more, applications that had begun with one main aim, such as selling books or streaming music, started to include commenting and sharing capabilities, allowing users to interact with each other. Cross-platform sharing options were also added, encouraging further interpersonal connections, until people's personal networks became a fundamental part of the architecture of the online world.

Such is the prominence of social media today that there are now scores of niche and idiosyncratic social media sites, tailored to all types of interests. These include the Swedish Fishbrain,[3] which gives fishing enthusiasts a forum in which to bond over their catches; and Ravelry, which brings together a community of knitters, crocheters and anyone else working in the medium of yarn.[4] There was even, for some reason, a short-lived social network built around ex-*Knight Rider* and *Baywatch* actor David Hasselhoff, known as HoffSpace.[5]

A couple of years after emoji went mainstream, there was a short spate of emoji-only social networks. The first of these was Emojicate, which developed its own custom-made range of characters with which its users were encouraged to communicate.

This was followed by Emojli, where messages, usernames and even the interface itself were all in emoji (the standard Unicode versions, this time). Then there was Steven, named after a cat belonging to one of the developers' girlfriends.[6] None of these really caught the public imagination.[7] They were a little too gimmicky, even for the internet. When the online news site TechCrunch wanted to write about the launch of Emojli, for example, its developers said they'd only be interviewed through the medium of emoji.[8] A proposition which highlighted quite how limited the site was as a viable social media platform.

The link between social media and emoji in general, though, is an important and enduring one. Emoji were born to fulfil precisely the sort of need that results from the purpose and practicalities of social media. Sites like Facebook are founded on people connecting and engaging with each other. They're used as much for what's known as 'phatic communication' – talking about trivial issues such as the weather or sports as a means of social bonding – as they are for conveying information. The shift to the 'social' internet thus opened the way for more conversational exchanges between users and the need for the sorts of written language resources we've been looking at in previous chapters: the sorts of resources which parallel the non-verbal communication that accompanies speech and that provide some of the social glue which can be lost with online writing but which, as the name implies, are one of the main purposes of social media. In other words, emoji are a solution to a social problem that technology has created. But tellingly they're a *technological* solution, and as such they have a number of interesting characteristics that other types of language don't have to contend with.

Upgrade Culture

Words can fall out of fashion for a number of reasons: an alternative word can come along to describe the same concept; the phenomenon to which the word refers can slip into obscurity; or the word can simply lose its popularity. As part of the research that goes into keeping dictionaries up to date, lexicographers track both new words that enter the vocabulary and existing words that are no longer used so often. Once these neglected words fall below a certain usage threshold, they get marked as obsolete. This means they're likely to be dropped from the smaller dictionaries to free up space for the new words.[9]

Take 'snollygoster', for example. In nineteenth- and early twentieth-century America, this was regularly used to refer to a shrewd but dishonest person, particularly one involved in politics. It was a favourite of Harry Truman, apparently, who frequently used it to describe members of the Republican Party. But its popularity has waned since then – so much so that, a few years ago, it was delisted by Merriam-Webster from their popular *Collegiate Dictionary*.

Another example is 'wittol', meaning a man tolerant of his wife's unfaithfulness or, as the *Oxford English Dictionary* puts it, 'a contented cuckold'. This hasn't been in current usage since the 1940s, which is why, in 2011, *Collins Dictionary* decided to drop it from their pages in order to make space for a batch of new words.[10] In the same cull they also got rid of 'alienism' (an alternative for 'psychiatry'), 'cyclogyro' (an aircraft with rotating blades sticking out from its side) and 'cassette player'.

Words thrive or wither based on a process of natural selection, with their popularity – as well as the shades of meaning they have – dependent on the community who use them. If enough people were to start using 'wittol' again, in the same way that some people have re-embraced 'cuckold' (particularly in the context of US politics), it could yet have a second lease of life. It all depends on the impulses of the communal imagination.

For emoji the situation is rather different. Their existence, and the factors that govern their creation and evolution, are quite unlike anything that other forms of language experience. They're less a product of natural selection than of genetic engineering. And because they're native-born to technology, they're prey to the same dynamics that govern the existence and evolution of all technology in today's consumer society. In particular, this involves a mixture of two factors which have had a massive influence on the mindset of modern-day life.

The term 'planned obsolescence' is used in industrial design to refer to the way that products are often created to have a limited lifespan. After a certain period, they'll either no longer function in the way they once did or have gone out of fashion. Either way, consumers are prompted to replace them sooner than they should strictly need to. The phrase dates back to the 1930s, when the property developer Bernard London wrote a pamphlet entitled 'Ending the Depression Through Planned Obsolescence'. It was then popularised in the 1950s by the industrial designer Brooks Stevens, who used it as a sort of catchphrase. His definition of it was an ideology that would instil 'in the buyer the desire to own something a little newer, a little better, a little sooner than is necessary'.[11] Throughout the latter half of the twentieth century and into the twenty-first, this idea became second nature to consumerist culture.

If we combine this with Moore's Law, we have a good approximation of the digital environment in which we live these days. Moore's Law is the prediction, first made by the electrical engineer Gordon E. Moore, that the number of transistors one can fit into a computer chip will double every two years. He proposed a version of this idea as far back as 1965, and it's pretty much held true ever since.[12] Its significance lies in the fact that it doesn't simply describe the rate at which computer chips increase in power but also the way that technology more generally advances at an exponential rate year on year.[13] Processing speed, memory capacity, size and price – all these things are continually growing or shrinking. And this means that the devices we have in our pockets, on our desks or in our homes are constantly increasing their capabilities, constantly offering more and faster functions.

The dramatic impact that has resulted from this 'law' is not confined to the technology sector alone. A knock-on effect can be felt across all aspects of our lives. It's altered the technology we use to communicate, which in turn has changed the ways in which we relate to each other and organise ourselves as communities. It's altered the information technology that underpins the way the financial sector works and the diagnostic and pharmaceutical equipment that's now a central part of modern medicine. Even the everyday household objects that provide the basic texture of our lives are the result of computer-facilitated product design.

And while the innovations that stem from this technology are usually seen as synonymous with progress, the implications they have aren't always positive. Issues such as the erosion of privacy and the increase in surveillance culture can be related directly back to the pervasiveness of mobile and networked technology, both of which have been made possible by the increased power and speed of computers.

Another consequence of the technology-driven changes in today's world is that we're constantly having to adapt to new ways of doing things. This is nowhere more noticeable than with communication. From mobile technology meaning that we're now always potentially contactable to the way that specific platforms such as Facebook, Twitter and Snapchat all offer us slightly different options for inter-acting with each other – and refine their services on an almost-weekly basis – digital tech means that interpersonal communication is now a rapidly and unceasingly evolving process.

Emoji, as we've seen, are a response to this process of change. In one sense they're born from the consequence that Moore's Law has had for communication and the way that technological change (the era of the smartphone) has led to social change (a move towards informal text-based chatting), which requires us to adapt our ways of doing things. But because emoji are a techno-logical solution, they've become pulled into this accelerated cycle of change themselves – and they too are characterised by a sort of built-in obsolescence. They've become part of the upgrade culture that characterises today's society.

As discussed earlier, emoji's existence relies entirely on the software that sustains them. It's the software on individual devices which gives them their physical presence. On a yearly basis, the Unicode Consortium adds a further set of anywhere from sixty to a hundred emoji to the total, which the tech companies then gradually roll out to their own devices. From the Consortium's perspective, this is part of the ongoing enhancement and maintenance of the system. It allows them to respond to feedback about cultural representation, about their overall usefulness and so on. But this yearly upgrading has also become an attractive reason for people to upgrade their devices more generally. It's now seen as a marketing opportunity for the tech companies – yet another way to persuade people to buy something a little newer and better, a littler earlier than necessary.

And it's not just a matter of keeping up with digital fashions. If the software is out of date, holes start appearing in the system. Aliens in boxes, or unspecified question marks, start showing up in your messages. It doesn't matter if you yourself are content with creating your messages from an older, impoverished set of emoji: if your friends have upgraded to the latest set, you're still going to end up running into communication problems.

In some ways this is just a new twist on an age-old issue. Language is always tied in subtle – and sometimes not-so-subtle – ways to economic factors. It always involves certain people having access to communicative resources that are closed off to others. Yet for the most part this happens in less tangible ways. A good education, for example, will help give you the sort of literacy skills that are valued in the job market. Being educated at certain schools, or in certain affluent areas, will give you the sort of accent which is highly valued in society. The lottery of being brought up in an English-speaking country means that your native language has both prestige and use-value across the globe. 'Resources' such as these are never equally distributed across the population, yet they can have far-reaching implications for people's life chances.

Not having access to the latest set of emoji is not quite in the same bracket as facing daily prejudice and discrimination because of your accent, of course. But, given the way that technology is playing an ever-greater role in the way we communicate, the issues represented by emoji in this respect are perhaps an indication of the future of linguistic inequality.

A Proposal for Correcting, Improving and Ascertaining Emoji

The logic of the market is one major influence in the everyday life of emoji, then. But how about that other inescapable instrument of control over our everyday actions and behaviours: government or institutional regulation? Are emoji subject to the same sort of authority that tries to dictate the shape and usage of many of the natural languages around the world?

Despite satirising the ambitions of people like Thomas Sprat and John Wilkins, Jonathan Swift did actually hold strong beliefs about the need for English to be regulated. He wrote a letter to the prime minister suggesting that 'some Method should be thought of for ascertaining and fixing our Language for ever'. His idea was that a panel of experts be appointed to advise on this, following the model of the *Académie française*, which had been overseeing the French language since 1634.

> In order to reform our Language, I conceive, My Lord, that a free judicious Choice should be made of such Persons, as are generally allowed to be best qualified for such a Work, without any regard to Quality, Party, or Profession.[14]

The idea never came to anything. On the death of Queen Mary in 1694, Swift returned to Ireland, and today he's remembered for shaping the language and culture through his writing rather than through regulation and reformation.

English is unusual among European languages in not having a regulative body. From the late sixteenth century onward, when the *Accademia della Crusca* of Florence was founded, one after another of the major European nations has established something similar. Today, everything from Chinese to Cherokee and Filipino to Finnish has an academy. There are language academies for invented languages such as Esperanto (the *Akademio de Esperanto*); and for dead languages like Latin (the Pontifical Academy for Latin in Vatican City).

So what does a language academy do? If we take the *Académie français* as an example, among its principal tasks are the production of a national dictionary (the *Dictionnaire de l'Académie française*) and the general promotion and oversight of the language, particularly in terms of its role as a fundamental part of French identity. This includes advising the government on usage and new terminology. Over the last few decades, much of this has focused on trying to stem the influence of English on the language.[15] To this end, the *Académie* devises a list of 'what to say, and what not to say', where it offers home-grown alternatives to Anglicisms that are creeping into the language. For example, rather than say 'La prolifération des **fake news**', it suggests you try 'La prolifération des contre-vérités'. And if you want to talk about being kept in the loop, you shouldn't say 'Gardez-moi **dans la loop**' but rather 'Gardez-moi informé'.[16]

Emoji, as we've discussed, are overseen by the Unicode Consortium. So how does the Consortium's role compare to a language academy? Are there similarities between the two which can help us to understand how emoji work as a system of communication and how their role in society is regulated?

Unlike language academies, the Unicode Consortium isn't a national body. Its ambitions, in fact, are expressly international: it aims to support writing systems from across all the globe. Despite this, however, it's very heavily weighted towards an American influence. Based in Mountain View, California, it has twelve voting members, the majority of which are US-based firms such as IBM, Apple, Microsoft and Facebook. The other voting members include the Chinese telecommunications company Huawei and the German software corporation SAP. Plus the Sultanate of Oman, for some doubtless perfectly logical reason. The result is that, as we'll see later, a Western bias tends to creep into the way certain decisions are made, even when the Consortium is trying its hardest to be culturally inclusive.

Although the Consortium standardises the representation of all text for computers around the globe, the popularity of emoji means that their oversight has become one of its most high-profile focuses over the last few years. In fact, so much has this become the case that there have been criticisms recently that resources and attention are being diverted from more marginalised writing systems.[17]

Among the issues the Consortium decides upon are the order in which the different characters should be listed (they don't have a conventional order in the way that an alphabet does, after all) and which new characters get included in the yearly updates.[18] The process for creating a new emoji works as follows. Someone (and it can be pretty much anyone) comes up with an idea for a new character and puts together a proposal. The Consortium then evaluates this based on a variety of factors. These include whether or not there's a need for the new symbol, how useful it's likely to be and whether it's going to have a global uptake (rather than being relevant to only a select group of users).[19] There are also a number of factors which can disqualify proposals from consideration. The new symbol can't be a logo or brand, for example; it can't be a specific person or a god; and it can't be something which is likely to be too culturally ephemeral. A good example of a character which ticks all these criteria is the dumpling emoji, which was introduced in 2017.[20] A dumpling clearly isn't a brand, god or something with limited longevity potential. On the other hand, it does have global appeal and is likely to be widely used – as the proposal for the emoji noted, dumplings are popular all around the globe, whether in the form of Polish *pierogi*, Russian *pelmeni*, Japanese *gyoza*, Italian *ravioli*, Georgian *khinkali*, Korean *mandu*, Spanish *empanadas*, Chinese *jiaozi*, etc. – so surely the virtual world should have one as well.

Over the last few years, there have been a number of high-profile campaigns for emoji that people felt were lacking from the current system. All of these are related, in some respect or other, to specific social issues – to the type of world that emoji reflect and the biases that have been inadvertently built into the system. For example, in 2015 the American long-distance runner Molly Huddle proposed the addition of a female runner because, at the time, athletics was only represented by a male character. As she commented, for her this was a small but significant act for addressing gender equality, 'sort of like when a little girl asks for a doll that looks more like her'.[21] Similarly, Rayouf Alhumedhi, a fifteen-year-old student living in Germany, proposed the 'woman wearing a hijab' emoji, as again this more accurately represented the cultural world that she and millions of others lived in.[22]

Jennifer 8. Lee, who led the campaign for the dumpling emoji, has since gone on to set up Emojination with the ecosystem architect Jeanne Brooks and the artist Yiying Lu, an organisation whose mission is to 'give voice to the people about emojis' and to counter the fact that '[t]he decision makers along the way are generally male, white, and engineers. They specialise in encoding. Such a review process certainly is less than ideal for promoting a vibrant visual language used throughout the world.'[23] And their initiative has had a definite effect on widening the cultural vocabulary of emoji. Along with the dumpling and hijab symbols, Emojination have since gone on to create a sauna emoji in collaboration with the Finnish government, a broccoli emoji (aimed, particularly at the vegetarian community), a red envelope emoji with the Chinese tech company Baidu and a DNA emoji.

We'll return later to the surprisingly complicated issues about exactly how representative and inclusive emoji can be. For the moment, the important point to note is the process by which new symbols are created and how this differs from the ways that new words are coined in natural languages. In a language like English, a new word, or neologism, becomes part of common usage when it's picked up by the community and starts being used on a regular basis. If, for example, the population at large began spontaneously using 'refudiate' in everyday conversation, it would, within time, become a recognised part of the English lexicon. There'd be no need for Sarah Palin to submit a written proposal to a language academy, arguing for the cultural importance of her word and entreating them to recognise it as an official addition to the language.

Emoji, on the other hand, are entirely dependent for their existence on what the Unicode Consortium thinks will be popular or useful. Yes, anyone can propose a new symbol. But for it actually to become a reality it needs to pass through the convoluted committee process to then be adopted across the different operating systems, which then release their own distinct design for it as part of a software update – all of which can take well over a year.

The fact that all new additions are what the Consortium thinks will be popular and believes reflect the interests of society is, arguably, somewhat similar to what the *Académie français* does when it recommends various alternatives to the Anglicisms it feels are polluting French. But the *Académie* has no power to actually enforce its recommendations. If the population at large prefer to use 'fake news' rather than 'contre-vérités', there's little the academicians can do about it. Whereas once the Unicode Consortium decides that a dumpling symbol is needed, this will turn up on your phone at some stage whether you want it or not 🥟.

Malevolent Literary Devices

The other major role performed by the *Académie français* is the production of a national dictionary. According to the satirist Ambrose Bierce, a dictionary is a 'malevolent literary device for cramping the growth of a language and making it hard and inelastic'.[24] As he was quick to add, though, his own project *The Devil's Dictionary* – in which this definition appears – is of course 'a most useful work'. The problem he had with the rest of the genre was the way works aimed to 'fix' the language. Before the very first dictionaries had been invented, back in the

> golden prime and high noon of English speech; when from the lips of the great Elizabethans fell words that made their own meaning and carried it in their very sound; when a Shakespeare and a Bacon were possible, and the language now rapidly perishing at one end

and slowly renewed at the other was in vigorous growth and hardy preservation – sweeter than honey and stronger than a lion – the lexicographer was a person unknown, the dictionary a creation which his Creator had not created him to create.

It could be argued that there's no need for an emoji dictionary. Their popularity, after all, is based on the fact that they're intuitive to use. Each character means what it looks like. Creating an annotated list that tells you that 🍎 = 'apple', 🥊 = 'boxing glove', 🛶 = 'canoe' would be rather redundant.

But there's a little more to it than this, of course. The way people actually use emoji, often improvising as they go along, results in meanings being created on the fly. People draw on visual metaphors, on puns and word play. In fact, much of the appeal of emoji is that they allow for a range of creative meaning-making. To adapt Bierce's words, we're living in a time when emoji make their own meaning and carry it in their very appearance. Things aren't yet settled across the emoji lexicon. And they certainly aren't fixed.

This is why, for some people, there's a pressing need for a dedicated emoji dictionary. In contexts such as the law, where determining the exact meaning of a statement can have far-reaching consequences, a definitive record would be extremely helpful. As the *New York Times* journalist Amanda Hess writes, legal interpretations are challenging because emoji have 'no fixed emotional resonance, clear dictionary definition, or established grammatical rules for interpreting them in the various contexts in which they appear'.[25] For this reason Eric Goldman, professor of law at Santa Clara University, argues that the creation of an emoji dictionary is an imperative, given the way that online communication is evolving and the dominant role it now plays in so many people's lives.[26]

So what would an emoji dictionary look like? If we continue the comparison with language academies, the Unicode Consortium itself offers short annotations for each character which provide some indication of their intended meaning and usage, as well as a descriptive name. But, as the Consortium itself notes, this doesn't 'encompass all the possible meanings of an emoji character'. Indeed, 'in some cases', the Consortium warns, these basic definitions 'may even be misleading'.[27]

More helpful are a couple of the proto-dictionaries that exist online. The most useful reference point for almost everything emoji-related is the website Emojipedia.com. This catalogues the full range of different characters, gives information about their official names and the way they appear on the various different platforms (including how these have changed over the years) and provides some very brief information about meaning. What it doesn't do, for the moment at least, is offer anything approaching a comprehensive definition of the real-world meanings of the different emoji, based on evidence of how people actually use them.

Another notable proto-dictionary is the crowdsourced Emoji Dictionary, which encourages users to submit their own definitions[28] in much the way that Urban Dictionary does. In theory this would produce a more accurate picture of the meanings people actually assign to the different characters – Urban Dictionary, after all, has been cited as an authority in a number of law cases. But at the moment the project has a rather chaotic overall look and presents a very subjective view of what the different emoji might plausibly mean. It's not by any means the authoritative catalogue of meanings and usage that an established dictionary of English is.

So what would a dedicated emoji dictionary look like? The lexicographer Jane Solomon believes it would necessarily need to be one based on historical principles – i.e. including information about the history and cultural context of definitions, in the way that the *Oxford English Dictionary* does for English. This is because the meanings of emoji can depend upon how the characters are displayed at different times, as well as how they're displayed on different platforms. In both cases, differences in design can alter the way people use them, thus creating distinctive connotations. This is analogous to the way that variation in verbal language exists from place to place and community to community, such as the different spelling conventions between British and American English. But as we saw in the previous chapter, it also means that a universal interpretation of any one emoji is never entirely possible, despite the fact that they're 'standardised' by the Unicode Consortium.

An approach drawing on the way people actually use the symbols was the one chosen by Dictionary.com when they began including usage notes about certain emoji as part of their main dictionary in the spring of 2018.[29] For example, the definition they give of the 'sweat droplets emoji' 💦 highlights the way that in 'sexual contexts, [this symbol] is used to depict sexual fluids' before then going on to add that sometimes 'this emoji also represents actual sweat or water and is completely unrelated to sex'.[30]

To what extent the development of a comprehensive emoji dictionary along these lines would then begin to 'fix' the meaning of emoji is difficult to say. Dictionaries today are meant to describe rather than prescribe how a language is used, although invariably they end up doing the latter to some extent – especially when they're viewed as an authority on correct usage. This is precisely why Bierce complained of the way they made language hard and inelastic.

Although we don't at present have a full reference dictionary for emoji, there are already certain sorts of devices which prescribe meaning and structure the way emoji are used. Many operating systems today include emoji as part of their predictive texting options. Whereas you previously needed to switch keyboards when you wanted to insert an emoji, now you're automatically offered options for this as you type, giving you the chance to integrate characters directly and easily into the sentence. The important and relevant point in this context, though, is that the recommendations are based on an internal dictionary that the phone or computer uses which pre-empts the meanings of characters. If I type 'confused', for example, I'll get 😕. Or for 'okay' I'll be offered 👌. In other words the software companies are themselves beginning to prescribe the meanings of emoji and, in doing so, nudging us towards orthodoxy.

The Robot's Handwriting

The French surrealist writer Michel Leiris recounts an incident in his autobiography in which, as a child, he once ate too much alphabetti spaghetti, which, as he puts it, resulted in him suddenly bringing 'back up, to the great detriment of the tablecloth . . . an endless series of letters I had not incorporated'.[31] As the novelist Tom McCarthy comments, this is a perfect metaphor for the way that, 'far from being a tool for refining the world into concepts, language is what mixes with saliva in your mouth, gets kneaded by your tongue and teeth, repeats on you'.[32] In other words, language has a material quality to it. And this is the case for all language, not just that shaped out of canned foodstuffs. Language isn't simply a disembodied system of communication which allows thoughts to pass from one mind to another. It has a physical existence – be this in the sounds of our speech or the scratches we make when writing. And this physical element is important. It can modify or inflect the overall message we're communicating as well as acting as an index of our identity.

This is most obviously the case with spoken language, where the distinctive sound of our voice becomes part of our personality, as does everything from the speed and volume at which we speak to the particular words and phrases we tend to favour. But it also happens with written language. In fact, towards the end of the nineteenth century, a whole 'science' developed around this idea, led by books such as Rosa Baughan's *Character Indicated by Handwriting: A Practical Treatise in Support of the Assertion that the Hand Writing of a Person is an Infallible Guide to His Character*. Today, making sweeping statements about psychological traits based on someone's handwriting is considered little more than pseudoscience. Yet handwriting can still indicate a great deal about a person, including the history of their schooling and the mental state they were in when doing the writing – whether they were rushed, stressed and so on.

Handwriting is also seen as a sign of authenticity and immediacy, acting as a physical bridge between reader and writer. In the mid-twentieth century, the philosopher Martin Heidegger wrote an extended reflection on the way that machines – and specifically the typewriter – were changing the act of writing. His belief was that the existence and use of the hand was one of the main defining traits of what it meant to be human. 'No animal has a hand, and a hand never originates from a paw or a claw or talon,' he wrote. We use our hands to pray, to murder, to greet each other, to give thanks and to make oaths. And, of course, we use them to write. For Heidegger, the 'word as script is handwriting'. But the typewriter alters this direct bond between the written word and its creator. It 'conceals the handwriting and thereby the character', he lamented. 'The typewriter makes everyone look the same.'[33]

With the rise of computer-mediated communication, the physical relationship between person and text has become further obscured. And emoji are perhaps the perfect example of this. Despite the fact that their visual quality is such a key part of their identity, we, as writers, have no influence over this. The look and aesthetic of emoji are pre-given. What's more, they're always mediated by the computer. Emoji may be a communication system designed around the look of the body, but they exist entirely independently of the shaping properties of our own bodies. They exist entirely within the software. And for the sort of social media communication in which emoji are used, technology is slowly filtering out the human element of language. Language is no longer something we physically mould ourselves and which retains the imprint of our bodies: the distinctive sounds of our voice, the way we manipulate a pen. It's standardised to the point at which it becomes entirely disembodied.

But the computer's control over our use of language isn't restricted to its material quality. It's also beginning to encroach on how we place the letters of the alphabet together, how we put one word after another and which emoji we choose. We're approaching a situation now where the computer is meeting us halfway in the act of composition itself, with the algorithms that govern features such as autocorrect and autocomplete beginning to shape not only the form of language we use but also what we do with this language.

As with so much recent technology, these features have come a long way in a very short time. Autocorrect began as a spellchecker with a little executive power. If you typed something like 'mis-taek', it would automatically alter it for you. In 2007, Microsoft added the Grammar Checker, which would check spellings within their context, picking up on things such as incorrectly conjugated verbs within a sentence and then underlining them with a helpful wavy green line. It also began making corrections across separate words, so that 'All th ebest' would be unravelled to 'All the best'.

At the beginning of the 2010s, smartphones further trans-formed the writing experience by adding a more emboldened autocorrect, along with an autocomplete function. Suddenly your phone was instinctively replacing words it thought were spelt incorrectly and offering a range of options to save you typing out things in full. This had its pluses and minuses. Among the drawbacks was the fact that this new-found aggressiveness often ended up altering your messages in bizarre, confusing and some-times downright inappropriate ways.

Then there's predictive texting, which uses a form of artificial intelligence to calculate what you're likely to type next, based on grammatical patterns and your previous texting history. It even adapts its suggestions according to what it knows about the different styles you use in different contexts – informal for instant messaging with friends, formal for email with colleagues and so on. In other words, the computer is helping you heed the advice that Nietzsche gave about matching your style 'to the specific person with whom you wish to communicate'. In fact, it's coer-cing you into doing this.

Spelling isn't an issue for emoji, of course. But predictive language choice is. And, as we noted at the end of the previous section, this is something which can have an effect on the mean-ings that individual emoji have. If you type 'hugs' on an iPhone, for example, you'll be offered 😊 as a replacement. And it's not just verbal language that gets emojified. Emoticons are also seen as replaceable. Typing :-| prompts the software's internal dictionary to offer up an eclectic choice of bemused and embarrassed emoji faces, the thumbs up, haloes and sunglasses.

Nietzsche, like Heidegger, was highly sceptical of the typewriter and of how '[o]ur writing tools are ... working on our thoughts'.[34] The assistance we now get from algorithms is yet another way in which this happens – another way in which the act of writing doesn't offer the same form of expression it once did. That's not to say that written language today doesn't still express our individuality or that it isn't still endlessly diverse. It's true that the direct link between the distinctive actions of the hand and the written word may no longer be central to the process. But this has been replaced by the ease with which we can mix and manipulate words and images, the ways we can re-craft and circulate messages. While one element of the compositional process is becoming ever more standardised, other opportunities are opening up which allow us new and diverse ways to express ourselves.

Prêt-à-parler

Frigyes Karinthy hasn't been the only person to entertain the idea of converting Gulliver's adventures into science fiction. The creators of *Star Trek*, Gene Roddenberry and Herb Solow, were also inspired by the idea. At one stage they even briefly thought about calling their series *Gulliver's Travels* and naming the central character Captain Gulliver.[35] It was presumably the idea of exploring alternative worlds which could be used as a contrast to human culture that appealed to them – and this was something that found its way into the series even when they'd decided against borrowing so directly from Swift.

A good example of this sort of Swiftian cultural experimentation occurs in the *Star Trek: The Next Generation* episode 'Darmok'. In this, the crew of the Starship *Enterprise* make contact with a race of aliens known as the Tamarians, whose language is structured entirely around allegory.[36] Rather than describing things directly, the Tamarians allude to them by making references to scenarios from the cultural history they all share as a community. If they want to convey loneliness, for example, they refer to an incident in which one of their mythic heroes is all alone on the ocean; if they want to tell someone to be quiet, they talk about the stillness of a river in wintertime. Unfortunately, because this language relies so exclusively on allegory, the crew of the *Enterprise* can't understand what the Tamarians are saying, even though their universal translator can render all the individual words into English. Without a grounded knowledge of the culture to which the allegories refer, the speech is all but meaningless, and intercultural communication becomes impossible.

The reason this works as a conceit for science fiction is that it's based, however tangentially, on the way that human language itself works. Every language is interwoven with references to the culture and history of the groups who speak it. And many words and phrases draw their meaning directly from the stories which make up this culture. We can describe people as Scrooge-like or quixotic, relying on our audience's knowledge of these fictional characters to understand what we mean. English is littered with Classical and Biblical allusions, from *Spartan* and *narcissistic* to *philistines, good Samaritans, forbidden fruit* and *sodomy*. Literary and cultural allusions even underpin the meaning of some emoji, in symbols such as 🍑 and 🙈🙉🙊.

The set-up of the *Star Trek* episode pushes the idea to an extreme, of course. It takes one particular element of the way that language is meaningful and extrapolates this into a thought experiment in which cultural allusion is so integral to the way people communicate that they become imprisoned in their own myth-based worldview. Yet the extremes to which the idea is pushed here are also, in a way, strangely similar to the ways in which online communication is evolving. The speculative conceit behind the Tamarians' language has a great many parallels with meme-based communication.

Online memes are a mixture of the ready-made and the remix. They use fragments of shared culture – often in the form of visuals – as succinct chunks of meaning to express an attitude or a reaction to a situation. The concept was first coined by the author Mike Godwin back in 1993. (This is the same Mike Godwin of Godwin's Law: the prediction that the longer an online discussion continues, the greater the likelihood that someone will make a comparison that involves Hitler.) Godwin was adapting the concept that Richard Dawkins had proposed within the context of evolutionary biology: a cultural idea or practice that spreads, mostly through mimicry, from one person to another and thus through a community. The examples that Dawkins gave included everything from catch-phrases and fashion trends to ideological martyrdom – each of them an idea which somehow grabs the attention of the popular imagination and gets replicated across groups of people until it becomes part of the fabric of the culture.

As the journalist Amelia Tait has pithily noted, since Godwin first applied the term to online communication its use has broadened so that now it often seems to mean little more than 'funny internet picture'.[37] It's not just pictures, of course. The category also includes animated gifs, screenshots, cartoons, quotes, hashtags and stickers. In some cases memes can simply be single words or phrases which have been misspelt – the enigma that was 'covfefe', for example.[38] But whatever their format, the basic process by which they function is the same. Usually drawing on popular culture as a language of expression, they're ideas or fragments of information that spread via imitation and repetition across the internet, becoming a shared cultural phenomenon.[39]

So where do emoji fit with all this? The basic answer is that emoji can be seen as close cousins of memes. In certain contexts they function in a very similar way, being a form of ready-made communication which one selects from a menu then slots into a conversation. For example, one of the most common forms of meme communication is the reaction face. This is the use of a short close-up of someone's facial expression reacting to a situation, which is sent in place of a written reply in social media conversations. The clip is usually a fragment extracted from pop culture (from a film or TV show) and used as a way of expressing a response which would be difficult to convey in words alone.

Importantly, the use of reaction faces is facilitated by the technology available on smartphones or social media sites, which means they're very simple to incorporate into messages. For example, the online database Giphy allows people to search for and share animated GIFs with great ease:[40] you simply type in a word like 'confused' and get a range of clips of people giving exaggerated expressions of the emotion, which you then send as an illustration of your own current state of befuddlement.

Emoji – and emoticons before them – are used in a similar way, albeit with a more stylised and static representation of emotions. As was discussed earlier, they gesture towards human emotion rather than imitating it in any great visual detail. For the millions of users of the standard set of emoji, this works as a perfectly adequate way of expressing emotion. For some, however, it has its limitations. Artists Molly Young and Teddy Blanks, for example, found the cartoon-like quality of emoji too bland, so they decided to create a set of stickers using close-ups of faces from portraits by artists such as Frans Hals, Jan Steen and Lucas Cranach the Elder which, they felt, offered 'a wider, starker, more virulently passionate range of human emotions'.[41] In contexts such as this, then, emoji are one form of a more general practice of visual communication which has been made possible by today's technology.

There are also cases in which emoji themselves have become memes or where they replicate elements from popular memes. This is the case with the aforementioned facepalm – an action in which one places one's face in one's hand as a sign of despair at someone's absurd behaviour. The first manifestations of this took the form of photos from popular culture – a particularly widespread one shows Patrick Stewart, in the role of Jean-Luc Picard from *Star Trek: The Next Generation*, with his head disconsolately cradled in his hands. In the mid-1990s, 'facepalm' began also being used as a word, and by the second half of the 2010s it had its own emoji 🤦.

In this case, the emoji is replicating a pre-existing meme. But emoji can also become memes in their own right, as in the case of the 'Thinking Face' 🤔. As the journalist Glenn Greenwald tweeted, adding this to a conversation indicates that (you believe) you've 'made a very clever, original, wry and amusing' refutation of someone else's contention[42] – a sentiment which characterises a great deal of the interactional traffic on Twitter. In all these examples, the emoji acts as a counterpoint to the meaning articulated in the preceding sentence – a way of ironically commenting on, or undermining, the main sense of the message.

In essence, all the face or gesture emoji fall into the category of ready-made chunks of meaning which can be used to express a range of typical emotions. In some cases they're relatively transparent (e.g. the facial expressions, as discussed in Chapter 3); in others they're more culturally specific and have accrued a particular meaning in the way they've been used by others. And it's this cultural specificity – the dos and don'ts of using them, and how they've come to mean what they mean – which gives us a surprisingly insightful picture of how we relate to each other in today's world.

6 People, Politics and Interpersonal Relationships

How to Say 'Cockwomble' in Emoji 🐸 *An Arsenal of Linguistic Weapons* 🐸 *'Me Plus You Equals Frowny Face'* 🐸 *Mourning Becomes Emoji* 🐸 *Ruining the Frog Emoji*

How to Say 'Cockwomble' in Emoji

If you can order porn with emoji, you should also, presumably, be able to swear with them. And according to Buzzfeed, you certainly can.[1] In what has all the elements of an archetypal Buzzfeed post, the site provides a handy run-down of twenty-one useful emoji expletives. This includes staples such as 'bastard' 🐷🚫👶 and 'wanker' 💦👋⚓, along with a few useful compounds like 'bollock-faced shit licker' 🍒😊💩👅. Then there are the more esoteric terms like 'cockwomble' 🐓🐙 – a British epithet meaning an 'obnoxious or idiotic person',[2] which came to international prominence during protests which greeted Donald Trump's visit to Scotland back in 2016.[3]

Given that swearing is one of the most emotive forms of language use – and that a key motivating factor behind the development of emoji was to fill a need for emotional framing in online correspondence – this would seem a natural function for them. But are these examples really swearing in the same way that verbal language is? Can typing 🐓🐙 in a Whatsapp message have the same force as actually calling someone a 'cockwomble' when the atmosphere gets a little heated in a face-to-face conversation?

If one of the underlying principles of swear-words is that they work as a sort of linguistic weapon which automatically triggers negative emotions in the brain of the listener,[4] then emoji profanities of this sort don't qualify particularly well. This is because they're simply not direct enough. The roots of almost all swear-words refer to a limited number of concepts. These include religious or supernatural beings, bodily functions and the organs related to them, disease, sexuality, and groups which are held in contempt in certain parts of society. But emoji, with their limited and highly regulated set of symbols, have very few words native to their own writing system for any of these categories. As such, the Buzzfeed terms are all compounds, which rely on translations from the English.

For example, 🐹 is a calque: a word that's borrowed from another language through direct translation. In this case, the two component parts of the English word are rendered with the symbols that individually represent them (although with a bit of poetic licence being taken in the substitution of the 'hamster face' for a womble). 🤲⚓, on the other hand, is a rebus, with pictures representing the different parts of the word. The conjoined hands look roughly like a 'w', which is appended to 'anchor' to approximate the pronunciation of the English word. And 🐕🚫🛏 works by creating a mini-narrative from concepts suggested by the three symbols, which then represents the literal meaning of 'bastard'.

All three are therefore creative puzzles which need to be deciphered. And because of this they don't have the immediacy of swearwords, which reduces much of their pragmatic force. If your adversary has to spend time puzzling over what you're getting at when you send them a message punctuated with 🐕🚫🛏 and 🤲⚓, they're as likely to be amused as they are offended once they're cracked the code.

There's a standard convention of using certain symbols to imply expletives without actually having to spell them out. This is the use of the asterisk – or occasionally a mix of other random typographical marks, known as grawlix[5] – as a substitute for some or all of the letters in the chosen word. Writing f*** or @#$%&! allows you to use the expletive without actually harnessing its offensive power. It's the written equivalent of altering a component of the pronunciation in speech – saying 'fudge', 'flippin', 'silly beggar' and countless other phonetic euphemisms rather than the offending words themselves. And from 2017 this too became a part of the emoji lexicon, with the release of the 'Face with symbols over mouth' 😶.[6]

But while the Buzzfeed-type emoji combinations aren't meant as euphemistic evasions, they nevertheless depend on people interpreting them as rude or taboo to qualify as bona fide swear-words. A lot will depend on how conventions of use develop, of course, and the extent to which any of these terms become embedded in communication practices. If they begin to be used regularly as expletives – and, equally importantly, are avoided or stigmatised because of the way they're used – then they may yet acquire the pragmatic force of explicit swear-words.

A similar process appears to be happening in other contexts. For example, there are suggestions that emoji are now being used for sexual harassment,[7] particularly within the context of non-consensual sexting.[8] In scenarios such as this – where men are sending unwanted innuendo-laden or explicit messages to women – the fact that these messages are written in emoji rather than verbal language doesn't lessen their impact. There are also organisations offering legal advice on how to avoid the problematic use of emoji in the workplace.[9] So in both cases, the real-life consequences of how and what emoji are being used to communicate are colouring their cultural meaning.

Beyond the Buzzfeed-type compounds and the grawlix face, there are, in fact, two or three native emoji for swearing. In 2014 the Unicode Consortium introduced the middle-finger character 🖕, much to the excitement of the media.[10] (Prior to the release of this, people often used the cactus as a substitute 🌵.) As a direct iconic representation of the real-life gesture,[11] 🖕 is a fairly straightforward translation, and were you to use it in a message the meaning would be pretty transparent. Indeed, in certain countries such as the United Arab Emirates, sending this emoji has already been designated a criminal offence in exactly the same way as making the gesture in person is.[12] Even in more swear-happy cultures, its directness hasn't been to everyone's liking. The journalist Chris Plante, for example, wrote that, while he respected the emoji's straightforwardness, 'I've always enjoyed the creativity previous emoji collections have required of people who want to express disapproval or rage'.[13] In other words, although it's now perfectly possible to express this sort of meaning with blunt concision in emoji, doing so somehow goes against the playfulness and creativity that for many are essential parts of their character.

Offensive gestures are often very culturally specific, and one or two of the symbols that notionally have more wholesome purposes could also, in certain contexts, come off as abusive. The 'sign of the horns' gesture 🤘, for example, is usually associated with heavy metal in the Anglophone world. It was popularised in this context after Ronnie James Dio, Ozzy Osbourne's replacement in Black Sabbath, began using it as an onstage salute. But in many Mediterranean and Latin countries the same gesture, known as the 'corna', is used as an insult. It represents the idea of being cuckolded and so belittles the virility of the person you use it towards. Given that the English word 'cuckold' – and its diminutive 'cuck' – has been brought back into fashion as an insult by the alt-right in recent years,[14] presumably there's a possibility that this gesture might also be taken up for more offensive purposes at some stage as well. Again, it all depends on how conventions of use develop.

All of which brings us, finally, to the poop emoji 💩.[15] This again would seem to have the potential to be a native profanity. Yet it's a long way from being a straightforward translation of 'shit'. As the founder of Emojipedia, Jeremy Burge, commented to ABC News, you can pretty much 'use it anywhere, and people don't quite know what you mean by it. You can use it in any context' – and for a whole range of different meanings.[16]

This is borne out by the ways it's been taken up both online and off-. For example, you can buy a whole range of merchandise featuring the poop emoji, from earrings to slippers to sunglasses.[17] It's also been co-opted into political discourse, for both negative and positive purposes. When someone discovered a bug in Donald

Trump's website during the 2016 presidential campaign, the first thing they did was insert this emoji on his homepage.[18] At the other end of the spectrum, the charity Water Aid adopted it as part of a campaign to raise awareness of their work in providing clean water and toilets to the billions of people globally who lack them.[19] So it combines the attention-grabbing element of a profanity with a certain endearing quality. As the Unicode Consortium's FAQ says, 'people like to use [emoji] to add color and whimsy to their messages'.[20] And the pile of poop, with its broad smile and welcoming eyes, is perhaps the perfect symbol of how this sort of whimsy extends even to the unruly world of swearing.

An Arsenal of Linguistic Weapons

The difference between 💩 and 🦅 💯 is that one has a stable, clearly defined meaning while the other requires a little puzzling out. And this split between the transparent and the oblique is something that characterises communication via emoji generally. While individual characters can be used in intuitive and straightforward ways – an eggplant is, sometimes, just an eggplant – they can also be used in a range of figurative or cryptic ways. This is what makes them such fertile ground for creativity. But this also means they can be a little capricious as a reliable system of communication. And, in contexts such as the law, this proves problematic.

'Lawyers make their living by the written and spoken word. Their arsenal is the lexicon and a grasp of how to use the various weapons which lie therein.' This was an opinion posted to an online forum in a long-running political scandal in New Orleans in the early 2010s. It's an opinion which, paradoxically, describes perfectly the process that led to the downfall of the person who posted it. The saga, as related by the author Jack Hitt in the New Yorker,[21] involved a dispute between the city's attorney general and a prominent local businessman which centred around corruption and bribery allegations in the lucrative world of post-Hurricane

Katrina garbage disposal. As the dispute escalated, so it spilt over onto the internet. A series of anonymous posts began springing up, making increasingly fierce attacks on the businessman. This went on for six months, until the authors of the posts were finally unmasked. It turned out they were two high-ranking officials from the attorney general's own office – which severely compromised his position and led, almost inevitably, to his resignation.

The identity of the two anonymous posters was discovered through analysis of the language used in their messages, which was then matched to linguistic patterns in the correspondence between government officials. This is a type of forensic linguistics – the application of linguistic expertise to legal issues. Although the origins of this sort of detective work can be traced back centuries, it's only relatively recently that forensic linguistics has become an established science. In the United Kingdom it developed in the second half of the twentieth century through investigations into the authenticity – and thus reliability – of police statements. In the United States it was initially used to ensure that suspects were properly informed of their rights when being interrogated – which led to the development of the Miranda Warning.

Nowadays forensic linguistics covers a vast range of different issues, from trademark disputes to the identification of suspects (as in the New Orleans case) to determining precisely what someone might have meant when they uttered a particular string of words. And it's in this last category where it's beginning to expand to cover emoji.

If you were to use 🖕 in a message to an adversary, it would be fairly difficult to argue that it wasn't meant as an insult. As we've seen, in societies which have strict anti-profanity laws, such as the United Arab Emirates, it's already explicitly listed on the statute books as such. Writing 🐓🐖, on the other hand, would probably afford you a wider margin of deniability. You could simply be referring to two of the smaller farmyard creatures, after all. A prosecutor, in this respect, is more likely to have their work cut out trying to determine exact intent.

There have been a number of legal cases in which the meaning of emoji have played a pivotal role. Given the relative novelty of the technology, plus the implications it has for the changing face of modern society, these have received their fair share of media coverage. In one of the most publicised, a teenager from Brooklyn was charged with posting messages to Facebook which were considered to be of a threatening nature by the police. In January 2015, 17-year-old Osiris Aristy wrote a status update which read 'Nigga run up on me, he gunna get blown down 🔫👮👮👮'.[22] The post, along with other anti-police declarations and a selection of selfies of Aristy posing with guns, was noticed by what was described as routine Facebook monitoring by the police, and he was arrested. Despite not being addressed to, or referencing, any particular person, the message was nevertheless interpreted as a credible act of criminal intimidation, and Aristy was charged with, among other things, making terrorist threats.[23] In the end a grand jury decided against indicting him on this, but the incident sparked a media debate about how the courts should deal with this sort of communication.[24]

Other, similar cases include that of a 12-year-old girl from Virginia who was arrested for threatening her school by posting the gun, bomb and knife emoji to Instagram and was subsequently charged with computer harassment and threatening behaviour.[25] Then there was the British member of parliament Craig Mackinlay, who received a death threat via Facebook which read 'Another MP that needs … ' followed by a succession of gun and knife emoji.[26] The perpetrator in this instance was initially charged with 'sending offensive, indecent, obscene or menacing communications', although the case was later dropped by the Crown Prosecution Service.

It's not just cases involving the threat of violence where the interpretation of emoji have become an issue. In 2017 there was the case of a landlord in Tel Aviv who sued for breach of contract after a group of prospective tenants reneged on what, in his view, had been a clear statement of intent to take the flat he was advertising. They'd responded by text message, including a string of emoji (a flamenco dancer, bunny girls, the peace sign, a champagne bottle), which the judge ruled clearly 'convey[ed] to the other side that everything is in order'.[27]

So what issues does the law need to be taking into account when dealing with cases involving emoji? How, if at all, are they different from more established systems of communication?

Eric Goldman, professor of law at Santa Clara University, lists a number of things that could cause legal problems.[28] Most prominent is the way that emoji can have different appearances for sender and recipient because of the lack of consistency in design between the different platforms. As we saw in Chapter 1, in certain circumstances this can result in the recipient simply seeing a placeholder (an alien or question mark in a box), in which case they have no indication at all of what the intended meaning was. And it's not just discrepancies between different platforms that can cause this. The way that tech companies regularly update or change their emoji also means that the designs the two parties in a conversation see may differ depending on the version of the operating system they're using. From a legal point of view, what's important is that in either instance sender and recipient will be viewing subtly different messages without realising it – and without this fact having been disclosed to them. In other words, the technology can be altering the meaning of the message without any clear indication that it's doing so.

A particularly salient example of how this happens is the gun emoji. On the majority of platforms this takes the shape of a handgun. On Apple's operating system it's a water pistol. In 2016 the company switched their design in a symbolic move aimed at discouraging gun crime in society.[29] This was part of a general stance they'd taken against violent emoji – at one stage they completely blocked the gun, bomb and knife from showing up on their desktop operating system, and in 2016, along with Microsoft, they persuaded the Unicode Consortium to drop plans for a rifle emoji.[30] To what extent altering the look of the pistol will actually impact on gun culture is difficult to say. And for some, the emoji had, in fact, been used as a

resource in anti-violence campaigns. It was often used by support-
ers of Black Lives Matter, for example, when protesting against
police shootings.[31] But the point to note here is that, from a legal
perspective, Apple's loose interpretation of the Unicode Standard
means that consistency of message from person to person is clearly
stretched, opening up a definite possibility that senders and
recipients could misunderstand each other due entirely to the
intermediation of the technology.

This may be something that the community of emoji pro-
viders irons out someday soon, though. There are signs that
convergence across platforms may be on its way.[32] Back in
2013, for instance, there was a great deal of diversity across
the designs of the gun. While Apple and Samsung went with
a standard revolver, Microsoft opted for a phaser, and Google
for some reason were using an eighteenth-century-style flint-
lock pistol. By 2016, everyone had converged on the revolver
design – except for Apple, who had made the switch to the
water pistol. In 2018, Samsung then also switched to a bright-
green water pistol – and, given the dominance that Apple and
Samsung have in the market, the other companies soon followed suit (with Google, for some reason, preferring an
orange water pistol rather than a green one).

For the moment, however, the different design approaches
bring with them the very real possibility of mixed signals and
muddled interpretations. But Goldberg notes that despite this,
based on some early emoji-related opinions, courts seem to be
able to handle emoji interpretation perfectly well for the most
part. In other words, a lot of the issues are theoretical rather than
actual to date. He cites as an example a case where a smiling
character that was added to the end of a message signalled that the
whole thing was meant as a joke rather than being intended
literally, and the court had no difficultly in reading it as such.
Indeed, given what we've seen of the history of anxiety over the
signalling of ironic intent, the use of emoji may in fact make a
court's job easier in this sort of case.

'Me Plus You Equals Frowny Face'

In the context of the law it's the indeterminate meaning of individual symbols that can pose problems. In other contexts, it's the implications of using the system at all that stirs up debate and consternation and prompts reflective questions about the nature of modern social relationships.

In the days before Alec Baldwin started provoking the ire of Donald Trump by impersonating him on *Saturday Night Live*, he played another television executive flirting with the world of politics. His character in the sitcom *30 Rock* had, at one stage in the story, dated former Secretary of State Condoleezza Rice. And when he was in need of her political connections to help out with a North Korea-related scrape, he regretted the fact that he'd broken up with her via text message – and specifically that he'd done so by writing 'Me plus you equals frowny face'.[33]

Without wishing to labour an explanation of the comedy here, this is a classic example of the 'incongruity theory' of humour. As the philosopher Henri Bergson puts it, a 'comic effect is always obtainable by transposing the natural expression of an idea into another key'[34] – in other words, using a particular type of language in a context where a different type is expected. Here the joke works by flaunting expectations about the etiquette of breaking up with someone – especially if you're a fully grown adult mixing in circles which include prominent stateswomen.

In scenarios such as ending a relationship, the medium is often considered as important as the message. It's not just what you say: it's the means by which you say it. The online dating site eHarmony, for example, advises that breaking up via text or email, or by changing your relationship status on Facebook before letting the other person know, is 'just not a decent way' to conduct yourself.[35] It may get the job done, but it violates certain basic standards of decorum. The site's guidance doesn't mention the use of something along the lines of 🙍😵🌸✳️❤️🌀🦶, but one presumes this wouldn't be too highly recommended either.

Is this really the case though? Is the use of emoji for negotiating the demise of a relationship always and inevitably insensitive? The issue here is all to do with appropriateness – and the conventional beliefs that circulate in society about which media channels are best suited to what types of communication. Texting, instant messaging and the use of emoji are all considered informal. There's nothing intrinsic about their identity which renders them this way. But the fact that they're most often used for trivial conversations – for casual, everyday concerns rather than for anything serious or solemn – means that these associations rub off on the way they're perceived. And when you try to use them for something more formal, these associations persist in the background.

Ideas along these lines have deep roots. In his book on the history of attitudes towards communication, John Durham Peters discusses how Socrates, back in the fifth century BC, thought that the new technology of writing was a threat to intimacy because of the way it was altering how people related to each other.[36] True communication, he felt, was interpersonal in the most literal sense of the word: it involved face-to-face interaction. Writing, on the other hand, introduced emotional distance. It lacked the intimacy that comes from communing with someone who's physically present at the time of the conversation and whose feelings you can gauge and respond to as the dialogue unfolds. To an extent, beliefs like this still exist today. The advice for personal and emotionally charged conversations such as ending a relationship is that it's far better to do it in person than by writing.

The scepticism Socrates felt over the effects of technology gets repeated every time a new innovation comes along. As the anthropologist Ilana Gershon notes, each new technology alters the way we engage in dialogue with each other, thus 'introducing new possibilities and new risks'.[37] There's an initial wariness about the new innovation – at least in mainstream or conservative quarters. And in some cases, this can be with good reason. Twitter, for example, opened up a world of immediate and democratic conversation; but it also facilitated a flood of trolling and abuse and the proliferation of extremist beliefs. Its identity as a medium of communication is not quite what its designers envisaged. But it does have a very distinct identity, and people today use it for the sort of communication they think is best suited to this identity.

What counts as appropriate is not solely to do with the choice of media, however. It's also about the type of language you use. Here the concept of linguistic 'register' is important. Register is a metaphor originally taken from music, where it refers to the range that a voice or instrument can have. The same musical sequence can be played in different ways depending on the particular register that the performer has access to. When the idea is applied to language, it refers to the levels of formality that are associated with different contexts or scenarios. The same basic message can be expressed using a range of linguistic registers, and these con-tribute to the overall meaning. In some circumstances it might be best to say, 'I am writing to express my sincerest apologies for my insensitive and inappropriate behaviour', whereas in others sim-ply 'Sorry' or even 😩 would do. It all depends on the expectations associated with the context.

In terms of what's appropriate when breaking up with someone, the final element of the equation is how one perceives the relation-ship with the (soon-to-be-former) partner. Here again, commu-nications technology has had a huge influence on the value accorded certain types of romantic and sexual relationships within society. The journalist Nancy Jo Sales has written about the 'dating apocalypse' that Tinder and similar dating apps have ushered in.[38] One of the people she interviews, evolutionary biologist Justin Garcia, suggests that the advent of the internet marks the second major transition in heterosexual mating patterns to have occurred in the last four million years. Firstly there was the agricultural revolution, about ten millennia ago, when the species became more settled, marriage became a social norm and many of the ideas that underpin our beliefs about relationships today were first formed. But these norms are now being destabilised by a hit-it-and-quit-it culture, facilitated by 'ass-on-demand apps'[39] such as Tinder. In the currently evolving sexual marketplace, traditional ideas of communications etiquette are often simply no longer relevant. This is a world, after all, where 'pick-up artist' sites will advise you on how to incorporate emoji as a crucial part of your 'text game'.[40] One such site explains that use of the 'face blowing a kiss emoji' 😘 is 'a very good one to start getting intimate' with the object of your affection and that if, after a while, they start using it too, this is your signal that 'it's on; now you just have to continue [to] start throwing subtle sexual comments every now and then'. As the journalist Katie Glass says, compared with this sort of culture, the old-fashioned text break-up seems quite polite.[41]

In this context, then, beliefs about the rights or wrongs of using emoji are part of larger shifts in expectations and etiquette in society, as well as in the evolving nature of human relationships more generally. And as we'll see, just as this applies to love, so it also applies to death.

Mourning Becomes Emoji

The death of the Princess of Wales two decades ago led to a phenomenon known as the Dianafication of public mourning – the large-scale communal outpouring of grief that follows in the wake of a national tragedy.[42] In 1997, the year of Diana's death, the internet was still in its infancy, and digital social media was still several years from being developed. Today, mass shows of grief accompanying global tragedies are becoming ever more commonplace, and social media now plays a pivotal role in them. For some people, however, this type of online mourning has the effect of devaluing the meaning of public grief. Just as the Dianafication of mourning always contained an element that was more to do with the self-promotion of the individual than with deep-felt emotion, so the expression of online grief is also criticised for its lack of authentic feeling.[43] And here again, the use of emoji has become a touchstone for wider debates about changing norms in society and what's now considered appropriate – or inappropriate – when it comes to the expression of grief.[44]

For many people the use of emoji in messages of condolence, or for the discussion of tragic news, is problematic simply because they're associated with a type of light-hearted, even childish, expression, and this association colours the meaning they have in all contexts. For example, when a Cincinnati news station reported a child's suicide with a crying face emoji they were roundly criticised for their insensitivity.[45] The style of the report was seen as an attempt to keep on trend with contemporary forms of expression, but one which was woefully misjudged. Likewise, when the singer Cher included a bomb emoji in a tweet reacting to 2016's terrorist attack at Ataturk Airport in Istanbul, there was a swift backlash from her fan base on social media.[46] The tweet simply offered prayers for the victims of the attack, but it was punctuated at the end with the emoji combination 💣✨. It led to her hastily having to post a follow-up message apologising for the inadvertent insensitivity. In both these cases there was obviously no intention to offend, but the means of expression ended up overshadowing the sentiment.

For other people, however, there's a certain natural affiliation between the expression of difficult emotions and an image-based form of communication. The journalist Emily Harnett, for example, wonders whether 'a grief that withdraws into something pre-literate … has simply found its perfect expression' in emoji.[47] And certainly, the use of simple visual symbols has become such a standard part of the response to large-scale tragic events that the tech companies have begun incorporating features into the design of their platforms to facilitate this type of expression. For example, in 2015 Facebook introduced the temporary profile picture.[48] This was initially offered as a way of letting people superimpose a rainbow flag over their profile image as a show of support for gay rights. But it was soon expanded in the aftermath of the 2015 and 2016 terrorist attacks in Paris and Brussels to let people show solidarity for victims of the attacks by altering the picture to one showing the colours of the flags of the two countries. While on one level this may seem a rather shallow way to register solidarity – something akin to zero-effort acts of political engagement such as clicktivism –

it's been widely embraced and continues, for the moment at least, to be a standard feature on many social media platforms.

A similarly simple feature is the sad-face reaction that's available on Facebook for responding to posts and which was much used in discussions and updates about the 2016 Brussels attacks. This option was, in fact, specifically added following a request from users, who felt that the all-purpose Like button wasn't able to express the full range of sentiments they often had.[49] In this instance, then, an emoji is seen by users and designers alike as perfectly acceptable for reacting to traumatic news – even if, as the sociologist Natalie Pitimson writes, the way we're using such a small palette of cartoon images 'to respond to the most horrifying of spectacles' does suggest 'a rather empty form of grief'.[50]

Ruining the Frog Emoji

Law, love, death and, finally, politics. At the end of February 2017, Finland released a number of new additions to the emoji they produce to promote their national culture.[51] The new symbols included a set about Tom of Finland,[52] the artist known for his homoerotic drawings of highly masculinised fetish subjects. Published to mark the legalisation of same-sex marriage in Finland on 1 March that year, they celebrated the inclusive image the country wished to advertise for itself – and signalled the dramatic change that had occurred in social attitudes since the artist's early underground career.

Finland is, at present, the only European country that publishes its own bespoke emoji. Various political groups have tried to join the trend as a means of drumming up support for their candidates. There have been Jeremojis,[53] Berniemojis[54] and Hillarymojis,[55] among others. Quite how effective any of these are is difficult to say ('not very' is probably the answer).[56] But at a grass-roots level at least, political debate involving emoji is definitely growing.

In the Unicode update for 2017, the national flags of England, Scotland and Wales were finally released. Along with ginger-haired characters (which had to wait until 2018 for their official debut),[57] these national flags were apparently the most requested for inclusion in that year's update. This was supposedly due to people wanting to cheer on the home nations in sports events.[58] But it seems likely that the state of contemporary politics was also a factor. The year before, after all, had seen one of the most significant changes in the political identity of the United Kingdom in a generation. During the 2016 Brexit campaign, the Union Jack emoji was often used in tweets but without clear-cut political associations. According to research by the data scientist Hamdan Azhar, just over a third of tweets which used the union flag included the #VoteLeave hashtag, but then so also did a fifth of #VoteRemain tweets.[59] In the absence of a wider palette of national flags, both sides, it seems, were using the symbol to suggest that their perspective was a true reflection of British identity.

National flags always have contested meanings, of course. And in recent years this has been particularly the case for England's national flag, the St George's Cross. In research conducted in 2012, a majority of people living in England felt more affinity for the Union Jack than they did for the English flag. Almost a quarter of them felt England's Cross of St George had racist overtones.[60] The authors of the research report put this down mostly to the way that the 'extreme street hooligans' of the English Defence League had degraded its image by appropriating it for their extremist-nationalist agenda.

The flag hasn't always had this meaning. In the 1970s it was the Union Jack that had the racist overtones, having been adopted by the National Front and still retaining the symbolism of Britain's empire-building and colonialist history. In contrast, the St George's Cross at the time was able to represent a more multi-ethnic England.[61] In effect, the cultural meanings of the flags derive from who uses them and how, as well as the way this is then taken up or contested in society. And of course, underlying present debates about the flags in the United Kingdom is the more complicated issue about what 'Englishness' means in a radically shifting political landscape.[62]

So what does all this have to do with emoji? In many ways, emoji work in a similar way to the national flags. As we've seen, alongside their literal meaning they can also take on particular connotations through the way they're used. It's this aspect of their use that leads to hapless news reports about 'secret emoji codes' and the illicit topics that teenagers are covertly discussing with such codes. A much-lampooned instance of this was when a news station in Seattle attempted to demystify this secret language for their viewers by explaining, for example, that the hibiscus emoji meant drugs and that the frog could be used in cyber-bullying as a way of saying 'you're ugly'.[63]

While there's no compelling evidence to suggest that either are used this way, the frog emoji is, in fact, a good example of the way symbols can become appropriated to signal specific meanings. For a long time a frog was included in the Twitter name used by Richard Spencer,[64] the alt-right activist who gained mainstream notoriety when he was punched in the face on air during a rally at Donald Trump's inauguration.[65] In this context, the emoji was an explicit reference to the Pepe the Frog meme and a way of identifying Spencer with a particular far-right ideology.[66]

The cartoon Pepe began as a character in a comic by Matt Furie. It quickly took off as a meme – initially with an entirely apolitical meaning. But in 2016, its popularity began to be appropriated by the alt-right. This started off as a prank (the sort of provocation that lies behind a lot of alt-right memes) but quickly snowballed until the Anti-Defamation League actually decided to list it as a hate symbol[67] – which in turn standardised its meaning for the communities with which Spencer is associated. The alt-right have often used large, high-profile events in the United States to promote their message, and during the 2017 Super Bowl the frog emoji saw a spike in use,[68] after which Spencer responded sarcastically to someone on Twitter that ruining the frog emoji had been 'my greatest sin to date'.[69]

Spencer's comment sounds frivolous, but, as social media acts more and more as a site for political debate, so emoji are becoming a key part of this. The use of an emoji as part of one's Twitter name has become common on both sides of the political spectrum and often involves appropriating or re-appropriating a symbol that's already current in the culture but now becomes shorthand for one's political values. On the left there are traditional symbols such as the red rose, which has a long history for labour groups and in this context has come to represent the Democratic Socialists of America. There's also the Statue of Liberty, which is used by those promoting the idea that immigration is a positive part of the nation's identity. This became particularly popular as part of the resistance to Donald Trump's attempts to drastically alter immigration policy in the first year of his presidency. Likewise there's the raised fist, which was another symbol of resistance to Trump's anti-immigration rhetoric and policies in 2017.[70]

More popular still is the snowflake. The word itself started being used as derogatory slang to refer to people, particularly those on the left and usually millennials, who were considered overly sensitive about aspects of modern social interaction.[71] It comes from a reprimand in Chuck Palahniuk's novel *Fight Club* (and its later movie adaptation):[72] 'You are not special. You are not a beautiful and unique snowflake' – the idea being that the generation now entering adulthood had been brought up in an overly protective environment which has made them unsuited to the trials of everyday adult life. The term then broadened its meaning until it was being used to apply to anyone with a liberal bent complaining about the political state of the world.[73] Finally, it evolved to be re-appropriated by those it had originally targeted, thus turning into a symbol of communal resistance.

Another symbol which has been partially reclaimed by those it was originally used to attack is the globe 🌐. This was initially employed by a faction on the far right as a symbol for people they characterised as 'globalists' for opposing the nationalist 'America First' agenda. It has a specifically anti-Semitic element to it, based on the deep-rooted racist conspiracy that the global economy is run by Jews. But again, people have begun to re-appropriate it, so that some Jewish people now include it in their Twitter names as a symbol of cultural pride.

This process of appropriating and disputing the symbolic meanings of symbols of this sort is never static, of course, and to what extent any of these political meanings are likely to stick is difficult to say. In the case of Pepe, for example, Matt Furie (its original author) and the Anti-Defamation League launched a #SavePepe campaign at the beginning of 2017 to try to reclaim the character.[74] Richard Spencer meanwhile went on to change his Twitter name from a frog to a glass of milk, which is another supposed white supremacist symbol – in this case something to do with misguided beliefs that correlate white ethnic identity with the body's tolerance for lactose.[75] As Spencer said in an interview with the journalist Sasha Lekach, 'Like Pepe, milk is now a symbol of white identity, both ironical and serious'.[76]

This pattern of appropriating signs and turning them into hate symbols has become a standard technique of the alt-right. The modus operandi involves trolling the media into reporting on the way that an otherwise innocent symbol has white supremacist links. When the media then picks up on it (thus providing some form of outside legitimisation), the symbol then turns into an actual element of iconography for the group. For example, the trolling campaign over milk as a white supremacist symbol ended with the animal rights organisation PETA declaring it as such,[77] so that what began as an ironic joke morphed into an actual means of signalling support for the extreme nationalist cause at rallies and protests.

The more success groups have with this sort of thing, the more far-fetched the campaigns become. As Emma Grey Ellis writes in *Wired*, the cycle is to 'make a joke, perform the joke in real life [and then] watch the media report on the joke as a real menace'.[78] To this end there have been campaigns to co-opt the meaning of both the OK sign 👌 and the peace sign ✌, with the logic being that these are completely non-controversial signs of positivity in mainstream culture and thus ideal targets for this type of trolling – i.e. if these can be perverted, so can anything.

But this is not the only way that emoji get incorporated into political discourse. As social media is now used in all forms of social and professional life, so a specialised jargon evolves among the communities who use it in this way – and this includes metaphoric uses of emoji. For example, amongst the WhatsApp groups that flourish in diplomatic circles, it has, supposedly, become traditional to represent Vladimir Putin by the little grey alien emoji.[79]

Whether the UK national flags emoji that were introduced in 2017 do end up being co-opted into the nationalist politics of a post-Brexit Britain, and how this colours their cultural meaning, remains to be seen. What's clear is that emoji are beginning to evolve as a critical language and are being used to express and contest political meaning in the same way any other language does. And this extends also to identity politics and issues such as gender and race.

7 Diverse Identities

Ask Me About My Pronouns

The novel *Ancillary Justice*, by Ann Leckie, is set several thousand
years in the future, in a galaxy overseen by a totalitarian empire.
The book's narrator, Breq, speaks a language which makes no
distinctions between genders – everyone's referred to using the
same generic pronoun 'she'. As the character explains early in the
story when she has a run-in with a bar owner,

> She was probably male, to judge from the angular mazelike patterns
> quilting her shirt. I wasn't entirely certain. It wouldn't have mat-
> tered, if I had been in Radch space. Radchaai don't care much about
> gender, and the language they speak – my own first language –
> doesn't mark gender in any way.[1]

Leckie has said she didn't set out to examine how the use of
gendered pronouns influences the way we perceive society. 'But
then, isn't that one of the things science fiction is for?' she asks.
'Imagining strange and unfamiliar worlds, that maybe give us a
new and interesting way to think about our own?'[2]

The reason this little linguistic innovation creates a 'strange
and unfamiliar world' is simply down to the fact that English is a
language which *does* distinguish between genders in some aspects
of its grammar (we choose between 'she' and 'he' when referring
to a woman or man) but that doesn't have a straightforward
gender-neutral pronoun (one that stands for 'he-or-she') for use

in situations where we either don't know the person's gender or want to refer to some generic figure. Historically this deficiency has meant that the masculine pronoun gets used as the default. In a sentence such as 'emoticons require a reader to tilt his head to the right', the 'his' stands for any reader, irrespective of gender. By switching things around – by making 'she' the default – Leckie is able to defamiliarise what we take as the norm and draw attention to the way our language is embedded with specific (in this case patriarchal) cultural values.

The gender of English pronouns has been seen as problematic for over 150 years now. The linguist Dennis Barron cites an example from 1882, in an article in the *Memphis Free Trade*, which argued, 'As the laws of grammar now stand, the use of "he" when "she" may be meant is an outrage upon the dignity, and an encroachment upon the rights, of woman. It is quite as important that they should stand equal with men in the grammars as before the law.'[3]

The closest that standard English gets to a gender-non-specific third-person singular pronoun is the improvisational use of 'they'. But given that pronouns are supposed to agree in terms of both gender and number, if you say something like 'Everyone loves their mother' you're using what is, strictly speaking, a plural pronoun (their) with a single noun (everyone). The language is flexible enough to let you do this. People with outspoken views on 'correct' usage aren't always quite so accommodating.

In recent years, with the rise in advocacy politics around transgender rights, the issue of pronouns has also become a major focus of debate for the way that it offers a strict binary between 'he' and 'she'. In the same year that Oxford Dictionaries chose 😂 as their word of the year, the American Dialect Society opted for 'they' as a singular, gender-neutral pronoun as theirs.[4] This combatting of gender-restrictive language is a key political issue, particularly for the generation now in secondary or university education. One of the practices this has led to, on US college campuses especially, is sharing one's preferred pronouns as part of the etiquette of introduction.[5] At the University of

Vermont, for example, students are given a choice when they enrol between 'he', 'she', 'they', 'ze' (one of the most popular invented gender-neutral pronouns[6]) or 'name only' (i.e. they don't wish to be referred to by a pronoun at all).

Emoji have no pronouns, of course. This is a challenge in and of itself – making it very difficult, from a grammatical point of view, to convey a simple idea such as 'She sent me a message'. But these same issues around gender – both in terms of embedded patriarchal norms and non-binary representation – are as salient for emoji as they are for natural languages. And they've led to some of the most notable changes in the evolving look of the symbols since they first made their global debut.

The Rise of the Merpeople

Along with pronouns, one of the other most notable battlegrounds for current debates about gender representation are the signs used on public toilets. As pictographic symbols, toilet door signs are a much closer analogy for emoji. Dissatisfaction with the traditional designs – the stickman in a suit, the stickwoman in a skirt – again centres around the fact that they present what's seen as a straightforward binary distinction between the sexes. For certain parts of the culture, this is increasingly viewed as a problem. In addition, there's the graphic representation itself, especially the triangle-shaped skirt on the woman, which is partly stereotype, partly outmoded.

These traditional designs date back to the infographics developed by the transport system companies in the United States and the United Kingdom for major international events in the 1960s and 1970s.[7] With the rise of mass tourism and the USA's ever-expanding global influence, the symbols quickly spread around the world to become an international standard. In many of the contexts where they're used, however, the way they differentiate between genders has little to do with local styles of dress. The assumption that men wear trousers rather than robes, the fact that the skirt is knee-length rather than ankle-length – these are all primarily Western norms. While the signs might be pictographic in Paris (they look, a little bit, like archetypal Parisian men and women), they're more ideographic in Riyadh (they indicate the idea of men and women without really corresponding to an archetype of Saudi dress codes). Even in the West, the assumptions they're based on seem increasingly dated.

The evolution of emoji in the years since they became a global phenomenon has confronted a similar range of issues. In the first few years of their global spread, reductive stereotype was a prevalent feature in a host of different symbols. In 2016, for example, a group of Google employees petitioned the Unicode Consortium over the fact that a large proportion of the professions only featured men. Roles such as the doctor, the scientist and the mechanic were, up until that time, solely available in male versions. As the group's proposal read, altering this to make the symbols more inclusive could help 'empower young women ... and better reflect the pivotal roles women play in the world'.[8] The journalist Jennifer 8. Lee, who was behind the campaign for the dumpling emoji, has also spoken out about this gender bias. In an interview with Public Radio International she talks of how limiting it can feel 'when the only professional roles for women are bride, princess and *Playboy* bunny'. At issue is the fact that this 'becomes part of the coded vocabulary in the global visual language' and that, given their popularity, 'people see reflections of themselves in emojis'.[9]

Since then the way gender is represented has diversified significantly. In 2017 the Unicode Consortium introduced three new emoji – a child, an adult and an older person – who aren't gender-specific. As Paul D. Hunt, a member of the Consortium's Emoji Subcommittee, explains, 'I proposed the addition of the gender inclusive emoji characters in order to provide better representation for people who want to express themselves in emoji as exactly that: just people.'[10]

In the same update, the option to choose the gender of a character was expanded beyond simply the professions. A variety of fantasy creatures, from zombies to vampires, are now also available in both male and female versions. Not only is there now a mermaid, but there's also a merman. And there are plans that this diversity will expand to include androgynous emoji representations as well. In other words, the internal grammar of emoji will offer a third, gender-non-specific option for all human and anthropomorphic emoji – meaning that the merpeople are just around the corner.

Twenty-First-Century Grammar

In the summer of 2013 Katrina Parrot, then a former programme manager who had recently worked with NASA, created iDiversicons, an app which offers hundreds of emoji with different skin tones, as well as same-sex and interracial couples.[11] These were stickers rather than standardised emoji – to use them you had to copy and paste them into your message – but within a year the Unicode Consortium had taken note itself and introduced a range of modifiers which allowed people to alter the skin colour on many of the characters, as well as the aforementioned choice between genders. In 2015 they introduced a choice of six skin tones, based on what's known as the Fitzpatrick classification scale, a device originally devised by a dermatologist back in the 1960s as a means of estimating how different types of skin responded to ultraviolet light.

These modifiers are applied by using what are known as Zero Width Joiners (ZWJ): a part of the code originally developed to allow for the digital representation of scripts with joined-up letters, such as Arabic. When they're placed between two characters which wouldn't otherwise be connected, they meld them into a single whole. For example, when the Vulcan salute and the medium brown colour are combined, it results in the rendering of a hand with medium brown skin wishing you longevity and prosperity. In other words, the computer is assembling the character from different component parts, guided by the choices you make. In a sense this is a sort of under-the-hood grammar. In much the same way that we can choose to combine the words 'police' and 'woman' to create 'policewoman', so 🧕 is a sequence combining 👮 and 👩. The only real difference is that it's the computer doing the assembly, not you.

Different languages – along with different historical iterations of a language – can encode different types of social relations in their grammar. Take, for example, early modern English. In *Hamlet*, when addressing his friend Horatio, the prince uses the pronoun 'thou'. But when Horatio addresses Hamlet, he uses the pronoun 'you'. Back in Shakespeare's day, English had two possibilities for the second-person single pronoun, in the same way that French and Spanish still do. 'You' was formal, 'thou' informal. So when talking to a social inferior, as Hamlet is when speaking to Horatio, 'thou' would have been the norm, with the formula reversed for Horatio addressing Hamlet. Although the distinction is still found in some regional dialects, for the most part it has died out. So despite British society still being heavily influenced by the class system, there's little trace of this in standard British English grammar.

In this sense emoji are more flexible than English. In modern standard English, gender is the only social relation that can be marked in the grammatical composition of individual words – and only in a handful of these. It's not possible, as it is with emoji, to modify the form of a word to indicate the skin colour of the person it refers to. Does this make emoji a more useful or detailed system of communication than English in this respect? Not necessarily.

Despite all the concerns about embedded bias in the original set of emoji, the reaction to the way that increased diversity is now included hasn't been entirely positive. The problem, in a nutshell, is that the more inclusive they become in some respects, the more people complain they remain exclusive in others. For example, the tech journalist Aditya Madanapalle, writing at the time of the release of the female professionals, worried that '[g]endered emoji just introduce more complications, more characters, more stereotypes' while simultaneously alienating 'all of those who are not represented by these "diverse" emoji'. Instead, she argued, it would be better to 'implement each [representation] in a neutral gender and colour'[12] (as in the case of the bright-yellow smileys) so as to bypass the design issues involved in trying to cope with the infinite variety of humanity.

An example of the complications that can ensue from the current approach to diversity is the same-sex families. Same-sex couples were first introduced in the 2012 update, with families with same-sex parents following in 2015.[13] As people noted, however, in the designs used by the major tech companies such as Apple, all the members of these various family combinations were blond, with the men wearing blue and the women in pink.[14] So while the demographics of modern family relationship were now being reflected, representations of gender and race were still entirely stereotyped.

The writer Paige Tutt is another who feels that Apple's racially diverse emoji ended up 'even more problematic than before'.[15] By offering the choice of the different skin tones, the company were inserting issues of race and representation into messages where it never needed to play a part. The problem for her was that the designs could only do so much in indicating diversity. In effect, all the software now does, she wrote in an article for the *Washington Post*, is allow its users 'to make white emoji a different color'. That's to say, 'there's nothing specifically "black" about an emoji with browner skin. Deepening the skin color of a previously white emoji doesn't make the emoji not white.' Instead, she contends, it just results in 'a bastardized emoji blackface'.

The Colour Yellow

So how about Aditya Madanapalle's idea to go back to abstract, neutral characters? This was Paige Tutt's preferred solution as well: simply remove the racialised emoji. But even the 'neutral' emoji can be problematic. The default colour for all the people-emoji is bright yellow. This simply follows the default colour of the smileys, which in turn is a legacy from the original smiley design from back in the 1960s. Unicode itself doesn't specify colours. The templates it publishes are all black and white, with the guidelines for skin colour advising that '[w]hen a human emoji is not immediately followed by an emoji modifier character [i.e. one of the five classifications from the Fitzpatrick scale], it should use a generic non-realistic skin tone'.[16] The suggestions for 'generic non-realistic' skin tones are blue, silver-grey or bright yellow. The colour all the software companies have chosen is the bright yellow. The problem is, however, that within the context of these new options, the default yellow, when presented as one of six options with the other skin tones, now looks as if it's meant to be a skin tone itself. For a lot of people it suddenly stopped looking like an abstract, non-realistic colour and instead became an offensive stereotype for Asians.[17]

Sensitivities around issues of representation like this are part of a wider debate about racial stereotypes online and the way that new forms of communication such as gifs and memes appear simply to be reproducing age-old prejudices. And while the individual examples of these may at first look trivial, they expose the way certain perceptions about race are embedded very deeply within society. The phenomenon has come to be referred to as 'digital blackface': the way in which non-blacks choose to embody blackness online, in analogy with the nineteenth- and early twentieth-century theatrical tradition of whites exaggeratedly imitating black people as a burlesque entertainment. And it's something that's seen as particularly prevalent in the way people use reaction gifs.

As discussed earlier, reaction gifs are a way of using ready-made fragments of pop culture to express an emotion or feeling within a conversation. As their use has become more popular, so a trend has developed for people to prefer gifs depicting black people when they feel the need to express particularly exaggerated reactions. The critique of this is that, when black people get used as ciphers for broad or extravagant displays of emotion, this is, in a sense, a new take on the old practice of blackface.[18] However inadvertent it may be, it ends up reinforcing derogatory stereotypes around race and culture.

There have been a number of other, similar controversies over bizarrely tone-deaf representations of race online. For example, in 2016 Snapchat released a Bob Marley photo filter which allowed people to transform themselves into a crudely parodic clone of the singer by adding dreadlocks and a Rastafarian-style hat and darkening their skin. As people quickly pointed out though, this in effect constituted a very literal form of blackface. Then there was FaceApp's incredibly ill-conceived 'hot' filter. FaceApp is software that uses neural network technology to alter the look of people's faces in photos. It can make a face look as if it's smiling, change its gender, make it look younger or older – or, in the case of the 'hot' filter, supposedly make it better looking. The trouble was, one of the techniques it used to achieve this was by lightening the skin colour of black users.[19]

It's within this broader context, then, that while the motivations behind the expanded diversity of the emoji population are well-intentioned, finding design solutions that avoid inadvertent stereotyping remains a challenge. As Andrew Mcgill wrote in the *Atlantic*, 'More than 20 years after the birth of the Internet, it's striking to think some people once saw the online world as a raceless utopia, where a user could leave his or her physical identity behind and be judged solely on what he or she said.'[20] Emoji, as a specifically visual form of communication, are a touchstone for issues of representation. As these examples illustrate, despite their best intentions those responsible for devising and designing the system have often ended up reproducing many of the ideologies and stereotypes that are deeply embedded within society.

Symbols of Inclusion and Exclusion

In August 2017, a group of white supremacists protested the planned removal of a Confederate statue in Charlottesville, Virginia. The violence that followed, which culminated in the murder of an anti-fascist protester, sparked a period of soul-searching in American society about the extent to which extremism had penetrated the political mainstream. On Fox News, one commentator, the conservative journalist Star Parker, tried to justify the original demonstration by arguing that the Confederate flag was a symbol of an exclusionary and repressive politics only in the same way that the LGBT Pride flag was.[21] The Pride flag, with its symbolic rainbow of diverse colours, was designed by the artist Gilbert Baker back in 1978. The motivation behind it was a desire to find an alternative symbol for the gay community to the pink triangle, which had been used by the Nazis as a mark of stigma. But to Star Parker there was an irony in people complaining about far-right symbols because 'the same people that are demanding that the Confederate flag comes down are the same people that are insisting that the rainbow flag goes up. These two flags represent the exact same thing. That certain groups are not welcome here.'

These comments produced a mixture of outcry and mockery at the absurdity of the false equivalence Parker was trying to get away with. But the belief system behind her comments, and the way she felt justified in making them, perhaps explains something about the rationale behind the strategy used by Facebook when it introduced a rainbow flag icon to celebrate Pride Week earlier that same year.

As we've seen, from Apple's unilateral action over the pistol to Microsoft and Apple's lobbying of the Unicode Consortium against the inclusion of a rifle emoji to the way that the range of skin tones and gender representation has gradually been expanded, there's a purposeful agenda in the management of emoji to reflect a clear set of cultural values – values which could probably best be described as liberal and multicultural. But the decisions that are made about all of this are also related to the identities – and thus the business aims – of the companies involved. An insightful case in this respect – albeit away from the Unicode standard – was Facebook's roll-out of their own rainbow flag icon in June 2017.

This icon was added as a temporary option to the half-dozen reactions that people can choose from to respond to someone's post or comment – the like, wow, sad, et cetera. But the icon wasn't rolled out universally. It was only available to 'people in major markets with Pride celebrations' and those who followed the company's LGBT page.[22] Shortly prior to this, the company had released figures showing it now had two billion monthly users.[23] As people pointed out, this made its 'population' larger than that of China, the USA, Mexico and Japan combined. It also meant that it had very large communities of users in parts of the world which had different cultural attitudes towards – and laws about – homosexuality. And it was for this reason, the company explained, that they limited access to the icon in those countries.

Yet it wasn't only territories where LGBT rights are unprotected where access was limited. Using an algorithm which detected information about users such as their geographical location and interests (based on their past online behaviour), the site effectively chose who was to be given this feature and who wasn't. In the context of the United States, for example, this resulted in people from cities that had voted for Donald Trump in the 2016 election not getting it automatically unless their profile and past online behaviour suggested they aligned themselves with the LGBT community. Some commentators wondered whether this added up to a sort of 'algorithmic hypocrisy' on the part of the company – and whether it would lead to the creation of cultural filter bubbles, in that the feature was available predominantly in cities with a progressive politics and largely hidden in more rural, conservative areas.[24]

It's difficult to know the precise motivation behind the strategy employed by Facebook here. By selectively releasing the icon, the company were, very likely, aiming to protect individuals and communities in which persecution and harassment over the issue is rife. When, back in 2015, they offered people the chance to place a temporary rainbow filter over their profile picture to mark the Supreme Court decision that same-sex marriage was a constitutional right in the US, there was a backlash in Russia and various countries across the Middle East.[25] One Russian user even created his own filter which placed a Russian flag rather than the rainbow over profile pictures – an improvised feature which proved to be very popular as a counter-demonstration.[26]

But as J. Nathan Matias, Aimee Rickman and Megan Steiner speculated in the *Atlantic*, it was also probably motivated by careful management of the company's own image. By supporting gay rights in places where there's strong support for these values, but at the same time avoiding getting caught up in arguments about cultural politics in more conservative areas, Facebook could navigate a careful public relations balance. The strategy, in other words, was to support a cause they believed in without creating a political backlash which might have damaged the business.

This is only a solitary example, of course – and, as the company said at the time, the whole venture was something of an experiment. But it's part of a wider context in which both the media we use to communicate (e.g. Twitter, Facebook) and the symbolic resources themselves (e.g. emoji) are controlled at the point of production by private companies – and can be used by those companies as a way of supporting the type of cultural values they wish to identify with. The broader ramifications of this are something we'll return to in the final chapter of the book. But, before moving to that, it's worth stressing that just because a company might attempt to manage the cultural and political meaning of emoji, this doesn't mean that people aren't able to customise or subvert this meaning for their own ends. In fact, such is the nature of the social internet that finding ways to challenge and lampoon orthodoxy is one of its key characteristics. And as was suggested at the very beginning of the book, the way people actually go about using emoji highlights the intrinsic creativity at the core of all communication.

8 Creativity and Culture

Creative Constraints

The Prisoner's Constraint is a writing exercise which lays out very strict rules for the composition of a poem. The idea is to imagine you're a prisoner who's got a limited supply of paper and wants to exploit every last inch of it. You do this by being strategic in how you write and avoiding any letters of the alphabet which include ascenders or descenders – i.e. those which extend above or below the writing line. This means you've got to create your entire poem using only the letters a, c, e, m, n, o, r, s, u, v, w, x and z.

> as one can see
> an onerous
> move
> as concerns
> success

But one which can produce intriguing results, as illustrated in this extract from a poem by Bob Brightt:

> **mr moose**
>
> some morose moose
> mr romeo moose
> ran
> a
> zoo

mr moose mr moose
mr romeo moose

zoos ooze sex
our zoo sure oozes sex

caresses are ace
ace mr moose
sex

no

mores mr moose
or

romeo

m o r e s
we sue ravenous mooses
sure
we sue
so
mr romeo moose

no more zoos
no more zoos no more sex no more caresses[1]

The Prisoner's Constraint was an exercise devised by the Oulipo group, a French literary collective from the 1960s who dreamt up elaborate challenges which put strict constraints on the writing process. The name Oulipo comes from the French phrase 'Ouvroir de Littérature Potentielle', or 'Workshop for a Potential Literature'. The group's guiding principle was that creativity is encouraged by constraints. As the writer Andrew Gallix puts it, the 'Oulipians are into literary bondage'.[2] They highlight the fact that all language use is inhibited in some way or other – there are rules of grammar, of genre, of style. Rather than attempt to ignore this fact, the Oulipo embrace it. As the novelist Georges Perec wrote, 'I set myself rules in order to be totally free'.[3]

Perhaps the best known of the works from the group is the novel *La Disparition* by Perec himself, which was written entirely without the letter 'e' (and ingeniously translated into English using the same constraint by Gilbert Adair). Both this and the Prisoner's Constraint poems are lipograms – compositions in which the writer systematically leaves out particular letters of the alphabet. It's a practice which goes back to the Ancient Greeks and still attracts adherents today. There's Walter Abish's novel *Alphabetical Africa*, for example, in which chapter 1 has words which begin only with the letter A, chapter 2 only with the letters A and B, and so on – until chapter 26 where there are no constraints on the words he can choose. At which point he reverses the process and starts removing letters as he works his way back to A in chapter 52. Or there's Mark Dunn's *ella minnow pea*, in which the spelling of words becomes more impressionistic as more and more letters get omitted – the title's a phonetic rendering of five letters from the middle of the alphabet.

It wasn't just lipograms that the Oulipo experimented with. Another well-known early work from a member of the group is Raymond Queneau's *Exercices de Style*, in which the same short anecdote is retold ninety-nine times, each in a different style or genre. And then – although not strictly an Oulipian project – there's Padgett Powell's novel *The Interrogative Mood*, in which every single line is phrased as a question.

So what do the self-consciously abstruse exercises of an avant-garde literary movement from the 1960s have to do with emoji? Well, as the poet Brian Kim Stefans says, there's a good argument that '[p]erhaps we are all Oulipians now'.[4] What he means by this is that the sort of everyday acts of creativity that we play around with on social media are strikingly reminiscent of the exercises the Oulipo movement engaged in. Formulating 140-character Twitter posts (in the days in which that was the constraint), obsessively cataloguing the everyday elements of one's life in an Instagram feed, remixing fragments of pop culture into memes – these are exactly the sorts of practices that a decade or two ago used to be the preserve of performance artists or minimalist poets. Yet now they're a staple of everyone's everyday creativity.

Back in February 1987, for example, the photographer Karl Baden began taking a photo of himself every morning. Thirty years later he's still doing this, charting the way that age and identity evolve in the photographic record of his self-image. It's a fascinating artistic project. But today, in the era of the selfie, similar experiments are being carried out by all sorts of people – whether as a means of self-expression and the building of self-esteem[5] or simply as an innovative way to communicate with your grandchildren.[6] There are Reddit subgroups dedicated to everyday selfies[7] and even a purpose-built app based around the idea.[8] This is the mainstreaming of the avant-garde.

Or there's the hashtag #facesinthings which people use when posting photos they've take of buildings or everyday objects (door handles, plug sockets) which look like faces (a phenomenon known as pareidolia in psychology). This was the sort of improvised technique that Picasso used when he created his 'Bull's Head' out of the seat and handlebars of a bicycle, but, again, it's now an Instagram hashtag pastime.

Emoji fall squarely within this category. When not being used to express emotion, or as a shorthand for simple events like meeting up for a drink, their predominant function is a creative one. And arguably it's this that has driven much of their popularity.

This playful experimentation ranges from understated little projects like the 'Emoji Aquarium', a Twitter feed which posts small concrete poems made up of fish and plant emoji that resemble an ever-changing aquarium,[9] to obsessive follies such as 'translating' the whole of Hermann Melville's novel *Moby Dick* into emoji – producing the infamous *Emoji Dick*.[10] One online reviewer commented: 'Lovely, some of the lines are completely unintelligible, some delightfully so.'[11]

Underpinning all these projects is the constrained nature of emoji as a communicative system. In the words of radio producer P. J. Vogt, emoji's 'charm is in how broken and inadequate it is'.[12] Rather than an exhaustive Porphyrian tree of concepts to describe the natural world, we've got a random selection of disparate pictures, and thus we have to improvise ways to make them express what we want. The majority of the symbols aren't the result of a community-wide consensus about what would be most useful. Instead they're a product of the history of emoji evolution and the values and beliefs of those on the Unicode Consortium committees. But once they end up on the phone's keyboard, people work out ways to imbue them with meaning. The whole process of communication becomes a creative act. It becomes a contest of forging sense out of the symbols available – and, in doing so, reinterpreting what's involved in making meaning.

Defining Creativity

Creativity is a fundamental part of how we relate to each other. It's one of those abilities, like language, that you can have great proficiency in without having any understanding of how it works. It's also something which has an enduring and essential relationship with language: language is one of the most salient ways in which we can express our creativity, while creativity is a critical element in the way that language works.

There are several competing definitions of creativity. For the linguist Noam Chomsky, it's that property of language which allows people to express 'indefinitely many thoughts' and to react 'appropriately in an indefinite range of new situations'.[13] Although language is made up of finite means – written English, for example, has only twenty-six letters in the alphabet – you can combine them in ways to create sentences which have never been written before throughout the history of humankind; and people have the ability to understand these, despite never having heard them before.

While this pinpoints a remarkably productive capacity of language, it's a very specialised definition of creativity and not one which helps much when it comes to understanding its general everyday workings. A more useful definition is James Kaufman and Robert Sternberg's proposition that something is creative if it's novel, of high quality and appropriate to the task it's being used for.[14] This definition pinpoints three key factors which lie behind much of what we understand as creative in both high culture and everyday communication – and they apply as much to emoji as they do to verbal language.

The term 'creativity' itself has become something of a cliché of modern times. Until the 1930s it wasn't much used at all. Its popularity surged in the 1960s and then again in the 1980s.[15] Today, it's bandied around in all sorts of contexts, from business mantras to psychology studies. There's a certain irony to this overuse. After all, as the art director George Lois defines it, creativity is 'the defeat of habit by originality'.[16] It's a way of disrupting the settled ways we have of seeing the world, of mixing invention with presentation to create an effect that stands out against the everyday run of things. And it's this that Kaufman and Sternberg are referring to when they talk of 'novelty'.

So how is this achieved? An enduring idea here is what's known as defamiliarisation[17] – the production of an effect which makes people appreciate things in a new light. At the word or sentence level, this can be done by using tropes such as rhythm, rhyme and metaphor. With emoji, it can be done by finding ways to express an idea via an unusual visual metaphor or by rebus writing. At a discourse level, this can be done with plot and structure, by juxtaposing ideas or themes in unexpected ways or by translating from one mode to another – as in the example of *Emoji Dick*. In each case, manipulation of the language draws attention to itself, either to create a particular aesthetic effect or to foreground an element of the content.

Simply littering your prose with unusual metaphors or other poetic tropes is not, in itself, creative, however. Almost more important than novelty is the idea that creativity always serves some purpose. A slightly different way of expressing this idea comes from the artist Marcel Duchamp, who wrote, 'The creative act is not performed by the artist alone; the spectator brings the work in contact with the external world by deciphering and interpreting its inner qualifications and thus adds his contribution to the creative act.'[18] Think of Duchamp's most famous work, *Fountain*.[19] This consists of a urinal, exhibited on its back. But because it's viewed within the context of a gallery, the audience arrives with various preconceived ideas about art which become part of the way they process the experience of viewing it. Without the reaction of the audience – and how this has rippled through the art world – the piece wouldn't have the significance it does. And it probably wouldn't have been emojified a century later by the gallery Cantor Fine Art as one of the key works of twentieth-century art history.[20]

This brings us to the way the role of the reader or audience is closely related to how creativity is valued in society. The fact that the term is so prevalent these days shows that, as a general concept, creativity is something that modern society considers important. But different types of creativity are valued in different ways. The tropes we mentioned earlier – the use of metaphor, types of word play, etc. – are found in everyday conversation as much as they are in literature. Linguistic creativity of this sort is, in fact, a fundamental part of how we use language in any situation. Yet the purposes it's put to, and the value that's placed on it, will be different in, say, the context of a discussion down the pub or an article in the *New Yorker*.

Emoji, for the most part, are associated with the type of communication which doesn't have a particularly high status in society, and thus their creative use is not, *prima facie*, considered literary or artistic. There are exceptions – not least the fact that in 2016 the Museum of Modern Art in New York acquired the original set of Shigetaka Kurita's emoji designs for their collection.[21] But it's their roots in online culture which is the initial spark for most of the creative uses of emoji, as well as the way they become an extension of the sort of everyday language play that has flourished so extensively on the internet.

Neologasms and Emojian Slips

The internet has been a major driver of linguistic innovation from the time it went mainstream. Not only does it allow words to spread quickly and widely: its fascination for the unusual and the quirky, combined with an encyclopaedic desire to archive the world, leads to the compulsive circulation of listicles such as '28 Beautiful Words the English Language Should Steal'[22] and '27 Brilliant Words You Didn't Know You Needed'[23] – words like the Swedish *tidsoptimist*, meaning a person who's overly optimistic about the amount of time they have and is thus invariably late.

The social nature of the internet has also had a profound influence on practices such as lexicography. Not normally thought of as a populist mainstream pastime, there's a vibrant online community dedicated to documenting vocabulary and to maintaining and enhancing the language by coining new words. Whereas in the past lexicography was simply a process of reflecting conventional use, now it's a place for linguistic innovation – both cataloguing, editorialising and creating the vocabulary of the moment.

One of the most popular examples of this is, of course, Urban Dictionary. Begun way back in 1999 by Aaron Peckham, the idea was to create a web-based dictionary of slang to which users could submit their own entries. Two decades later, its store of definitions runs into the millions. Unlike traditional dictionaries, it records fleeting and everyday spoken language and gives definitions which are personal rather than authoritative. Words are pulled from everyday informal speech and are presented in an equally informal way: spelling is often non-standard (or simply full of typos), as are punctuation conventions. The result is something starkly different from traditional lexicography, as this definition intimates:

> Dictionary – What you're reading right now, but without all the assholes, anti-Americans, dumbass n00bs, atrocious grammar, made up words, slang, gibberish, and other crap. [Cyberquad, 6 April, 2004]

There's also a trend in the dictionary for the coining of entirely new words to describe aspects of modern life. Blends again are particularly popular and often reflect the lifestyle and preoccupations of the demographic who contribute to the dictionary (which is mostly teens and those in their early twenties). So you get things such as *intexticated* ('Driving while texting on a cell phone'); *neologasm* ('the pleasurable feeling from having coined a new word. Combination of neologism and orgasm'); and *emojian slip* ('when you send the wrong emoji in a text, constituting an unintentional error regarded as revealing subconscious feelings'). Used in this way, the coining of words itself becomes a form of communication and community-building, and the dictionary has a social function far beyond simply codifying and cataloguing the language. The creativity that sites such as this generate means that the internet becomes an unparalleled resource for engaging with language.

We've already looked at a few ways in which the same sort of creative reflection has turned its focus to emoji. There are genres such as the 'emoji review', which offers sardonic rundowns of the different designs for particular emoji. There are the countless Buzzfeed-type lists which provide primers on 'What Your Favourite Emojis Really Mean' – the formula usually being that it's something either sassy or sardonic, such as the Grimacing Face 😬 meaning 'I'm probably asking you a favour right now'.[24] Then there are examples of people contrasting pre- and post-digital communication, such as a sculpture by the artist Maya Ben-Ezer which substituted the keys of an early typewriter with emoji.[25]

But the creativity inspired by emoji isn't just in how people reflect on them as a type of 'language' – it's also the uses they're put to, and particularly the limits to which they can be pushed as a form of communication.

The following sentence is in English:

Λοβ ιζ ιν δι εαρ

Unless you're familiar with the Greek alphabet, however, you're going to have difficulty reading it. It's part of a phenomenon known as 'Engreek' – using the Greek alphabet to write out English words, usually as a way of adding a particular cultural slant to their meaning.

As we saw in earlier chapters, in the early days of the internet, before Unicode standardised character encoding, it was often difficult to write messages in anything other than the basic Roman alphabet. People would transliterate phrases from their local language into this alphabet, improvising as they went along. You'd have to write 'tha ertheis avrio?', for example, if you wanted to text a friend to ask if they were coming along tomorrow but your phone didn't support the Greek alphabet.

Now that most devices can switch painlessly between different writing systems, the pragmatic need for this practice no longer exists. Yet people still play around with the different systems, and the phenomenon of Engreek is one such example. The reasons they do this aren't simply about finding workarounds for the limitations of the technology anymore. Instead, there are various different motivations, most of them centring around the creative possibilities that modern technology makes available.

The same practice happens with writing systems other than
the Greek alphabet, of course – and this extends to emoji.
When BBC America tweeted an advert for an episode of
Doctor Who called 'Smile' in 2017, they did so entirely in
emoji.[26] The tweet was a way of highlighting the theme of the
episode, which saw the Doctor and his companion travel to a
future which was governed by robots who communicated
entirely in emoji. But the message itself, rather than using
the symbols in the conventional way, had them transliterating
an English sentence:

Improvising a sort of 'Emoglish' by using emoji as letters of the
alphabet, the sentence spells out 'Get caught up with last night's
new #DoctorWho on BBC America'.

The same technique was also used extensively by the actress
Carrie Fisher. Her Twitter feed was full of messages made up
entirely of transliterations of English words, with the odd extra
character inserted in the place of spaces. This, for example, is one
she sent out on 4 May, which is celebrated in certain circles as Star
Wars Day:[27]

Despite the fact that in many ways the meaning here is more
transparent than if the characters symbolised a combination of
ideas (which, as we've seen, can be a challenge to interpret because
of the lack of a conventionalised emoji grammar), deciphering
what she's saying can take a bit of work – so much so, in fact, that
one woman set herself up as a 'translator' dedicated exclusively to
rendering Carrie Fisher's tweets back into standard English
orthography.[28]

Returning to the original Greeklish example, for those who don't know the Greek alphabet, Λοβ ιζ ιν δι εαρ reads as 'Love is in the air'. This particular example is from a piece of graffiti found in the centre of Athens. The phrase is a common enough one in English – and one which has a certain international currency because of the John Paul Young song of the same name, which was then featured in the soundtrack to the film *Strictly Ballroom* and also performed as part of the closing ceremony of the 2000 Sydney Olympics. The motivation for writing this in Engreek might, therefore, have been an indirect comment on the way that English-language phrases such as this have flooded global culture. The linguist Tereza Spilioti has noted that Engreek is often used as a means of mocking the cosmopolitan aspirations of people who flaunt their English abilities or as a way of appropriating English as a global language by writing it with a 'Greek accent'. Fundamentally, though, it's a means of upsetting the normal rules of writing and being able to play with language. Much like doing a word puzzle, it allows people to engage in small acts of linguistic dexterity and to bounce these back and forth with their friends as a form of social bonding.

One of the motivations for doing this with emoji is a stylistic choice. The journalist Rebecca Hawkes writes of Carrie Fisher that her humour, outlook on the world and 'natural eccentricity' made her a perfect celebrity for the online era[29] – and her idiosyncratic use of emoji clearly contributed to this. While Engreek plays on the similarities between the sounds of Greek and English, in emoji the practice is far more focused on the visuals. It's about improvising a makeshift writing system based on the way that the shape of certain emoji roughly match letters of the alphabet and playing with the aesthetics of this alphabet.

As a form of creativity this is quite a niche use, however. More common are experiments to see what sort of meaning can be generated entirely from emoji in their normal guise as a picture-based writing system. Can genres such as fiction, poetry and comedy be rendered entirely in emoji? And if so, what does this tell us about our understanding of narrative, of style and of humour?

The Experimental Narrator

Writers have, over the years, experimented with the constraints of a variety of different types of digital media, exploring how they can provide an artistic catalyst for their work. In recent years, for example, the novelists Jennifer Egan and David Mitchell have both tried their hand at writing fiction for Twitter. The main constraint here is that every sentence needed (at the time they were writing) to be tailored to the 140 character limit. But there was also the way that the story was 'published' in a series of discrete sentences over an extended time period, which the reader then had to piece together into a coherent whole as they scrolled through their feed.

The Twitter stories of both authors work surprisingly well, with specific narrative motivations created to explain the structural constraints. Egan's story 'Black Box' was tweeted from the *New Yorker*'s Twitter account over nine days in the spring of 2012. The story is science fiction, and each tweets represents one of a series of what Egan describes as 'terse mental dispatches from a female spy of the future'.[30] In this way, both their truncated form and means of dissemination become part of the apparatus of the story itself.

Mitchell's 'The Right Sort', meanwhile, develops over 280 tweets to tell the story of a young teenager and his mother visiting a sinister house. In order to ease his anxiety about the trip, the boy has taken one of his mother's Valium. As the narrative unfolds he begins to experience ever-more-macabre incidents, which could be due either to the drugs or to some supernatural presence in the house. Mitchell uses the staccato sentence patterns to reflect the way in which the boy's mind is working – as one tweet explains, 'The pill's just kicking in now. Valium breaks down the world into bite-sized sentences. Like this one. All lined up. Munch-munch.'

In both cases, however, despite the rationale for the piece-meal delivery, the reading experience works best when the tweets are all collected together in one place. Indeed, both stories were subsequently published in a more traditional, complete form: Egan's in the *New Yorker*,[31] and Mitchell's in the *Guardian*.[32]

Playing with some of the different affordances of the medium, various other writers have taken more purposefully experimental approaches to social media fiction. The novelist Teju Cole, for example, published a short story called 'Hafiz' by getting a group of his friends to randomly tweet all the individual sentences from it, which he then retweeted in the correct order, thus joining them together in his own Twitter feed to make a coherent story.[33]

Then there's the British artist Simon Morris, who, inspired by an idea from Kenneth Goldsmith's book *Uncreative Writing*, decided to type out verbatim the entirety of Jack Kerouac's *On the Road*, one page at a time. He then posted each page of this to his blog, 'Getting Inside Jack Kerouac's Head'.[34] Over the course of ten months he typed the complete novel, which, presented as a blog, now read back to front (i.e. the most recent excerpts he'd typed were at the top of the page, and everything was archived in reverse order). At the end of the process he then published the whole thing back into book form.[35]

The relative merits of these different exercises depend on how you view the purpose of the creative process. Read as a story in the paper, David Mitchell's 'The Right Sort' is a traditional piece of fiction with plot complications, character progression and a coherent narrative. In fact, Mitchell later reworked the story to become the first chapter of his novel *Slade House*, which was published in entirely conventional form. Simon Morris's reworking of Kerouac, on the other hand, is much more of a conceptual project. In this case the ideas which motivated it and the execution of the idea are of greater relevance than the final product.

So how about the use of emoji as a resource for creative writing? Where do they fit along this cline? And why might people be interested in experimenting in this way? On the whole, emoji composition is more towards the experimental end of things. At the moment it's more a way of reflecting on the writing process – and on how semiotic systems are used to make meaning – than an authentically engaging medium for telling stories. There's the aforementioned *Emoji Dick*, for example. This was the brainchild of the data engineer Fred Benenson, who crowdfunded $3,500 to assemble a group of several thousand people to translate the 200,000-word novel into emoji. The result is a long-form piece of experimental art, testing the limits of emoji's expressive capabilities. It may have gained notoriety for being the first-ever emoji book entered into the Library of Congress's catalogue, but it's far closer to Simon Morris's Kerouac project than it is to David Mitchell's or Jennifer Egan's experiments with Twitter fiction.

The issue of if and how narrative can be rendered in emoji remains an interesting one, however. While emoji might not be ideally suited for translating five-hundred-page works of nineteenth-century fiction, they can perhaps still thrive as a medium for shorter attempts at storytelling. In 2015 the National Young Writers' Festival tried exactly this as an exercise, asking people to send in succinct emoji stories, each of 140 characters or less. The results they attracted could be grouped into three basic categories: straightforward narratives using line breaks, expressions and actions to tell a story; tableaux which worked along the lines of a narrative picture; and abstract or impressionistic compositions.[36]

But without a complex grammar, is it really possible to compose a serious narrative in emoji? And what can the issues and challenges around trying to use them as a medium for storytelling reveal about the way they work as a form of creative communication?

Emojifiction

Here's the opening to a famous short story, translated into emoji.

Given the fact that the grammar of emoji is so elemental at the moment, the way we attempt to interpret a text like this is to draw on our understanding of some of the fundamental elements of narrative and use these as scaffolding for the meaning that's encoded in the individual symbols. In other words, we're projecting onto the symbols the way the different concepts are linked together, and in this way we (try to) decode the story based on our understanding of how narratives work.

A traditional narrative usually starts with an abstract, which tells you how the story begins. It then lays out who or what's involved and where the action takes place. This is followed by the 'complicating action', which in turn leads to a resolution, explaining how everything worked out in the end.[37] In the case of the short-story opening, then, we understand the first two emoji to mean that it's night-time and that someone's asleep in bed. The thought bubble is a convention from comics, and in this case (as the person is asleep) we can interpret it as dreaming – or, given the devils and demons appearing in the man's dream, as having a nightmare. The line breaks then indicate the start of each new action in much the same way that sentences do in a verbal text. The transition from the first to the second line thus shifts from night-time to daybreak.

Neil Cohn, author of *The Visual Language of Comics*, has suggested that one of the key elements for interpreting a visual narrative is what he calls the *continuity constraint*.[38] This is the idea that we try to piece together some sense of continuity between symbols – we assume that symbols printed next to each other have a relationship to each other, and we thus look for a coherent meaning that connects them. If we see several faces lined up in a row, for example, we might assume this is meant to be the same person experiencing a range of different emotions (unless there's a particular context which suggests otherwise, such as a crowd scene). So we can read the three faces in the second line as the protagonist sleeping, waking up bleary-eyed and then being confronted by something which leaves him dumbstruck (so much so that his mouth metaphorically disappears).

Here's the opening of this story in its original verbal form (translated into English), which comes from Franz Kafka's 'The Metamorphosis'.

> One morning, as Gregor Samsa stirred awake out of unsettling dreams, he found himself transformed into a monstrous insect. He lay on his back, which was like a hard shell, and if he raised his head a little he could see his bulging, brown stomach, divided by hard, curved ridges; there was scarcely any stopping the duvet from sliding completely off the top of it. His numerous legs, which seemed pathetically puny in proportion to the rest of him, flickered helplessly before his eyes.[39]

In effect, the emoji translation only really covers the first line of the verbal text – a man awaking from a troubled sleep and finding himself transformed into an insect. It gestures, rather impressionistically, at the numerous legs flickering before his eyes. But it can't convey the detail or psychological perspective of someone trying to come to terms with the fact that his body has dramatically metamorphosised during the night.

Below is another short narrative, this time composed directly in emoji (i.e. it hasn't been translated from what was originally a verbal text). Again, this draws on the language of comics, specifically in the use of thought bubbles as a way of representing the interior concerns of the character, and line breaks working as a way of distinguishing between actions (i.e. operating as the equivalent of periods in verbal written sentences). Each line is only able to contain a fairly simple idea, though: mostly a subject and an action (e.g. the man imagines marrying the woman in line 6), so the overall story is rather simplistic. The syntax of these 'sentences' follows the conventional word order of English: the man (subject) speaks (verb) to the woman (object). Given these basic 'rules' of discourse and grammar, see how easy (or difficult) you find it to interpret.

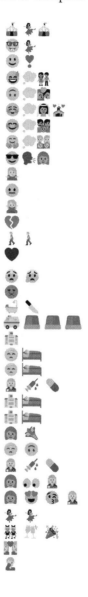

There are other constraints due to the medium which
influence the telling of this story. It only involves three
characters (male protagonist, dancer, doctor), and, as names
are difficult to render in emoji, all the characters are anonymous. It also relies on its being a fairly recognisable story;
i.e. there's an expected pattern which helps the reader to
anticipate the unfolding of the action. It would be far more
difficult to create something with more narrative complexity
because readers wouldn't be able to draw on their expectations to help them interpret it.

In cases such as the two quoted stories, the aim is to
translate elements of a verbal narrative into emoji. But perhaps there are other narrative forms which can draw more
on the specific affordances that emoji offer. The next narrative, for example, works in a way that's closer to a comic
than a written piece of prose, with each successive line
representing the same scene as it evolves over time. It's the
equivalent of a six-panel comic strip, with the basic picture
repeated in each and the story being told through the slight
differences between them. So rather than reading character-
by-character from left to right, as you would with a verbally
written text, you have to take each line as a complete whole,
imagining them representing different moments in time in
an unfolding narrative.

In terms of the component parts of a narrative, this mini-
story has a set-up, which includes the main actors: the scene as
shown in the first line with a tractor mowing a field of corn. It

has a complicating action: the collision between tractor and person that occurs in line 4. And it has a resolution: the final line in which the scene has been totally transformed. It doesn't have an opening introduction – an abstract – but if I were to give it a title, 'Deathly Harvest' maybe, this could operate as that.

Even this narrative feels more like an experiment than an authentic attempt at creative expression, however. Emoji, with their specific ties to social media, are probably better suited to forms of narrative which suit the affordances of social media – one of the most salient of which is concision. And indeed, it's improvisational approaches to narrative which fit with these sort of constraints that create the most interesting results. For example, when Hillary Clinton won the nomination for Democratic candidate for the presidency in June 2017, a strategist for the Democratic party, Laura Olin, optimistically tweeted the following (Figure 8.1).[40]

Although lacking many of the components outlined in the earlier emoji stories, this is still a narrative, condensing 227 years of US history into a single tweet. It resonated to such an extent that it inspired a number of sequels, including one in which, once the actual result of the presidential election was known, the final emoji of a woman was replaced with one of a clown.

*

Figure 8.1 Laura Olin's 'history of the presidency' tweet

Beyond storytelling, emoji have been embraced by a host of different literary forms and cultural practices, ranging from poetry[41] and stand-up comedy[42] to fashion and architecture. This includes a pair of sneakers from Betabrand decorated with a geometric pattern made of hundreds of interlocking poop emoji and Chanel's Autumn 2016 collection, which featured a series of printed fabrics decorated with the cat emoji, the peace sign, the four-leaf clover, and the thumbs up, as well as an emoji-style version of the Chanel logo itself.[43] Then there's the use of emoji as an architectural feature, as in a building in the Dutch city of Amersfoort designed by Changiz Tehrani, who decided to use the symbols as gargoyle-style decorations.[44]

To understand why emoji been adopted into culture – and particularly popular culture – so readily, it's probably easiest to simply swap the elements of the relationship around: it's not so much that emoji have been embraced by pop culture as it is that pop culture has been adapted as a means of communication. As we've seen, emoji have their origins – both in the way they look and the ideas they represent – in pop culture. But equally important is the fact that they're native-born to consumerism. Emoji are a writing system which was birthed into a culture of hyper-capitalism and privatised regulation. And it's this element of their existence which perhaps foreshadows the most important way in which technology is going to define the communication of the future.

9 The Emojification of Everyday Life

Six Emoji in Search of an Author 🐾 *Emojification* 🐾 *Get-Rich-Quick Schemes* 🐾 *Kitten Writing and Heavenly Dogs* 🐾 *Everyday Revolutions*

Six Emoji in Search of an Author

A week prior to the release of the much-hyped *The Emoji Movie* in 2017, its marketing department tweeted an advert parodying the television adaptation of Margaret Atwood's *The Handmaid's Tale*. The advert showed a bright yellow female emoji smiling broadly from behind one of the restrictive bonnets worn by the handmaidens in the series. Atwood's novel is set in a dystopian future, in which women are stripped of their rights by a totalitarian government and ritually raped by the elite of society. Unsurprisingly, the tone-deaf use of this allusion in the film's advertising didn't go down well with the public at large.[1] As one person on Twitter put it, 'Oh you've got jokes on the subjugation, rape and societal betrayal of women! Can't wait to take my kids!'[2]

When it finally came out, *The Emoji Movie* was almost universally panned by critics. According to Charles Bramesco in the *Guardian*, it was 'a force of insidious evil';[3] for *Vox*'s Alissa Wilkinson it was 'less of a movie and more of an insult';[4] and for Peter Sobczynski at *RogerEbert.com* it was 'a demonstration of artistic abdication at its most venal'.[5] On the review site Rotten Tomatoes, after the first twenty-eight appraisals had been processed, its rating was an unequivocal 0 per cent.[6]

The reason that people found it almost offensively bad, though, points to the paradox that underpins emoji and drives their role as the standard-bearer for the future of communications technology. As we've discussing throughout this book, what from one perspective look like colourful, uncomplicated little symbols are also the advance guard for the way that technology – and, more importantly, technology companies – are taking an ever-greater control over the ways in which we relate to each other today. And in this context, the invocation of a dystopian world that the misguided *Handmaid's Tale* parody invoked was perhaps more apt than was intended.

As we've seen, emoji have a split personality in modern culture. On the one hand they are, without doubt, a very helpful resource for online communication. They offer a way of restoring the layer of meaning that's conveyed by tone of voice, gesture, glance and so on – of simply and easily injecting some emotional framing back into the conversation. Then there's the creative potential they offer. Social media, as we saw in the previous chapter, has become a cradle for everyday language play, and this is a major part of the social bonding that takes place online. Again, emoji, with their eclectic vocabulary and their pictorial nature, are a perfect resource for this.

From these two perspectives, emoji are far from being a step back for civilisation or a dumbing-down of culture. But there's also a far more ambiguous side to them. Unlike any other type of language we use, emoji's existence depends entirely on technology and the huge multinational corporations which produce that technology. Although in theory emoji are public-domain entities, the whole system is regulated by a small consortium of representatives from the major tech companies. And each of these companies produces – and owns – their own designs for emoji, which are constantly being updated as part of the general refresh cycles which keep people buying new phones every few years. Their existence, in other words, is tied directly to the marketing strategies of a handful of the biggest corporations in the world. And this is what *The Emoji Movie* illustrated so painfully.

It was almost inevitable that Hollywood would embrace emoji as a movie concept. In many ways they're ideal for adaptation into a drama. After all, they have a ready-made cast of stock characters who look like, and to an extent are based on, cartoons. They're something of a modern equivalent of the characters from the *commedia dell'arte*, the sixteenth-century Italian theatre genre with fixed sets of stock characters – foolish old men, scheming servants, sentimental lovers – which could be endlessly mixed and improvised into stories for performance.

Then of course there are the commercial opportunities. You've got both pre-existing global character recognition and a huge range of possible brand tie-ins to exploit. Unfortunately for *The Emoji Movie*, they went overboard on the second part of this equation while failing to exploit the first.

Sony, which produced the film, had some form here, with 2016's *Angry Birds Movie*. But *The Emoji Movie* pushed the strategy to ever greater extremes. It became simply a conveyor belt of tech product placement, from YouTube, Instagram and Twitter to WeChat (for that all-important Chinese market), Candy Crush and Dropbox, which is cast as a bizarre Shangri-La for the intrepid emoji adventurers in the film.

In the dystopian world of George Orwell's *Nineteen Eighty-Four*, one of the ways in which the totalitarian government controls the population is by controlling its language. By manipulating the meaning of words, they're able to manipulate people's thoughts and behaviour. In the case of emoji, it's not the government who has control over the content of the 'language' – it's corporations. They don't, on the whole, manipulate emoji in order to manipulate the political beliefs of the population – although, as we've seen in earlier chapters, cultural representation in emoji is a lively political issue. They do, however, co-opt them into their overall commercial strategies. Emoji, in other words, are a product, just like any other technological feature is. This is what *The Emoji Movie* exposes in such a disconcertingly honest way. And for something which has become such a ubiquitous part of modern-day culture, this co-dependence between language, commerce and technology could well prove to be a major turning point in the evolution of human communication.

Emojification

On Sunday, 17 July, 1955, the original Disneyland in California opened with a special International Press Preview event.[7] The day turned out not to be the most auspicious of starts for the theme park.[8] Construction on several of the attractions was barely complete, there were traffic jams all across the neighbourhood, and there was a severe lack of food and water on what was one of the hottest days of the summer. In the months leading up to this, the banks who were backing the project, along with Walt Disney's brother Roy, who was financial director of the film studio, were all deeply worried that it was going to end up a commercial catastrophe. But despite all the pre-launch pessimism, the gamble taken by Disney to create this sanitised fantasy world turned out, of course, to be a huge success. It was instrumental in the Disney brand becoming so ubiquitous across the globe and ending up as byword for a particular ethos of corporate entertainment.

17 July also happens to be 'World Emoji Day', an annual event created 'to promote the use of emojis and spread the enjoyment that they bring to all of those around us'.[9] The reason it's marked on this particular day is because this happens to be the date displayed on the iPhone's calendar emoji. And the link to large corporations such as Apple is in full effect on World Emoji Day. In 2016, for example, Sony used it for announcements about the aforementioned *The Emoji Movie*, Google unveiled a set of more 'inclusive' emoji, and companies such as General Electric, Twitter and Coca-Cola all tied their own promotions to it. As, in fact, did Disney.

It's mere coincidence that Disneyland and emoji share the same ceremonial birthday, of course. There's no actual connection between the two. Yet there are certain similarities in the way the influence that the former has had on society parallels that of the latter – and how the Disneyfication ethos finds a modern equivalent in the emojification of society.

Disneyfication is a term used to describe the way in which mainstream culture is being transformed in ways which resemble a Disney theme park. The idea – initially called 'Disneyization' – was popularised by the social scientist Alan Bryman in his book *The Disneyization of Society*. It's used to imply a homogenisation of culture, founded around consumption and merchandising: one which presents an artificially 'perfected' image of society based on a bourgeois ideal of American values. Issues such as class, race and gender inequality are all airbrushed out, as are references to anything that could be considered negative. In their place is presented a manufactured image of the world free of poverty, discord or any other social malaise, all glossed over with a romanticised and tourist-friendly façade.

Disneyland doesn't, of course, pretend to be real life. It's meant to be an escape from the mundanity and travails of everyday reality. It was for this reason that the philosopher Jean Baudrillard asserted that it was actually the most 'real' place in America, as it embraces the fiction that's at the heart of all society. Society, according to Baudrillard, is based on various economic and religious ideologies, on cultural beliefs such as national identity and capitalist progress, and on countless other narratives which shape the way we organise our lives and communities. 'Disneyland,' he writes, 'is presented as imaginary in order to make us believe that the rest is real, when in fact all of Los Angeles and the America surrounding it are no longer real, but of the order of the hyper-real and of simulation.'

In what ways might emoji be similar to this? Like Disneyland, emoji offer an overwhelmingly positive spin on the things we may want to communicate. Not only are their designs brightly coloured and cartoon-like, but the content is skewed very much towards the generally upbeat. It's only in the last few years that a few more disgruntled and pained faces have been added to the rostrum – things like the mouth of swear symbols 🤬, the vomiting face 🤮, the exploding head 🤯. And even these, in the exaggeration of their design, are comic burlesques of the real emotions related to nausea or irrepressible rage.

This isn't to say that we're constrained to positive and life-affirming messages because of the range of symbols on offer. Despite a tightly controlled character list, this is not George Orwell's Newspeak, where people are only able to articulate ideas for which there's a word in the dictionary. Whereas in the world of *Nineteen Eighty-Four* deleting a word from the dictionary banishes it from people's working vocabulary, real-life communication doesn't work like that. As we've seen, even in the absence of swear words or sexually explicit vocabulary, these ideas can still be conveyed in emoji with a bit of creative juxtaposition.

Another similarity with Disneyfication is the strong, centralised regulation of the product. Unlike almost any other form of language, emoji's entire existence now is overseen by this one small, non-elected consortium of people, based in the United States and dominated by large transnational (although largely US-based) corporations. And this, unsurprisingly, gets reflected in the values represented in the symbols. While these are more socially liberal that those promoted by Disney, they are, nevertheless, a particular cultural worldview, as we saw in the debates over gender and race representation.

Then there's the way that Disney famously saw everything as a constant branding opportunity. This again has striking parallels with the way emoji are promoted in society; and again marks a break with nearly all other systems of everyday communication.

Get-Rich-Quick Schemes

The phrase 'Make America Great Again' was first used by Ronald Reagan as part of his 1980 presidential campaign. Foolishly, Reagan didn't bother to trademark the slogan and so never managed to monetise it. When Donald Trump was looking for a slogan for himself – an essential first step in his plans for a run for the White House – he initially considered using the slightly truncated 'Make America Great'. The only problem was that this somehow suggested that America had never previously achieved true greatness – that, two centuries into the great American project, it had only ever really managed mediocrity. This obviously didn't play to the narrative he was pushing, that a once-powerful nation had been run into the ground by eight years of Barack Obama. Adding 'Again' at the end of the short string of words solved this problem. Plus, as an added bonus, it turned out that not only had Reagan failed to trademark the phrase, but neither had anyone else.[10] So he did, securing exclusive rights to its use for political promotion and fundraising. And almost immediately he began monetising it through a variety of 'MAGA'-themed goods and trinkets: the red baseball cap, of course, but also collector's items such as a '24 karat gold-finished' Christmas tree decoration[11] and 'Official Trump-Pence Mini Megaphones (Set of 2)'.[12]

The copyrighting of particular slogans or catchphrases is one of the most obvious ways in which language can be tied to economics. One could argue, however, that *all* language is bound up with economics in today's society. When people learn a foreign language in order to improve their employment opportunities, as many people around the world do with English, they're 'investing' in language skills in the hope that these will lead to financial gain. And it's not just foreign language skills: the standard English one learns at school is often an important basic criterion for finding a good job. In these ways, language is a commodity in the same way that education is. But the way that emoji are related to economic issues, and specifically the way they're owned and exploited by a small number of very large companies, makes them a curious, almost unique, phenomenon in the history of communication.

The origins of the iconography around which emoji are built have very specific corporate roots. The yellow smiley face, now such a universally recognisable part of modern-day culture, was initially created as a PR stunt for a merger between two American insurance firms. It was designed by a commercial artist named Harvey Ross Ball who, in the early 1960s, was hired by the State Mutual Life Assurance Company of Worcester, Massachusetts, when they bought out their rivals at Guarantee Mutual of Ohio.

All the upheaval caused by the merger led to a slump in worker morale, and as part of a scheme to combat this the company's management asked Ball to come up with an image which would promote a sense of wellbeing and positivity across the office. Ball's solution, simple yet effective, was a little yellow smiling face with one eye ever-so-slightly bigger than the other. He was paid $45 for his work.

Just like Ronald Reagan, Ball foolishly didn't trademark his creation. And this has led to various battles down through the years over the commercial rights to the symbol. For example, the retail giant Walmart, who've used the image on employee uniforms since the mid-1990s, tried to trademark it in the early 2000s.[13] They ended up in a protracted legal battle with the French journalist and copywriter Franklin Loufrani, who owns the rights to the image in several countries around the world – although not, importantly, in the United States. Loufrani runs a company called SmileyWorld, which explains in its mission statement that the smiley is 'more than just an icon, a brand and a lifestyle: it is now a spirit and a philosophy, reminding people just how powerful a smile can be'.[14] Working from this premise, the company is able to generate a yearly turnover in excess of $265 million while selling more than 23 million products annually.[15] Having the legal rights to a yellow circle with two dots and a curved line has proved to be a highly lucrative business.

There have been other examples of people trying to monetise new forms of communication over the years, but with far less success. One of the most infamous is the ill-fated SarcMark, an initiative formulated by a father and son from Michigan, Paul and Douglas Sak. Like many of the punctuation inventors we encountered earlier, the Saks felt that the world was in need of a dedicated sarcasm mark. 'The written word,' they opined, 'has question marks and exclamation points to document those thoughts, BUT sarcasm has NOTHING! In today's world with increasing commentary, debate and rhetoric, what better time could there be than NOW, to ensure that no sarcastic message, comment or opinion is left behind.'[16]

Having identified this gap in the market, and designed a suitable symbol to represent it – something resembling a back-to-front 6 with a dot in the middle (which the tech journalist Nick Broughall memorably described as looking like 'an inverted foetus'[17]) – they then rolled out a plan to charge people for the privilege of using it. In June 2008 they filed a patent, and eighteen months later they made a public announcement about their invention. People who wished to use the SarcMark for non-commercial purposes could do so for the competitive price of $1.99; business users were urged to email the Saks directly for details of the commercial rates.

Somewhat unsurprisingly, the public reaction wasn't overwhelmingly positive. Within a month of the initial press release, an insurgency movement had developed. 'Of late', this movement wrote on its website, 'the forces of Big Sarcasm have brought forth onto the internet the idea that sarcasmists everywhere must license and download their proprietary new "punctuation" … in order to clarify sarcasm in their writing.'[18] The rebel group called instead for an Open Sarcasm initiative, which would counter the 'greedy capitalists of Sarcasm, Inc.' wherever they tried to sell their wares.

Emoji aren't quite in this category, of course. You don't have to directly hand over a small sum of money whenever you want to use them. Yet their status is much more closely linked to commercial concerns than the letters of the alphabet are, or indeed all the other punctuations marks to which we have access. As was discussed earlier, the actual renderings of all the emoji are owned by the technology companies which design them, and they're often used very explicitly as marketing motivation for software and hardware updates. Stickers, meanwhile, are a hugely lucrative business, not only for the social media apps which sell them but also as a promotional tool for companies. Several brands have created their own emoji keyboards for sharing themed stickers. These range from IKEA emoji – which include chests of drawers and a tower of meatballs with a Swedish flag resting on top of it[19] – to the World Wide Fund for Nature creating an endangered species sticker set to raise money for animals at risk of extinction.[20]

Then there's the business model practised by Twitter, who create their own custom emoji to accompany major events such as the Super Bowl or the US election – but who also sell these bespoke symbols for promotional purposes, with companies like Coca-Cola and Starbucks reputedly paying in excess of a million dollars for online campaigns based around their own branded Twitter emoji.[21] In this respect, emoji are the perfect manifestation of a communications system tailor-made for the neoliberal times in which we live.

Kitten Writing and Heavenly Dogs

The English language is spoken at some level by around 1.75 billion people worldwide. That's one in every four members of the global population. For the British Council, who operate as the United Kingdom's official promoter of British culture overseas, this creates a huge potential audience. And they're very explicit about their desire to take full advantage of this as a way to raise the profile of the country. 'The English language is perhaps the United Kingdom's greatest and yet least-recognised international asset,' they write on their website. 'It is a cornerstone of our identity and it keeps us in the mind of hundreds of millions of people around the world, even when they are not talking to us.'[22] Such is the status of the language across the globe that it provides great economic – but also diplomatic – contributions to the United Kingdom's prosperity. Or to put it another way, it's an ideal instrument for the leverage of soft power.

The concept of 'soft power' was coined by the political scientist Joseph Nye to describe the way that a group or nation can use culture rather than force or economic strength to boost their status on the world stage. The idea is that it's possible to shape the perception people have of a country by presenting its culture in an appealing and attractive light. Nye coined the term in his 1990 book *Bound to Lead: The Changing Nature of American Power*, in which he argued that by exporting its language, values and ethos by means of cultural products, the United States would be able to maintain and reinforce its status in the world. The process is one which has long been practised to great effect in American culture – not least in Hollywood and through advertising and branding – although mostly this has been without the explicit backing of government policy.[23] Nye's contention was that this same process should become an overt part of international diplomacy.

In these terms, the British Council's strategy to further promote the use of English – and with it, English-language culture – around the world is an archetypal soft-power initiative, aiming to exploit a resource which already has global standing. Given the profile that emoji now have (with a global reach easily equivalent to English), could they not also be used for similar purposes? Is their heritage something that Japan could capitalise on as a way to spread and promote a positive image of its culture around the world?

There is, as it happens, a notable precedent for the use of a visual communication system as a means of promoting Japanese cultural capital to an international audience. When Japan first hosted the Olympic Games, in 1964, they approached the event as an opportunity for emphasising the country's recovery from the war and presenting a national identity that was both modern and peaceful.[24] Japan was originally supposed to have hosted the 1940 Summer Olympics, but, following the outbreak of war with China in 1937, Tokyo forfeited the Games, which were instead moved to Helsinki (although they were then cancelled completely when World War II broke out). Twenty-four years later, the Japanese government looked to the Games as an excellent chance to be symbolically accepted back into the international community.

Central to their plans for showcasing this desired image of modernity and technological advancement was the use of graphic design. The aim was to create a particularly modern Japanese aesthetic in the design of logos, signs, posters and all the other visual paraphernalia which announced the Games. In order to do this, they drew for inspiration on the notion of the isotype, a means of presenting information in an entirely visual way through icons. Isotype (standing for International System Of Typographic Picture Education) is a set of pictorial symbols which are used to visually represent concepts and ideas related to the social sciences. It was developed at the beginning of the twentieth century by the Social and Economic Museum of Vienna, which wanted a way of easily explaining elements of its collection to the public. As its primary inventor, the philosopher Otto Neurath, said, 'To remember simplified pictures is better than to forget accurate figures.'[25]

Given that the thousands of tourists visiting the country for the Olympics were unlikely to speak much Japanese, the creation of a visually based system of communication was an ideal solution. But alongside this practical need for a form of universally comprehensible communication, the designers also wanted to create something which would represent modern-day Japanese culture. They were determined to move away from stereotypes of geisha, cherry blossoms and Mount Fuji. Instead they opted for an aesthetic based on abstracted, geometric designs – which thus became the first instance of pictograms being used as part of the image of the Olympic Games.[26]

Emoji weren't conceived in the context of an international audience, of course. They were a local initiative for a local market. Politics, in the early days of their development, played little part in their story. Nevertheless, their roots are deeply embedded in Japanese culture, and much of this still shows through in both their general aesthetic and the range of individual symbols – all of which makes for some interesting cultural identity issues, now they've been embraced by a global community. We've discussed, for example, the influence of manga on the way that meaning is encoded in some of the pictures. Another notable but submerged element of their lineage is what's known as *koneko ji* (小猫字), or 'kitten writing' – a particular style of handwriting which was the craze among teenage girls in the 1970s. This consisted of large, rounded characters, which were often decorated with hearts, stars and cartoon faces.[27] This in turn became part of a broader trend for cute or *kawaii* culture, which went on to become one of the defining features of Japanese youth culture over the last three decades – and is another of the cultural antecedents that fed into the development and overall look of emoji.

The Japanese roots of the system can also be seen in the way that a vast array of Japanese culture is explicitly referenced in the symbols themselves. We touched on a number of these earlier: emoji such as ▦▦▦▦, all of which include specific language elements of Japanese (either written or gestural). But there are several more symbols, covering Japanese customs, culture and various natural features. For a start, Japan is the only country which has its own emoji map ▦. Then there are all the Japanese-specific foods, such as sashimi, curry rice, bento boxes, *o-nigiri* (rice cakes), *sembei* (rice crackers) and green tea. While most of these will be recognisable to an international audience, there are a few which are less well known outside Japan itself, such as *oden* (egg, fish cakes, radish) and *dango* 団子, a rice-flour sweet which is coloured by red bean and green tea ▦▦. Then there's the *narutomaki* (なると巻き) ▦, a type of fish paste which takes its name from the pink spiral pattern running through its centre (and whose name is also incidentally a slang term for the @ sign in Japanese).

There are various slightly more subtle references to Japanese culture in the design of certain objects: the bright red satchel, for instance, known in Japanese as a *randoseru* (ランドセル) and which is an intrinsic part of the uniform for elementary school kids. Then there are practices which are common in Japan and other parts of Asia, though much less so in the West, such as wearing a surgical mask when one has a cold ▦. Or the phenomenon of the love hotel ▦ – the sort of establishment where you can hire rooms by the hour for pursuing the type of private liaisons which would otherwise be rather difficult in a society where cramped family accommodation is the norm.

Some of the standard ideographs that are used in Japanese society are also transferred directly into emoji. There's the *onsen* (温泉) or hot springs symbol ▦, for example; and the *shoshinsha* mark (初心者マーク) 🔰, which symbolises a beginner driver but is also used for any type of neophyte. A few of the characters depict very specific Japanese traditions, such as the *koinobori* (鯉幟), or carp streamers 🎏 which are flown from flagpoles on Children's Day (5 May); and the dolls for the *hinamatsuri* (雛祭り) holiday on 3 March 🎎, which is dedicated to the health and wellbeing of young girls.

Finally there are the ogre 👹 and goblin characters 👺. The former of these is *Namahage* (生剥),[28] a folkloric creature traditionally associated with New Year celebrations when men dress up in his mask and wear long straw capes. The latter is *Tengu* (天狗), or 'heavenly dog', a legendary supernatural being often depicted with an unnaturally long nose, whose mask is once again worn during festivals and celebrations.

For many global users, the specific provenance of many of these symbols probably barely registers. Emoji such as the *narutomaki* or *koinobori* will simply remain unused, while *Namahage* and *Tengu* can represent any generic ogres and goblins, either literally or metaphorically. In certain cases, however, the Japanese-centric nature of these symbols has led to isolated incidents of corporate censorship. Due to long-standing political frictions between Japan and South Korea, for example, Samsung (a Korean company) temporarily removed three of the Japan-specific emoji – the Map of Japan, the Crossed Flags 🎌 and the Chart Increasing With Yen 💹 – from the symbols available on the software on their devices. For a while they even changed the two crossed Japanese flags to a pair of South Korean flags, although in a later update they reverted to the original and in the end restored the other emoji as well.[29]

While these many examples are a legacy of the origins of emoji, in recent years – since they emigrated to America and set up home in California – the influence of Western culture has begun to spread more and more throughout the system. In some cases this simply involves removing the specific Japanese cultural reference points. For example, the design of the rucksack, originally based on the distinctive *randoseru*, was altered to a much more standard backpack in Apple's 2016 software release. And often nowadays a Western bias applies even when Unicode are seemingly attempting to make the range of symbols more internationally inclusive. When they introduced two Chinese-themed emoji in 2017, for instance, the objects it chose – a fortune cookie and a takeaway box – were, in fact, Westernised elements of Chinese culture. As the designer Yiying Lu –the Chinese-born, American-based artist who designed them both – noted in an interview with the *Atlantic*, the 'Chinese takeout box is completely invented in the West. And the fortune cookie was invented by a Japanese person, but it was popularized in America.'[30] In other words, globalisation, in these instances, is, in fact, a subtle form of Americanisation. If anything, then, emoji are operating more as yet another instrument of American soft power than as an opportunity for Japan to broaden its cultural appeal across the world.

Everyday Revolutions

There's a religious community in Japan, founded by an illiterate weaver at the end of the nineteenth century, whose members revere as one of their gods a Jewish ophthalmologist from Poland called Ludovic Lazarus Zamenhof.[31] In 1887 Zamenhof wrote a book laying out his design for an international language. He published this under the pseudonym Dr Esperanto – a word which, in time, came to be applied to the language itself. The ideals of this language chimed so well with those of the newly formed Japanese sect that they declared it the language of heaven. And when Zamenhof passed away they deified his spirit.[32]

Esperanto is the most well-known, and successful, of what are referred to as International Auxiliary Languages (IALs). Created specifically for the purpose of international communication, these are the close cousins of the philosophical languages that John Wilkins and his contemporaries were inventing back in the seventeenth century. But whereas the primary aim for Wilkins was to build a language which could better serve the purposes of science, the ambitions of language inventors in the late nineteenth and early twentieth centuries were more political. Technological changes were creating an ever-more-interconnected world, while at the same time a wave of nationalism was stirring up military conflict across Europe. The hope for those who backed the various International Auxiliary Language projects was that cultural and political differences could be overcome with a globally shared means of communication.

Zamenhof's motivation was his personal experience of marginalisation and cultural struggle growing up in the Eastern European environment in which he did. 'If I had not been a Jew from the ghetto,' he wrote, 'the idea of uniting humanity … would never have entered my head.'[33] For Zamenhof, language was both the 'prime motor of civilisation' and also 'a cause of antipathy, nay even of hatred, between people'.[34] Linguistic diversity fed cultural prejudice. It created divisions between communities. It was one of the root causes of the strife and disorder that bedevilled the world. So he decided to devise a language which wouldn't be tied to any one nation or culture – one which could help unite rather than divide humanity. The tragic irony of his story is that the language he invented went on to be persecuted by one totalitarian regime after another. Under Hitler it was seen as the language of international Jewish conspiracy (and all three of Zamenhof's children were killed by the Nazis[35]). Under Stalin it was demonised as a tool for espionage.

Esperanto itself remains extremely popular, with a speech community which now runs into the hundreds of thousands, if not millions. But it never became a truly universal language in the way that Zamenhof envisaged. Today, the interest in creating IALs has all but died out. There are occasional suggestions that emoji have emerged as a modern equivalent – that they've developed into a universal form of communication which is not tied to any one culture or nation (despite the various caveats outlined in this book).[36] As we've seen, though – and as we'll discuss in further detail – they're not a full language in the way that something such as Esperanto is. A closer parallel might be the universal visual 'language' invented by another Central European, also motivated by his personal experiences of the political turmoil of early twentieth-century Europe.

Karl Kasiel Blitz was born in a city in the east of the Austro-Hungarian Empire, in what is now Ukraine. In 1938, when the Nazis annexed Austria, he was sent to a concentration camp: Dachau initially, then Buchenwald. After intense lobbying by his wife (who was a German Catholic), the authorities released him, but he had to leave the country. He ended up in the United Kingdom where, given the unfortunate connotations of his name, he adopted the surname Bliss. With his wife now having escaped Germany herself and living in Shanghai, Bliss followed her out there. As with Zamenhof, the mixture of these traumatic personal experiences along with the tragic events convulsing the world as a whole sowed the seed in his mind that the reason people 'hated each other [was] mainly because they spoke and thought in different languages'.[37]

The story goes that while living in Shanghai Bliss learnt to interpret meaning from the Chinese characters he saw around him without ever learning Chinese itself. As an ideographic script, it was possible to decipher a little sense from the writing without any knowledge of the spoken language. Yet this meaning obviously remained both limited and muddled given that Chinese characters have evolved substantially from their original ideographic roots. Prompted by this, however, he decided that he'd invent his own visual-based language system, in which the symbols looked like the things they were meant to represent. This, he argued, would produce a 'logical writing for an illogical world'[38] and would offer a truly universal communication system for humankind.

The system he created – which he named Blissymbolics – stuck very closely to the ideals he initially devised. His approach, similar in its fundamentals to the seventeenth-century philosophical languages, was to divide the world up into its elemental, constituent parts, each of which was represented by an icon, and then build complex concepts by combining these. As Wilkins found, however, nature itself is not ordered systematically, so the formula for combinations was never entirely intuitive. Plus there was the fact that the icons themselves, which might have had a passing similarity to the concepts they were meant to represent, were necessarily very stylised. The result was a language which fulfilled some of the aims he had for it but never quite managed to be the fully logical and transparent form of communication of which he'd dreamt.

Blissymbolics did, however, achieve a relative amount of success in one particular area: it was embraced by an institution in Canada as an educational system which could help children with learning difficulties – a purpose for which its visual nature proved to be ideal. For Bliss, however, who was a complex and contrary man, this wasn't the purpose for which the language had been devised. And it certainly wasn't the world-encircling status he'd envisaged for it. He thus spent much of the end of his life fighting against the very people who were trying to embrace its possibilities.

The aim of this brief sketch about the pioneers of two universal language projects is to show that it's not necessarily the form or structure of a communication system that determines the role it comes to play in society. Other factors, such as global and personal politics, can be equally important in deciding the fate of a language. As noted, one of the ideas frequently mentioned in the media for emoji is that they're a universal form of a communication which could, perhaps, provide a solution to the need for an international auxiliary language in the way that attempts such as Esperanto never quite managed. As a visual-based form of communication, they could evolve into the sort of system that Bliss was trying to create – i.e. a self-sufficient language of pictographs and ideographs which is unaffiliated with any pre-existing spoken language.

In many ways emoji have succeeded where Blissymbolics or even Esperanto struggled, spreading and flourishing on a truly global scale. But the reasons for their success are as much to do with chance as with design. As we've seen, they were a mixture of a long-standing weakness in written language which became newly important with the changes in communication practices that were brought about by technology; and a solution to this need that was likewise the result of technological change. The enduring dream of a way to indicate irony (along with other moods and stances) became a pressing concern for the social media age, and it just so happened that the ability to punctuate written messages with minute pictures happened to evolve in the right place at the right time.

Then there's the aspiration that all the International Auxiliary Languages have of getting adopted by governments and civic institutions around the world and in this way gaining the sort of backing which would allow them flourish on a global scale. To date this has never quite happened, which is one of the main reasons for their failure to fulfil the mission envisaged by their inventors. Paradoxically, this sort of international backing is precisely what *has* happened with emoji – albeit not in the form of governmental patronage, but through corporate support underpinned by a standardisation institution. In this way they're a mixture of commerce, chance, history and technological evolution, all of which have combined at the right time to propel them to their current global prevalence.

But despite emoji having achieved what the International Auxiliary Languages never fully managed, this isn't to say that they are or ever can be a solution to the Babel of different languages which so complicates international communication. There remains a major difference between the IALs and emoji, and this is that they fulfil notably different communicative purposes. Emoji are not designed to substitute for natural languages. As we've explored throughout this book, they do something quite different, supplementing verbal language in diverse ways for the expression of mood, emotion, humour and creative play.

So what can we take from this about how they'll continue to evolve? And, more importantly, what this evolution might indicate about the future of human communication? For the present, emoji continue to flourish. In 2017, for example, five billion were being sent each day on Facebook's Messenger alone.[39] Unicode, meanwhile, is designed with forward compatibility in mind, so in this way at least emoji won't suddenly become obsolete as technology continues to develop. New characters are added to the code in such a way that they don't undermine anything in previous versions of the standard. This means that the system allows continuity for all the writing systems we use: those which date back thousands of years and those which were born just half a dozen years ago. At this stage in our historical evolution, almost 90 per cent of all internet data that's written and exchanged is encoded in the Unicode Standard. As the Consortium write, it would 'require a complete collapse of the information technology structure worldwide for all that stored information to suddenly become uninterpretable'.[40] Emoji, in other words, are now a secure part of the recorded inventory of human writing systems. Their history is secure, even if their future remains unknown.

*

Thirty-six years from now we'll have tipped into the second half of this century. Millenials will be middle-aged, and we'll be commemorating the centenary of the untimely death of Alan Turing. When he was adapting the short story 'The Minority Report' by Philip K. Dick for the cinema, Steven Spielberg gathered together a think tank of futurologists to imagine what society would look like in what would be, from today, precisely thirty-six years into the future. The production designer on the film, Alex McDowell, drew up what the group referred to as the '2054 bible': an 80-page document outlining everything from the architecture and technology, to the economics and politics of this imaginary future.[41] The film *Minority Report*, which was released in 2002, is a detective story based around the idea of what would happen to the concept of free will if technology were to develop to a point where it can access a map of all future actions. The world it imagines is one in which technology has penetrated into every aspect of people's lives, so much so that privacy no longer exists and your behaviour is constantly being scanned. Your location is continuously pinpointed by computers, your identity incessantly checked and evaluated. There's an aspect of classic Big Brother dystopian-ism here, but the motivation behind it all is primarily commercial: corporations being able to target you precisely with their market-ing. A society of universal surveillance run for corporate means, with the information then being passed across to government agencies when they request it.

It's almost twenty years since this think tank took place – and still over three decades from the time it was envisaging. But already elements of this future are beginning to penetrate our present. The ubiquity of technology, its ties to commerce and marketing, its use for surveillance and the way this is eroding privacy and perhaps even some parts of individual agency – all these have begun to become an ordinary part of our everyday lives.

One major element of life in the future which *Minority Report* doesn't attempt to reimagine is language. The characters for the most part speak Standard American, punctuated with the occa-sional newly coined word to refer to technological innovations. But the other trends it predicts, and which we're now seeing taking hold, are themselves having an influence on the way we communicate. Here again the ubiquity of technology, its ties to commerce and marketing, its use for surveillance and the way this is eroding privacy and perhaps even some parts of individual agency – these are all issues we've discussed in this book which relate now to the modern resources we use to talk to each other.

As I wrote at the very beginning, this book will almost invari-ably be out of date by the time you come to read it. The details of how emoji are used, what they look like, how they're integrated into the various means of digital communication – all this is changing at such a rapid pace that the 'old media' publishing cycles involved in getting a manuscript into press and then out into the world mean that aspects of the content are likely to seem dated even while the ink is still fresh on the page. But then again, this book has been as much about the relationship between com-munication and society as it has been about emoji themselves. It's been as much about the way that developing technology is influencing forms of communication as it has been about emoji alone. I've used emoji as a prism through which to look at various broader questions concerning human interaction and human society. As I said at the outset, emoji – which are at once both frivolous and serious – are a perfect cipher for the paradoxes that result from rampant technological change. In this respect, while some of the superficial details are shifting and evolving on a daily basis, the issues that underpin the way technology is having an impact on our interactions, our relationships and our society are likely to be far more enduring.

The revolution we're experiencing at the moment, in other words, is centred around digital communication, the internet and mobile technology. It's this which is changing society in profound and far-reaching ways – whereas emoji themselves are something between a cultural trope, a fad and an entirely ordinary mutation in the evolution of human communication. It seems highly likely that within a few years' time they'll have faded from public consciousness, replaced by a very different type of technology-enabled communication. But while they're not perhaps a full revolution in their own right, they are the current poster child for the way that computer-mediated communication is slowly but surely altering our experience of the world in which we live. And in taking a close look at where emoji have come from, how they work and the legacy they're likely to leave, we can get a far clearer picture of the real techno-communicative insurgency that's taking place around us, with all the manifold implications it has for our everyday lives.

Notes

1 The What, the Why and the Where of Emoji

1. Meet the Female Recruiters of ISIS, http://nymag.com/daily/intelligencer/2014/09/meet-the-female-recruiters-of-isis.html (accessed 1 May 2018).
2. The Emoji Infographic: Stats to Back Up Your Obsession, www.meltwater.com/uk/blog/the-emoji-infographic-stats-to-back-up-your-obsession/ (accessed 1 May 2018).
3. Who Needs Words When You Have Emojis? www.emarketer.com/Article/Who-Needs-Words-You-Have-Emojis/1012466 (accessed 1 May 2018).
4. Word of the Year: Frequently Asked Questions, https://en.oxforddictionaries.com/word-of-the-year/word-of-the-year-faqs (accessed 1 May 2018).
5. Sarah Palin Calls on 'Peaceful Muslims' to 'Refudiate' Their Own Religion, http://littlegreenfootballs.com/article/36769_Sarah_Palin_Calls_on_Peaceful_Muslims_to_Refudiate_Their_Own_Religion (accessed 1 May 2018).
6. Word of the Year 2010, http://blog.oxforddictionaries.com/2010/11/noad-2010-word-of-the-year/ (accessed 1 May 2018).
7. Sarah Palin Stands by Made-up Word 'Refudiate,' Compares Self to Shakespeare, http://ew.com/article/2010/07/19/sarah-palin-refudiate/ (accessed 1 May 2018).
8. Recent Updates to the OED, http://public.oed.com/the-oed-today/recent-updates-to-the-oed/ (accessed 1 May 2018).
9. There's Now a Frida Kahlo Emoji Collection, www.dazeddigital.com/artsandculture/article/35179/1/there-s-now-a-frida-kahlo-emoji-collection (accessed 1 May 2018).
10. Catholic Emojis Are Something to Love about the iOS 10 Update, www.catholicnewsagency.com/blog/catholic-emojis-are-something-to-love-about-ios10-update (accessed 1 May 2018).

11. St. Drogo, www.catholic.org/saints/saint.php?saint_id=2989 (accessed 1 May 2018).

12. St. Polycarp of Smyrna, www.catholic.org/saints/saint.php?saint _id=5532 (accessed 1 May 2018).

13. Barney, S., Lewis, W. J., Beach, J. A., and Berghof, O. (eds and trans.) (2006) *The Etymologies of Isidore of Seville*, Cambridge University Press, p. 404.

14. What Is the Plural of Emoji? http://observer.com/2014/11/what-is-the-plural-of-emoji/ (accessed 1 May 2018).

15. Female, www.etymonline.com/index.php?term=female (accessed 1 May 2018).

16. SwiftKey Emoji Report April 2015, www.scribd.com/doc/ 262594751/SwiftKey-Emoji-Report (accessed 1 May 2018).

17. The Emoji Infographic: Stats to Back Up Your Obsession, www .meltwater.com/uk/blog/the-emoji-infographic-stats-to-back-up-your-obsession/ (accessed 1 May 2018).

18. Building 8 @ F8: The After Action Report, www.facebook.com/ photo.php?fbid=343078196094625 (accessed 1 May 2018).

19. Tinder and the Dawn of the 'Dating Apocalypse', www.vanityfair .com/culture/2015/08/tinder-hook-up-culture-end-of-dating (accessed 1 May 2018).

20. You Need an Emoji Strategy, https://sprintworks.se/blog/emoji-strategy/ (accessed 1 May 2018).

21. A Swedish Non-Profit Created New Emoji To Help People Talk About Abuse, www.thefader.com/2015/05/26/a-swedish-non-profit-created-new-emoji-to-help-people-talk-about-abuse (accessed 1 May 2018).

22. Emoji Is Dragging Us back to the Dark Ages – and All We Can Do Is Smile, www.theguardian.com/artanddesign/jonathanjonesblog/ 2015/may/27/emoji-language-dragging-us-back-to-the-dark-ages-yellow-smiley-face (accessed 1 May 2018).

23. Unicode & Emoji, www.unicode.org/emoji/slides.html (accessed 1 May 2018).

24. More than Words: Are 'Emoji' Dumbing Us Down or Enriching Our Communications? www.independent.co.uk/life-style/gad gets-and-tech/features/more-than-words-are-emoji-dumbing-us-down-or-enriching-our-communications-8610767.html (accessed 1 May 2018).

25. What Does the Alien Emoji Mean on iOS? http://blog.getemoji .com/post/116839074745/what-does-the-alien-emoji-mean-on-ios-its-an (accessed 1 May 2018).

26. Emoji Unicode Tables, http://apps.timwhitlock.info/emoji/tables/ unicode#note3 (accessed 1 May 2018).

27. Full Emoji List v11.0, http://unicode.org/emoji/charts/full-emoji-list.html (accessed 1 May 2018).

28. More Emoji Fragmentation, https://sixcolors.com/link/2017/01/ more-emoji-fragmentation/ (accessed 1 May 2018).

29. The Pope Now Has His Own Set of Emojis, Just in Time for His First U.S. Visit, www.adweek.com/digital/pope-now-has-his-own-set-emojis-just-time-his-first-us-visit-166800/ (accessed 1 May 2018).

30. Hieroglyphics Release Emoji Pack, http://hiphopdx.com/news/ id.36850/title.hieroglyphics-release-emoji-pack# (accessed 1 May 2018).

31. 80 Hatsune Miku emoticons free download, https://chinesefontde sign.com/80-hatsune-miku-emoticons-free-download.html (accessed 1 May 2018).

32. www.trumpoji.com (accessed 1 May 2018).

33. Popemoji, http://apps.swyftmedia.com/popeIsHope (accessed 1 May 2018).

34. EMOJEW: The First Jewish Emoji App, https://lbbonline.com/ news/emojew-the-first-jewish-emoji-app/ (accessed 1 May 2018).

35. Bernie Sanders Has Got His Own Set of Emojis, www.indepen dent.co.uk/news/world/americas/bernie-sanders-has-got-his-own-set-of-emojis-10487691.html (accessed 1 May 2018).

36. The Secret Language Of Line Stickers, https://techcrunch.com/ 2015/07/10/creepy-cute-line (accessed 1 May 2018).

37. Branded Stickers Are the New Branded Emoji Keyboards, http:// digiday.com/marketing/branded-stickers-new-branded-emoji-key boards (accessed 1 May 2018).

38. Why Emojis and Stickers Are Big Business, www.forbes.com/sites/ vivianrosenthal/2016/08/19/why-emojis-and-stickers-are-big-busi ness (accessed 1 May 2018).

39. The History of the Royal Society of London for the Improving of Natural Knowledge, www.royalcollection.org.uk/collection/ 1057783/the-history-of-the-royal-society-of-london-for-the-improving-of-natural-knowledge (accessed 1 May 2018).

40. Swift, J. (2001 [1726]) *Gulliver's Travels*, part 3, chapter 5, Penguin, p. 172.

2 Emoji and the History of Human Communication

1. Descartes, R. (1960 [1637]) *Discourse on Method and Meditations*, Bobbs-Merrill, p. 42.
2. The Evolution of Writing, https://sites.utexas.edu/dsb/tokens/the-evolution-of-writing/ (accessed 1 May 2018).
3. Borges, J. L. (1998) *Collected Fictions*, trans. A. Hurley, Penguin, p. 285.
4. The Origin of our Alphabet, www.nuspel.org/alphabetx.html (accessed 1 May 2018).
5. The Decipherment of Hieroglyphs, www.bbc.co.uk/history/ancient/egyptians/decipherment_01.shtml (accessed 1 May 2018).
6. Borges, J. L. (1999) *Selected Non-Fictions*, trans. E. Allen, S. J. Levine and E. Weinberger, Penguin.
7. The Discovery of a World in the Moon by John Wilkins, www.wired.com/beyond-the-beyond/2016/11/discovery-world-moon-john-wilkins/ (accessed 1 May 2018).
8. Irony & Sarcasm marks, www.shadycharacters.co.uk/2011/09/irony-sarcasm-marks-part-1-of-3/ (accessed 1 May 2018).
9. https://twitter.com/yesthatsthejoke (accessed 1 May 2018).
10. Grice, P. (1975) Logic and Conversation, in P. Cole and J. L. Morgan (eds.), *Syntax and Semantics 3: Speech Arts*, Elsevier, pp. 41–58.
11. Poe's Law, www.christianforums.com/threads/big-contradictions-in-the-evolution-theory.1962980/page-3#post-17606580 (accessed 1 May 2018).
12. Smiley Lore, www.cs.cmu.edu/~sef/sefSmiley.htm (accessed 1 May 2018).
13. Trotsky, L. (1972 [1907]) 1905, trans. A. Bostock, Vintage, p. 85.
14. The New £5 Note Has a Major Grammar Blunder … But Have You Spotted It? www.telegraph.co.uk/news/2017/04/27/new-5-note-has-major-grammar-blunderbut-have-spotted/ (accessed 1 May 2018).
15. What Is the Origin of the Question Mark? https://en.oxforddictionaries.com/explore/origin-of-question-mark (accessed 1 May 2018).

16. The History of the Exclamation Point, www.smithsonianmag.com/smart-news/the-history-of-the-exclamation-point-16445416 (accessed 1 May 2018).
17. Graham, S., and Frank, G. (1958) *Beloved Infidel*, Henry Holt.
18. Crystal, D. (2016) *Making a Point*, Profile, p. 180.
19. Ironic Serif: A Brief History of Typographic Snark and the Failed Crusade for an Irony Mark, www.brainpickings.org/2013/09/27/shady-characters-irony/ (accessed 1 May 2018).
20. The Point of Exclamation, https://opinionator.blogs.nytimes.com/2012/08/06/the-point-of-exclamation/ (accessed 1 May 2018).
21. Smiley Lore, www.cs.cmu.edu/~sef/sefSmiley.htm (accessed 1 May 2018).
22. Original Bboard Thread in which :-) Was Proposed, www.cs.cmu.edu/~sef/Orig-Smiley.htm (accessed 1 May 2018).
23. The Collected Works of Ambrose Bierce, www.worldcat.org/title/collected-works-of-ambrose-bierce/oclc/3246573 (accessed 1 May 2018).
24. Nabokov's interview, *The New York Times*, 1969, www.lib.ru/NABOKOW/Inter11.txt_Ascii.txt (accessed 1 May 2018).
25. Smileys, http://shop.oreilly.com/product/9781565920415.do (accessed 1 May 2018).
26. The Canonical Smiley (and 1-line Symbol) List, http://marshall.freeshell.org/smileys.html.
27. http://knowyourmeme.com/memes/crying-laughing-emoji (accessed 1 May 2018).
28. Flipping Tables, http://knowyourmeme.com/memes/flipping-tables (accessed 1 May 2018).
29. A Second Winter Storm Is Coming. How Much Snow? ¯_(ツ)_/¯, www.nytimes.com/2018/03/06/nyregion/winter-storm-quinn-noreaster.html (accessed 1 May 2018).
30. 16 Characters From Other Languages That Make Great Emoticons, http://mentalfloss.com/article/56495/16-characters-other-languages-make-great-emoticons
31. 囧, http://knowyourmeme.com/memes/囧 (accessed 1 May 2018).
32. What Does /s Mean? www.reddit.com/r/OutOfTheLoop/comments/1zo2l4/what_does_s_mean/ (accessed 1 May 2018).
33. Derks, D., Bos, A. E. R., and von Grumbkow, J. (2008) Emoticons and Online Message Interpretation. *Social Science Computer Review*, 26, 379–388. Attardo, S., Eisterhold, J., Hay, J., and Poggi, I. (2003)

Multimodal Markers of Irony and Sarcasm. *Humor – International Journal of Humor Research*, 16, 243–260. Walther, J. B., and D'Addario, K. P. (2001) The Impacts of Emoticons on Message Interpretation in Computer-Mediated Communication. *Social Science Computer Review*, 19, 324–347.

34. Walther, J. B., and D'Addario, K. P. (2001) The Impacts of Emoticons on Message Interpretation in Computer-Mediated Communication. *Social Science Computer Review*, 19, 324–347.

3 Making Faces

1. 'To Mersenne, 20 November, 1629' in Descartes, R. (1991) *The Philosophical Writings of Descartes*: Volume 3, The Correspondence, Cambridge University Press, p. 13.

2. Wilkins, J. (1668) *An Essay towards a Real Character and a Philosophical Language*, Royal Society, p. 156.

3. Borges, J. L. (1999) *Selected Non-Fictions*, trans. E. Allen, S. J. Levine and E. Weinberger, Penguin, p. 231.

4. How Many Words Are There in the English Language? https://en.oxforddictionaries.com/explore/how-many-words-are-there-in-the-english-language (accessed 1 May 2018).

5. The Words in the Mental Cupboard, http://news.bbc.co.uk/1/hi/magazine/8013859.stm (accessed 1 May 2018).

6. Rousseau, J. J., Scott, J. T., and Scott, J. T. (2000) *Essay on the Origin of Languages and Writings Related to Music*, Dartmouth College Press.

7. How Many Languages in the World Are Unwritten? www.ethnologue.com/enterprise-faq/how-many-languages-world-are-unwritten-0 (accessed 1 May 2018).

8. Understanding Poker Tells, www.pokerology.com/lessons/poker-tells/ (accessed 1 May 2018).

9. Rousseau, J. J., Scott, J. T., and Scott, J. T. (2000) *Essay on the Origin of Languages and Writings Related to Music*, Dartmouth College Press.

10. Eckman, P. (2003) *Emotions Revealed: Recognizing Faces and Feelings to Improve Communication and Emotional Life*, Weidenfield and Nicolson.

11. Emoji Recognition Chart, http://gorgeoustaps.com/emojiautism (accessed 1 May 2018).

12. This Artist Uses Emoji to Explore Empathy, Autism, and How We Connect, www.wired.com/2013/12/emoji-autism-spectrum/ (accessed 1 May 2018).
13. The Naked Face, www.newyorker.com/magazine/2002/08/05/the-naked-face (accessed 1 May 2018).
14. Personal interview.
15. Comic Book Urban Legends Revealed #110, www.cbr.com/comic-book-urban-legends-revealed-110/ (accessed 1 May 2018).
16. Astro Boy A Japanese Citizen? www.animenewsnetwork.com/news/2003-03-20/astro-boy-a-japanese-citizen (accessed 1 May 2018).
17. Cohn, N. (2013) *The Visual Language of Comics*, Bloomsbury.
18. Poker Face, www.newyorker.com/magazine/2013/05/20/poker-face (accessed 1 May 2018).
19. Andreas-Salomé, L. (1988) *Nietzsche*, Black Swan Books.
20. Miyake, K (2007) How Young Japanese Express Their Emotions Visually in Mobile Phone Messages: A Sociolinguistic Analysis, *Japanese Studies*, 27:1, 53–72.
21. In Praise of Emoji as Tactful Conversation-Enders, www.slate.com/blogs/future_tense/2016/06/30/emoji_are_perfect_and_polite_ways_to_cut_off_a_written_interaction.html (accessed 1 May 2018).

4 Metaphors and Moral Panics

1. These Are the Very Best Vagina Emoji for Sexting, www.theverge.com/2015/10/9/9486103/flirtmoji-sexting-sex-vagina-emoji-design (accessed 1 May 2018).
2. London Restaurant Launches Menu Written in Emojis, www.standard.co.uk/goingout/restaurants/london-restaurant-launches-menu-written-in-emojis-a3295511.html (accessed 1 May 2018).
3. Ordering Cocktails via Emoji Is a Thing You Can Do Now, www.independent.co.uk/life-style/food-and-drink/news/ordering-cocktails-via-emoji-is-a-thing-you-can-do-now-10444066.html (accessed 1 May 2018).
4. Are Emojis Going to Replace Pin Codes? www.theguardian.com/technology/2015/jun/15/emojis-pin-numbers-passcodes (accessed 1 May 2018).

5. Booty Call? Grindr's New Emojis Are as Outrageous as You'd Expect, www.gaytimes.co.uk/news/65476/grindr-launches-own-emoji-collection-2017/ (accessed 1 May 2018).
6. Flirtmoji, https://flirtmoji.co/info (accessed 1 May 2018).
7. Flirtmoji Designer Admits Some Vulva Emoji Were Inadvertently Plagiarized, www.theverge.com/2015/10/16/9550865/flirtmoji-vulva-emoji-plagiarized-erin-tobey (accessed 1 May 2018).
8. Emoji 4 Porn, www.pornhub.com/emoji (accessed 1 May 2018).
9. Search by Emoji on YouPorn, www.youporn.com/emoji (accessed 1 May 2018).
10. The Peach Emoji Doesn't Look Like A Butt Anymore and People Are Devastated, www.buzzfeed.com/juliareinstein/rip-peach-emoji (accessed 1 May 2018).
11. Apple Concedes, Returns Peach Emoji to Butt Form, www.dailydot.com/unclick/apple-peach-butt-emoji-fix (accessed 1 May 2018).
12. Brand Guidelines, https://cdn.cms-twdigitalassets.com/content/dam/brand-twitter/asset-download-zip-files/Twitter_Brand_Guidelines.pdf (accessed 1 May 2018).
13. Twitter Creator Jack Dorsey Illuminates the Site's Founding Document, http://latimesblogs.latimes.com/technology/2009/02/twitter-creator.html (accessed 1 May 2018).
14. How 'Show Me the Receipts' Became a Catchphrase for Holding the Powerful Accountable, https://slate.com/human-interest/2016/07/how-show-me-the-receipts-became-a-catchphrase-for-holding-the-powerful-accountable.html (accessed 1 May 2018).
15. The Secret Ska History of that Weird Levitating Businessman Emoji, http://europe.newsweek.com/secret-ska-history-man-business-suit-levitating-emoji-442192?rm=eu (accessed 1 May 2018).
16. The 2 Tone Label, http://2-tone.info/articles/label.html (accessed 1 May 2018).
17. Tag Archives: Man in Business Suit Levitating, www.theparisreview.org/blog/tag/man-in-business-suit-levitating (accessed 1 May 2018).
18. 9 Emojis that Look Completely Different on Other Phones, http://mentalfloss.com/article/70879/9-emojis-look-completely-different-other-phones (accessed 1 May 2018).
19. The Best New Genre of Blog is 'Emoji Review', www.theverge.com/tldr/2017/5/11/15616064/tumblr-emoji-review-blogs (accessed 1 May 2018).

20. Horse Face Emoji Review, http://turing-tested.tumblr.com/post/155826171580/horse-face-emoji-review (accessed 1 May 2018).

21. Grammar and Her Children: Learning to Read in the Art of the Twelfth Century, http://merg.soc.srcf.net/journal/09education/cleaver.php (accessed 1 May 2018).

22. John of Salisbury (1962) *The Metalogicon of John of Salisbury: A Twelfth-Century Defense of the Verbal and Logical Arts of the Trivium*, trans. by D. D. McGarry, University of California Press, p. 61.

23. Emoji and Pictographs, http://unicode.org/faq/emoji_dingbats.html (accessed 1 May 2018).

24. Here Are Rules of Using Emoji You Didn't Know You Were Following, http://time.com/2993508/emoji-rules-tweets/ (accessed 1 May 2018).

25. The example comes from Gunther Kress.

26. Gun Emoji Pairings, www.lexicalitems.com/blog/gun-emoji-pairings (accessed 1 May 2018).

27. Assassin Targeting Kim Jong Un's Half-brother Wore 'LOL' Shirt, http://nypost.com/2017/02/15/assassin-targeting-kim-jong-uns-half-brother-wore-lol-shirt (accessed 1 May 2018).

28. Happy 25th Birthday to LOL, www.slate.com/blogs/lexicon_valley/2014/05/23/lol_s_25th_anniversary_origins_of_still_popular_internet_abbreviation_trace.html (accessed 1 May 2018).

29. OMG! It Started in 1917 with a Letter to Churchill, www.wsj.com/articles/omg-it-started-in-1917-with-a-letter-to-churchill-1504882081 (accessed 1 May 2018).

30. New Initialisms in the OED, www.oed.com/public/update0311#new (accessed 1 May 2018).

31. Sean Spicer Largest Audience To Ever Witness Inauguration Period, www.youtube.com/watch?v=X2VKQfX5tSE (accessed 1 May 2018).

32. In the Beginning, There Was Fan Fiction: From the Four Gospels to Fifty Shades, www.theguardian.com/books/2012/aug/13/fan-fiction-fifty-shades-grey (accessed 1 May 2018).

33. How #Hashtags Changed the Way We Talk, www.tintup.com/blog/how-hashtags-changed-the-way-we-talk/ (accessed 1 May 2018).

34. The Word of the Year? 'Squeezed Middle' Says Oxford Dictionary, www.independent.co.uk/news/uk/this-britain/the-word-of-the-year-squeezed-middle-says-oxford-dictionary-6266506.html (accessed 1 May 2018).

35. Revealed: The X-rated Meanings Behind Popular Emojis that Will Make You Think Twice Before Sending Your Next Text, www.daily mail.co.uk/femail/article-4200384/The-X-rated-meanings-popular-emojis.html (accessed 1 May 2018).

36. Eggplant, http://emojipedia.org/aubergine/ (accessed 1 May 2018).

37. The Complete (and Sometimes Sordid) History of the Eggplant Emoji, http://firstwefeast.com/features/2015/06/eggplant-emoji-history (accessed 1 May 2018).

38. A Beginner's Guide to Sexting with Emoji, www.dailydot.com/irl/sexting-emoji/ (accessed 1 May 2018).

39. Move Over, Banana, www.slate.com/articles/technology/users/2015/04/eggplant_rising_how_the_purple_fruit_surpassed_the_banana_as_the_most_phallic.html (accessed 1 May 2018).

40. #FreetheDick, Bring Back #EggplantFriday, http://jezebel.com/freethedick-bring-back-eggplantfriday-1679948818 (accessed 1 May 2018).

41. http://mediatakeout.com/shock-exclusive-chris-browns-eggplant-pics-leaked-and-were-sorry-for-calling-him-pencil-dck-that-man-is-packing-warning-graphic/ (accessed 1 May 2018).

42. Netflix Wins Bidding War for 'Eggplant Emoji' From Ben Stiller, 'Workaholics' Creators, www.hollywoodreporter.com/news/netflix-wins-bidding-war-eggplant-emoji-ben-stiller-workaholics-creators-968990 (accessed 1 May 2018).

43. Durex 'Launches' Eggplant-flavoured Condoms, www.newshub.co.nz/home/world/2016/09/durex-launches-eggplant-flavoured-condoms.html (accessed 1 May 2018).

44. https://eggplantmail.com (accessed 1 May 2018).

45. Emojibator, https://emojibator.com/products/emojibator (accessed 1 May 2018).

46. This Emoji Vibrator Is the Only Eggplant You Need, www.cosmopolitan.com/sex-love/news/a63262/emoji-vibrator/ (accessed 1 May 2018).

47. Weale, J. (1854) *The Pictorial Handbook of London Comprising its Antiquities, Architecture, Arts . . . and Scientific Institutions*, H. G. Bohn, pp. 656–657.

48. *The Peterborough Chronicle*, cited in Freeborn, D. (2006) *From Old English to Standard English*, Macmillan, p. 36.

49. 'Blatherers – Do They Talk Webbish at the Expense of Welsh? E-mail, Text Messaging and the Internet Is Changing Language at

an Unprecedented Rate but What Effect Will It Have on Welsh?'
Daily Post, 26 September 2001, p. 9. Cited in Thurlow, C.
(2006) From Statistical Panic to Moral Panic: The Metadiscursive
Construction and Popular Exaggeration of New Media Language
in the Print Media, *Journal of Computer-Mediated Communication*
11, 667–701, p. 672.

50. Icelandic Has the Best Words for Technology, https://gizmodo
.com/icelandic-has-the-best-words-for-technology-1702697272
(accessed 1 May 2018).
51. Celebrating Language Warriors, www.huffingtonpost.com/k-david-
harrison/endangered-languages_b_1290171.html (accessed 1 May
2018).
52. Humphrys, J. (2007) I h8 txt msgs: How Texting Is Wrecking Our
Language, *Daily Mail*, 24 September.
53. Crystal, D. (2008) *Txting: The gr8 db8*, Oxford University Press.
54. Emojis Are Ruining Civilization, http://nypost.com/2015/10/14/
emojis-are-ruining-civilization/
55. Are Emoticons and Emojis Destroying Our Language? www.huffing
tonpost.com/joan-gage/emoticons-and-emojis-destroying-our-lan
guage_b_7950460.html (accessed 1 May 2018).
56. Emoji Is Dragging Us Back to the Dark Ages – and All We Can Do Is
Smile, www.theguardian.com/artanddesign/jonathanjonesblog/
2015/may/27/emoji-language-dragging-us-back-to-the-dark-ages-
yellow-smiley-face (accessed 1 May 2018).
57. Emojis: The Death of the Written Language? www.cnbc.com/2015/
06/24/emojis-the-death-of-the-written-language.html (accessed 1
May 2018).
58. Thurlow, C. (2006) From Statistical Panic to Moral Panic: The
Metadiscursive Construction and Popular Exaggeration of New
Media Language in the Print Media, *Journal of Computer-
Mediated Communication* 11, 667–701, p. 671.
59. Plester, B., Wood, C., and Bell, C. (2008) Txt Msg N School Literacy:
Does Mobile Phone Use Adversely Affect Children's Written
Language Attainment? *Literacy*, 42:3, pp. 137–144.
60. Plester, B., and Wood, C. (2009) Exploring Relationships Between
Traditional and New Media Literacies: British Preteen Texters at
School. *Journal of Computer-Mediated Communication* 14, pp.
1108–1129.

61. Emoji Grows as an Educational Tool, www.abc.net.au/am/content/ 2016/s4654046.htm (accessed 1 May 2018).

62. Using Eemoji as a Tool to Support Children's Well-being from a Strength-based Approach, www.achper.org.au/2017/program/con ference-schedule/area?command=record&id=175&cid=89 (accessed 1 May 2018).

63. Samsung's New App Uses Emojis to Help People with Language Disorders Communicate, https://techcrunch.com/2017/04/24/ wemogee/ (accessed 1 May 2018).

5 The Shaping Force of Digital Technology

1. Karinthy, F. (1966). *Voyage to Faremido/Capillaria*, trans. P. Tabori, Living Books.

2. Three and a Half Degrees of Separation, https://research.fb.com/ three-and-a-half-degrees-of-separation/ (accessed 1 May 2018).

3. http://fishbrain.com (accessed 1 May 2018).

4. https://www.ravelry.com (accessed 1 May 2018).

5. Thousands Sign up to Hoff Space, http://news.bbc.co.uk/newsbeat/hi/ entertainment/newsid_7487000/7487300.stm (accessed 1 May 2018).

6. Former Twitter Chief Scientist Launches Steven, an Emoji-Based Social App, https://techcrunch.com/2014/09/04/former-twitter-chief-scientist-launches-steven-an-emoji-based-social-app (accessed 1 May 2018).

7. The Rise and Rise of Emoji Social Networks, www.theguardian .com/technology/2014/sep/12/emoji-social-networks-app-emojli-emojicate-steven (accessed 1 May 2018).

8. Now There's Not One, But Two Emoji-Only Social Networks, https://techcrunch.com/2014/08/04/emoji-only (accessed 1 May 2018).

9. Dictionary Compilers Create Endangered Words List, www.theguar dian.com/books/2011/aug/21/endangered-words-collins-diction ary (accessed 1 May 2018).

10. Dictionary Makers Kill the Cassette Player to Make Room for the Mankini, www.slate.com/blogs/browbeat/2011/08/19/concise_ox ford_english_dictionary_what_words_got_dropped_to_make.html (accessed 1 May 2018).

11. Industrial Strength Design, https://mitpress.mit.edu/books/indus trial-strength-design (accessed 1 May 2018).
12. The End Of Moore's Law? Why the Theory that Computer Processors Will Double in Power Every Two Years May Be Becoming Obsolete, www.independent.co.uk/life-style/gadgets-and-tech/news/the-end-of-moores-law-why-the-theory-that-computer-processors-will-double-in-power-every-two-years-10394659.html (accessed 1 May 2018).
13. Big Idea: Technology Grows Exponentially, http://bigthink.com/think-tank/big-idea-technology-grows-exponentially (accessed 1 May 2018).
14. Swift, J. (1712) A Proposal for Correcting, Improving and Ascertaining the English Tongue, https://andromeda.rutgers.edu/~jlynch/Texts/proposal.html (accessed 1 May 2018).
15. Can the Académie française Stop the Rise of Anglicisms in French? http://blog.oxforddictionaries.com/2014/03/academie-francaise/ (accessed 1 May 2018).
16. Dire, ne pas dire, http://www.académie-française.fr/dire-ne-pas-dire/neologismes-anglicismes (accessed 1 May 2018).
17. How the Appetite for Emojis Complicates the Effort to Standardize the World's Alphabets, www.nytimes.com/2017/10/18/magazine/how-the-appetite-for-emojis-complicates-the-effort-to-standardize-the-worlds-alphabets.html (accessed 1 May 2018).
18. Emoji and Pictographs, http://unicode.org/faq/emoji_dingbats .html (accessed 1 May 2018).
19. So You Want to Propose an Emoji to Unicode? Here's How … www.emojione.com/blog/so-you-want-to-propose-an-emoji-to-unicode-heres-how
20. The Dumpling Emoji Project, www.dumplingemoji.org (accessed 1 May 2018).
21. Runner Girl Emoji, http://blog.saucony.com/runner-girl-emoji-molly/ (accessed 1 May 2018).
22. The Hijab Emoji Project, www.hijabemoji.org (accessed 1 May 2018).
23. http://www.emojination.org (accessed 1 May 2018).
24. Bierce, A. (2003 [1906]) *The Devil's Dictionary*, Bloomsbury, p. 179.
25. Exhibit A: ;-) www.slate.com/articles/technology/users/2015/10/emoti cons_and_emojis_as_evidence_in_court.html (accessed 1 May 2018).
26. Surveying the Law of Emojis, https://papers.ssrn.com/sol3/papers .cfm?abstract_id=2961060

27. Emoji and Pictographs, http://unicode.org/faq/emoji_dingbats
    .html (accessed 1 May 2018).
28. Emoji Dictionary, https://emojidictionary.emojifoundation.com
    (accessed 1 May 2018).
29. A Major Dictionary Has Officially Added Emoji, http://time.com/
    5186512/emoji-dictionary/ (accessed 1 May 2018).
30. Sweat Droplets Emoji, www.dictionary.com/e/emoji/sweat-dro
    plets-emoji/ (accessed 1 May 2018).
31. Leiris, M. (2017) *Scratches: The Rules of the Game*, Yale University
    Press, p. 40.
32. McCarthy, T. (2017) *Typewriters, Bombs, Jellyfish: Essays*, New York
    Review of Books.
33. Heidegger, M. (1992 [1942–1943]) *Parmenides*, trans. A. Schuwer
    and R. Rojcewicz, Indiana University Press, pp. 80–81.
34. Quoted in Kittler, F. A. (1999) *Gramophone, Film, Typewriter*,
    trans. G. Winthrop-Young and M Wutz, Stanford University
    Press, p. 200.
35. Solow, H. F., and Justman, R. H. (1991) *Inside Star Trek: The Real
    Story*, Pocket Books, pp. 18–19.
36. Tamarian Language, http://memory-alpha.wikia.com/wiki/
    Tamarian_language (accessed 1 May 2018).
37. Thanks to Social Media, Ordinary People Can Now Influence
    Elections More Than Tabloids, www.newstatesman.com/politics/
    elections/2017/06/thanks-social-media-ordinary-people-can-now-
    influence-elections-more (accessed 1 May 2018).
38. 'Covfefe': Trump Invents New Word and Melts Internet, www.bbc
    .co.uk/news/world-us-canada-40104063 (accessed 1 May 2018).
39. Shifman, L, (2013) Memes in a Digital World: Reconciling with a
    Conceptual Troublemaker, *Journal of Computer-Mediated
    Communication*, 18:3, pp. 362–377.
40. Meet Giphy, a GIF-lover's New Best Friend, www.dailydot.com/
    unclick/giphy-gif-search-review/ (accessed 1 May 2018).
41. Old Masters for the Digital Age, www.sothebys.com/en/news-
    video/blogs/all-blogs/past-masters/2016/11/old-masters-for-the-
    digital-age.html (accessed 1 May 2018).
42. https://twitter.com/ggreenwald/status/831665575755649025
    (accessed 1 May 2018).

6 People, Politics and Interpersonal Relationships

1. 21 Glorious Ways to Swear Using Emojis, www.buzzfeed.com/robi
   nedds/21-glorious-ways-to-swear-using-emojis (accessed 1 May
   2018).
2. Cockwomble, https://en.wiktionary.org/wiki/cockwomble (accessed 1
   May 2018).
3. Upping Our Insult Game, http://languagelog.ldc.upenn.edu/nll/?
   p=26396 (accessed 1 May 2018).
4. Steven Pinker: The Language of Swearing, www.youtube.com/
   watch?v=1BcdY_wSklo (accessed 1 May 2018).
5. Grawlix, https://en.wiktionary.org/wiki/grawlix (accessed 1 May
   2018).
6. Face with Symbols on Mouth on Emojipedia 5.0, http://emojipedia
   .org/emojipedia/5.0/serious-face-with-symbols-covering-mouth/
   (accessed 1 May 2018).
7. The Eggplant Emoji Is the Next Frontline of Online Harassment,
   www.vocativ.com/culture/society/the-eggplant-emoji-is-the-next-
   frontline-of-online-harassment/ (accessed 1 May 2018).
8. Non-Consensual Sexting: The Hot New Way to Make Someone
   Really Uncomfortable, http://time.com/77540/non-consensual-sext
   ing-the-hot-new-way-to-make-someone-really-uncomfortable/
   (accessed 1 May 2018).
9. EMOJI-GOSH! How Emojis in Workplace Communications Can
   Spark a Lawsuit (Or Make It Harder to Defend One), www.btcur
   rentsemployment.com/emoji-gosh-how-emojis-in-workplace-com
   munications-can-spark-a-lawsuit-or-make-it-harder-to-defend-
   one/ (accessed 1 May 2018).
10. Everyone Is Downloading iOS 9.1 for the Middle Finger Emoji, www
    .theguardian.com/technology/2015/oct/22/ios-91-middle-finger-
    emoji-uk-launch-apple-news-security-updates (accessed 1 May
    2018).
11. The Finger, or 'Bird Is the Word', https://stronglang.wordpress
    .com/2015/03/24/the-finger-or-bird-is-the-word/ (accessed 1
    May 2018).
12. The Middle Finger Emoji Could Land You in Jail in the UAE,
    https://motherboard.vice.com/en_us/article/the-middle-finger-
    emoji-could-land-you-in-jail-in-the-uae (accessed 1 May 2018).

13. iOS 9.1 Will Let You Send People the Middle Finger Emoji, www
    .theverge.com/2015/9/10/9301529/middle-finger-emoji-ios-
    iphone (accessed 1 May 2018).

14. Why Angry White Men Love Calling People 'Cucks', www.gq.com/
    story/why-angry-white-men-love-calling-people-cucks (accessed 1
    May 2018).

15. Poop Emojii, http://knowyourmeme.com/memes/poop-emoji
    (accessed 1 May 2018).

16. Why Are We so Passionate About the Smiling Poop Emoji? www
    .abc.net.au/news/2016–12-10/the-popularity-of-the-poo-emoji/
    8102762 (accessed 1 May 2018).

17. Poop Emoji, www.etsy.com/uk/market/poop__emoji (accessed 1
    May 2018).

18. You Can Apparently Leave a Poop Emoji – Or Anything Else You
    Want – on Trump's Website, www.slate.com/blogs/the_slatest/
    2016/11/08/someone_hacked_trump_s_website_and_left_a_poo
    p_emoji_on_it.html (accessed 1 May 2018).

19. There's a Problem No One's Talking About, www.wateraidamerica
    .org/news/its-time-to-give-a-shit (accessed 1 May 2018).

20. Emoji and Pictographs, www.unicode.org/faq/emoji_dingbats.html
    (accessed 1 May 2018).

21. Master of the Sock Puppets, www.newyorker.com/news/news-desk/
    master-of-the-sock-puppets (accessed 1 May 2018).

22. That ;) You Type Can and Will Be Used Against You in a Court of
    Law, www.wired.com/2015/02/emoji-in-court-cases/ (accessed 1
    May 2018).

23. Terrorist Charge Dropped Against Teen Accused of Emoji Threats
    to Police, www.dnainfo.com/new-york/20150203/bushwick/terror
    ist-charge-dropped-against-teen-accused-of-emoji-threats-police
    (accessed 1 May 2018).

24. Brooklyn Teen Arrested for Alleged Facebook Threat to Officers
    Using Emoji, http://newyork.cbslocal.com/2015/01/23/brooklyn-
    teen-arrested-for-alleged-facebook-threat-to-officers-using-emoji/
    (accessed 1 May 2018).

25. 12-year-old Girl Facing Criminal Charges for Posting Gun, Bomb
    and Knife Emojis on Instagram, www.ibtimes.co.uk/12-year-old-
    girl-facing-criminal-charges-posting-gun-bomb-knife-emojis-insta
    gram-1546646 (accessed 1 May 2018).

26. Man Charged Over Facebook 'Death Threat' Sent to MP Will Not Face Trial, www.theguardian.com/law/2016/aug/18/facebook-death-threat-man-will-not-face-trial-jo-cox (accessed 1 May 2018).
27. Emojis Prove Intent, a Judge in Israel Ruled, https://qz.com/987032/emojis-prove-intent-a-judge-in-israel-ruled/ (accessed 1 May 2018).
28. Goldman, E. (2017) *Surveying the Law of Emojis*, Santa Clara University Legal Studies Research Paper, pp. 8–17.
29. Water Pistol Emoji Replaces Revolver as Apple Enters Gun Violence Debate, www.theguardian.com/technology/2016/aug/02/apple-replaces-gun-emoji-water-pistol-revolver-violence-debate (accessed 1 May 2018).
30. Water Pistol Emoji Replaces Revolver as Apple Enters Gun Violence Debate, www.huffingtonpost.co.uk/2015/10/13/hunting-rifle-emoji-_n_8283972.html (accessed 1 May 2018).
31. In Defense of the Gun Emoji, www.fastcodesign.com/3062610/in-defense-of-the-gun-emoji (accessed 1 May 2018).
32. 2018: The Year of Emoji Convergence? https://blog.emojipedia.org/2018-the-year-of-emoji-convergence (accessed 1 May 2018).
33. Everything Sunny All the Time Always, https://en.wikipedia.org/wiki/Everything_Sunny_All_the_Time_Always (accessed 1 May 2018).
34. Bergson, H. (2008 [1911]) *Laughter: An Essay on the Meaning of the Comic*, Arc Manor, p. 61.
35. The Decent Person's Guide to Breaking Up, www.eharmony.com/dating-advice/relationships/the-decent-persons-guide-to-breaking-up (accessed 1 May 2018).
36. Peters, J. D. (1999) *Speaking into the Air: A History of the Idea of Communication*, University of Chicago Press.
37. Gershon, I. (2011) Un-Friend My Heart: Facebook, Promiscuity, and Heartbreak in a Neoliberal Age, *Anthropological Quarterly*, 84:4, pp. 865–894.
38. Tinder and the Dawn of the 'Dating Apocalypse', www.vanityfair.com/culture/2015/08/tinder-hook-up-culture-end-of-dating (accessed 1 May 2018).
39. Here's a Handy Tinder Glossary, http://nymag.com/thecut/2015/08/heres-a-handy-tinder-glossary.html (accessed 1 May 2018).
40. Emojis 101 On Text Game: How to Use Them with Girls, www.badboylifestyle.com/text-game-emojis-101-importance-use (accessed 1 May 2018).

41. How to Dump Someone by Emoji, https://katieglass.net/2014/04/18/ column-how-to-dump-someone-by-emoji/ (accessed 1 May 2018).

42. Dianafication, www.waywordradio.org/dianafication_1/ (accessed 1 May 2018).

43. Social Media Can Bring out the Worst in Public Mourning, Says an Expert on Digital Grief, www.thejournal.ie/grief-online-2965296-Sep2016/ (accessed 1 May 2018).

44. 5 Times You Should Never, Ever Use an Emoji, www.bustle.com/ articles/131182–5-times-you-should-never-ever-use-an-emoji (accessed 1 May 2018).

45. Local 12 Used an Emoji to Describe a Suicide, www.cincinnativse veryone.com/local-12-used-an-emoji-to-describe-a-suicide (accessed 1 May 2018).

46. Istanbul Airport Attack: Cher Apologises for Bomb Emoji in 'Insensitive' Tweet, www.independent.co.uk/news/people/turkey-istanbul-airport-attack-bombing-cher-twitter-tweet-latest-news-a7109371.html (accessed 1 May 2018).

47. Death and Emojis: How Grief Manifests on Social Media, https:// broadly.vice.com/en_us/article/death-and-emojis-how-grief-mani fests-on-social-media (accessed 1 May 2018).

48. Rep a Cause with Facebook's New Temporary Profile Pics, https:// techcrunch.com/2015/09/11/facebook-temporary-profile-picture (accessed 1 May 2018).

49. Facebook Introduces Reactions Alongside Like Button, www.chica gotribune.com/bluesky/technology/ct-facebook-reactions-20160224-story.html (accessed 1 May 2018).

50. Coming to Terms with Digital Grief: Hashtags and Emojis Are Here to Stay, https://theconversation.com/coming-to-terms-with-digital-grief-hashtags-and-emojis-are-here-to-stay-57087 (accessed 1 May 2018).

51. Finland's National Emojis Feature Headbanger and Naked Sauna-Goers, https://www.theguardian.com/world/2015/nov/04/finland-launches-national-emojis-of-typical-characters-like-the-headban ger (accessed 1 May 2018).

52. Tom of Finland, https://finland.fi/emoji/tom-of-finland/ (accessed 1 May 2018).

53. Jeremoji, http://jeremoji.getforge.io (accessed 1 May 2018).

54. Berniemojis, www.nashbox.com/portfolio/berniemojis/ (accessed 1 May 2018).

55. Hillarymoji, http://hillarymojiapp.com (accessed 1 May 2018).
56. Can Emojis Win Elections? www.newstatesman.com/politics/uk/ 2016/08/can-emojis-win-elections (accessed 1 May 2018).
57. Redhead Emoji Finally on the Table After Campaign for Ginger Equality, www.telegraph.co.uk/technology/2017/01/20/redhead-emoji-finally-table-campaign-ginger-equality/ (accessed 1 May 2018).
58. Flags of England, Wales and Scotland Given Thumbs up by Emoji Chiefs, www.telegraph.co.uk/news/2016/12/11/flags-england-wales-scotland-given-thumbs-emoji-chiefs/ (accessed 1 May 2018).
59. Here Are the Most Popular Emojis from the #Brexit Reaction, https://motherboard.vice.com/en_us/article/the-emojis-of-great-brexit (accessed 1 May 2018).
60. St George's Flag is a Racist Symbol Says a Quarter of the English, www.telegraph.co.uk/news/uknews/9217620/St-Georges-flag-is-a-racist-symbol-says-a-quarter-of-the-English.html (accessed 1 May 2018).
61. Patriot Games: How Toxic Is the England Flag Today? www.theguardian.com/uk-news/2014/nov/26/patriot-games-battle-for-flag-of-st-george-english-identity (accessed 1 May 2018).
62. The Many Faces of Englishness: Identity, Diversity and Nationhood in England, www.ippr.org/juncture/the-many-faces-of-englishness-identity-diversity-and-nationhood-in-england (accessed 1 May 2018).
63. Presenter Explaining 'Secret Emoji Codes' Report Sparks Hilarious Responses, www.telegraph.co.uk/news/2017/02/03/presenter-explaining-secret-emoji-codes-report-sparks-hilarious (accessed 1 May 2018).
64. https://twitter.com/RichardBSpencer/status/829122739734794240 (accessed 1 May 2018).
65. Richard Spencer, Alt-Right Leader and White Nationalist, Punched in Face at Trump Inauguration, www.independent.co.uk/news/world/americas/richard-spencer-alt-right-punched-donald-trump-inauguration-a7538746.html (accessed 1 May 2018).
66. How 'Pepe the Frog' Went from Harmless to Hate Symbol, www.latimes.com/politics/la-na-pol-pepe-the-frog-hate-symbol-20161011-snap-htmlstory.html (accessed 1 May 2018).
67. Nazi Pepe Controversy, http://knowyourmeme.com/memes/events/nazi-pepe-controversy (accessed 1 May 2018).
68. The Top Super Bowl Emoji Was an Alt-Right Frog Symbol, www.axios.com/super-bowl-dominated-by-alt-right-frog-emoji-on-social-2243088480.html (accessed 1 May 2018).

69. https://twitter.com/RichardBSpencer/status/829122739734794240 (accessed 1 May 2018).
70. The Resistance Will Be Emojified, http://blog.emojipedia.org/the-resistance-will-be-emojified/ (accessed 1 May 2018).
71. No, 'Snowflake' as a Slang Term Did Not Begin with 'Fight Club', www.merriam-webster.com/words-at-play/the-less-lovely-side-of-snowflake (accessed 1 May 2018).
72. Fight Club: A Beautiful or Unique Snowflake, www.youtube.com/watch?v=EP5aqAC8PPY (accessed 1 May 2018).
73. Michael Gove Calls Boris Johnson's Critics 'Snowflakes' After He Compares French President to WW2 Guard, www.huffingtonpost.co.uk/entry/jeremy-corbyn-wild-and-inappropriate-downing-street-defends-boris-johnsons-theatrical-comparison-of-francois-hollande-to-ww2-prison-camp-guard-fawlty-towers-dont-mention-the-war_uk_587f7c97e4b0831b7c6e6948 (accessed 1 May 2018).
74. Pepe Creator's Brilliantly Succinct Response to Alt-Right Leader Getting Punched, http://www.huffingtonpost.com/entry/pepe-creator-comments-on-alt-right-leader-richard-spencer-getting-punched_us_58862a57e4b070d8cad3e30f (accessed 1 May 2018).
75. Milk, a Symbol of Neo-Nazi Hate, https://theconversation.com/milk-a-symbol-of-neo-nazi-hate-83292 (accessed 1 May 2018).
76. The Real Meaning of All Those Emoji in Twitter Handles, http://mashable.com/2017/06/03/emoji-twitter-handles-meanings/#iEmBYRmGBkqH (accessed 1 May 2018).
77. Why Cow's Milk Is the Perfect Drink for Supremacists, www.peta.org/blog/cows-milk-perfect-drink-supremacists/ (accessed 1 May 2018).
78. The Alt-Right's Newest Ploy? Trolling with False Symbols, www.wired.com/2017/05/alt-rights-newest-ploy-trolling-false-symbols/ (accessed 1 May 2018).
79. The Rise and Rise of International Diplomacy by WhatsApp, www.theguardian.com/technology/2016/nov/04/why-do-diplomats-use-this-alien-whatsapp-emoji-for-vladimir-putin (accessed 1 May 2018).

7 Diverse Identities

1. Leckie, A. (2013) *Ancillary Justice*, Orbit, p. 3.
2. He Said, She Said, www.orbitbooks.net/2013/10/01/said-said (accessed 1 May 2018).

3. The Gender-Neutral Pronoun: 150 Years Later, Still an Epic Fail, https://blog.oup.com/2010/08/gender-neutral-pronoun (accessed 1 May 2018).

4. 2015 Word of the Year is Singular 'They', www.americandialect.org/2015-word-of-the-year-is-singular-they (accessed 1 May 2018).

5. Beyond 'He' and 'She': The Rise of Non-Binary Pronouns, www.bbc.co.uk/news/magazine-34901704 (accessed 1 May 2018).

6. The Need for a Gender-Neutral Pronoun, https://genderneutralpronoun.wordpress.com/tag/ze-and-zir/ (accessed 1 May 2018).

7. Ciochetto, L. (2003) Toilet Signage as Effective Communication, *Visible Language* 37:2, pp. 190–205.

8. Expanding Emoji Professions: Reducing Gender Inequality, http://unicode.org/L2/L2016/16160-emoji-professions.pdf (accessed 1 May 2018).

9. One Way to Escape the Tyranny of Gendered Languages: Emojis, www.pri.org/stories/2016–08-09/one-way-escape-tyranny-gendered-languages-emojis (accessed 1 May 2018).

10. What is Gender and Why Does it Matter to Emoji? http://blog.emojipedia.org/what-is-gender-and-why-does-it-matter-to-emoji/ (accessed 1 May 2018).

11. www.idiversicons.com (accessed 1 May 2018).

12. Gendered Emoji Alienates Transgenders, Genderqueer and Stereotypes Men and Women, http://tech.firstpost.com/news-analysis/gendered-emoji-alienates-transgenders-genderqueer-and-stereotypes-men-and-women-330377.html (accessed 1 May 2018).

13. Gay Families Are Coming to the Emoji Keyboard, www.huffingtonpost.com/2015/02/24/gay-family-emojis-apple_n_6743968.html (accessed 1 May 2018).

14. The Missing Emojis We'd Like to See, http://www.bbc.co.uk/newsbeat/article/32233469/the-missing-emojis-wed-like-to-see (accessed 1 May 2018).

15. Apple's New Diverse Emoji Are Even More Problematic Than Before, www.washingtonpost.com/posteverything/wp/2015/04/10/how-apples-new-multicultural-emojis-are-more-racist-than-before/ (accessed 1 May 2018).

16. Unicode® Technical Standard #51: Unicode Emoji, http://unicode.org/reports/tr51/ (accessed 1 May 2018).

17. Asians Are Not Impressed with Apple's 'Diverse' Yellow Emoji, https://qz.com/349561/asians-are-not-impressed-with-apples-diverse-yellow-emoji/ (accessed 1 May 2018).
18. We Need to Talk About Digital Blackface in Reaction GIFs, www.teenvogue.com/story/digital-blackface-reaction-gifs (accessed 1 May 2018).
19. FaceApp: Selfie App Accused of Racism for Whitening Users' Skin, www.independent.co.uk/life-style/gadgets-and-tech/news/faceapp-selfie-app-racism-filter-whitens-users-skin-viral-photo-a7701036.html (accessed 1 May 2018).
20. Why White People Don't Use White Emoji, www.theatlantic.com/politics/archive/2016/05/white-people-dont-use-white-emoji/481695/ (accessed 1 May 2018).
21. Conservatives Say Rainbow Flags Are Just as Oppressive as Confederate Statues, www.newsweek.com/fox-news-gay-pride-rainbow-flags-racist-confederate-statues-same-exact-thing-650992 (accessed 1 May 2018).
22. Facebook Celebrates Pride Month, https://newsroom.fb.com/news/2017/06/facebook-celebrates-pride-month/ (accessed 1 May 2018).
23. Facebook Now Has 2 Billion Monthly Users . . . and Responsibility, https://techcrunch.com/2017/06/27/facebook-2-billion-users/ (accessed 1 May 2018).
24. Who Gets to Use Facebook's Rainbow 'Pride' Reaction? www.theatlantic.com/technology/archive/2017/06/facebook-pride-reaction/531633/ (accessed 1 May 2018).
25. Who Came out Against Facebook's Rainbow Flags? www.bbc.co.uk/news/blogs-trending-33313807 (accessed 1 May 2018).
26. A Russian Man Created a Tool to Counter All the Pride Profile Pics on Facebook, www.buzzfeed.com/maxseddon/facebooks-pride-flag-is-driving-some-russians-crazy (accessed 1 May 2018).

8 Creativity and Culture

1. This poem, written for this book, is gratefully reproduced here with permission from the author.
2. Meet Twitter's Weird and Brilliant Longform Emoji Storyteller, http://kernelmag.dailydot.com/issue-sections/features-issue-sections/11752/mr-bikferd-emoji-storyteller-twitter/ (accessed 1 May 2018).

3. Literary Bondage: A Workshop for Potential Literature, www
   .kissthewitch.co.uk/seinundwerden/spring14/introduction.html
   (accessed 1 May 2018).

4. Gaming the System: On the Oulipo, https://lareviewofbooks.org/
   article/gaming-the-system-on-the-oulipo (accessed 1 May 2018).

5. What I Learned Taking A Selfie Every Day For A Year, www.life
   hacker.com.au/2016/08/what-i-learned-from-taking-a-selfie-every-
   day-for-a-year (accessed 1 May 2018).

6. This Grandma Sends Her Granddaughter a Selfie Every Day for the
   Cutest Reason, www.countryliving.com/life/a41861/grandma-
   sends-granddaughter-selfies

7. www.reddit.com/r/selfieaday (accessed 1 May 2018).

8. Selfie A Day – Everyday Photo, https://itunes.apple.com/us/app/selfie-
   a-day-everyday-photo-diary/id877133105 (accessed 1 May 2018).

9. https://twitter.com/emojiaquarium (accessed 1 May 2018).

10. http://www.emojidick.com (accessed 1 May 2018).

11. Emoji Dick Soft Cover, www.lulu.com/shop/fred-benenson/emoji-
    dick-soft-cover/paperback/product-12555956.html (accessed 1 May
    2018).

12. 250 New Emoji Characters Announced, www.wnyc.org/story/250-
    new-emojis-announced (accessed 1 May 2018).

13. Chomsky, N. (1965) *Aspects of the Theory of Syntax*, MIT Press, p. 6.

14. Sternberg, R. J., and Kaufman, J. C. (2010) Constraints on
    Creativity: Obvious and Not So Obvious, in J. C. Kaufman and R.
    J. Sternberg (eds.), *The Cambridge Handbook of Creativity*,
    Cambridge University Press, pp. 467–482.

15. Ngram viewer: Creativity, https://books.google.com/ngrams/graph?
    content=Creativity&year_start=1920&year_end=2030&corpu
    s=15&smoothing=3&share=&direct_url=t1%3B%2CCreativity%3B
    %2Cc0 (accessed 1 May 2018).

16. Lois, G., and Pitts, W. (1977) *The Art of Advertising: George Lois on
    Mass Communication*, H. N. Abrams.

17. Russian Formalism and Defamiliarization, https://onworldlitera
    ture.wordpress.com/2014/06/11/russian-formalism-and-defamiliar
    ization/ (accessed 1 May 2018).

18. The Creative Act: Marcel Duchamp's 1957 Classic, Read by the
    Artist Himself, www.brainpickings.org/2012/08/23/the-creative-
    act-marcel-duchamp-1957/ (accessed 1 May 2018).

19. Marcel Duchamp: Fountain, www.tate.org.uk/art/artworks/duch amp-fountain-t07573 (accessed 1 May 2018).
20. The Ultimate Fine Art Emoji Collection for Art Lovers Everywhere, www.konbini.com/us/inspiration/cantor-gallery-fine-art-emoji/ (accessed 1 May 2018).
21. The Original Emoji Set Has Been Added to the Museum of Modern Art's Collection, https://stories.moma.org/the-original-emoji-set-has-been-added-to-the-museum-of-modern-arts-collection-c6060e141f61#.8cdna05cu (accessed 1 May 2018).
22. 28 Beautiful Words the English Language Should Steal, www.buzz feed.com/danieldalton/ever-embasan (accessed 1 May 2018).
23. 27 Brilliant Words You Didn't Know You Needed, www.buzzfeed .com/danieldalton/nom-nom-nomonym (accessed 1 May 2018).
24. Let's Be Honest, This Is What Your Favorite Emojis Really Mean, www.buzzfeed.com/kirstenking/this-is-what-your-favorite-emojis-really-mean (accessed 1 May 2018).
25. An Emoji Art Show Heads to Eyebeam Art+Technology Center, www.papermag.com/an-emoji-art-show-heads-to-eyebeam-arttech nology-center-1427171676.html (accessed 1 May 2018).
26. https://twitter.com/DoctorWho_BBCA/status/856270963440320513 (accessed 1 May 2018).
27. https://twitter.com/carrieffisher/status/728034201442889728 (accessed 1 May 2018).
28. https://twitter.com/thecarrielator (accessed 1 May 2018).
29. Twitter's Funniest Princess: How Carrie Fisher Ruled the Internet, www.telegraph.co.uk/films/2016/12/28/twitters-funniest-princess-carrie-fisher-ruled-internet/ (accessed 1 May 2018).
30. Coming Soon: Jennifer Egan's 'Black Box', www.newyorker.com/ books/page-turner/coming-soon-jennifer-egans-black-box (accessed 1 May 2018).
31. Black Box, www.newyorker.com/magazine/2012/06/04/black-box-2 (accessed 1 May 2018).
32. The Right Sort, David Mitchell's Twitter Short Story, www.theguar dian.com/books/2014/jul/14/the-right-sort-david-mitchells-twit ter-short-story (accessed 1 May 2018).
33. Teju Cole Writes a Story a Tweet at a Time, www.npr.org/2014/01/ 16/262473432/forget-the-new-yorker-storyteller-turns-to-twitter (accessed 1 May 2018).

34. On the Road, http://gettinginsidejackkerouacshead.blogspot.co.uk/ 2008/06/31-may-2008.html (accessed 1 May 2018).

35. Getting Inside Jack Kerouac's Head, http://www.informationasma terial.org/portfolio/getting-inside-jack-kerouacs-head/ (accessed 1 May 2018).

36. Storytelling with a Wink and a Smile: The Arrival of the Emoji-pocalypse, https://theconversation.com/storytelling-with-a-wink-and-a-smile-the-arrival-of-the-emoji-pocalypse-48308 (accessed 1 May 2018).

37. Labov, W. (1997) Some Further Steps in Narrative Analysis, *Journal of Narrative and Life History*, 7:1–4, pp. 395–415.

38. The Visual Language of Comics: Introduction to the Structure and Cognition of Sequential Images, www.visuallanguagelab.com/ vloc.html (accessed 1 May 2018).

39. Translation by Frank Monaghan.

40. This Woman Brilliantly Celebrated Hillary Clinton's Historic Moment with a Meme. Then Men Took Credit for It, http://the week.com/speedreads/628833/woman-brilliantly-celebrated-hil lary-clintons-historic-moment-meme-men-took-credit (accessed 1 May 2018).

41. Stephanie Berger & Carina Finn, https://smokinggluegun.com/ 2013/06/01/stephanie-berger-carina-finn/ (accessed 1 May 2018).

42. A Comedy Gig Entirely in Emoji? Only at the Edinburgh Fringe Festival, www.scotlandnow.dailyrecord.co.uk/lifestyle/comedy-gig-entirely-emoji-only-6206528 (accessed 1 May 2018).

43. There Were EMOJIS on This Season's Chanel Catwalk, www.cosmo politan.com/style-beauty/fashion/news/a55059/there-were-emojis-on-this-seasons-chanel-catwalk/ (accessed 1 May 2018).

44. Emoji Replace Gargoyles and Kings on New Amersfoort Building, www.dutchnews.nl/news/archives/2017/04/emoji-replace-gar goyles-and-kings-on-new-amersfoort-building/ (accessed 1 May 2018).

9 The Emojification of Everyday Life

1. The Emoji Movie Tried to Emoji-fy The Handmaid's Tale and Obviously It Backfired Horribly, www.independent.co.uk/arts-entertainment/films/news/the-emoji-movie-release-date-trailer-

handmaids-tale-tweet-marketing-bad-reactions-bad-a7858431
.html (accessed 1 May 2018).

2. https://twitter.com/KikiHavens/status/889608292179341312
(accessed 1 May 2018).

3. The Emoji Movie Review – a Big Thumbs Down, www.theguardian
.com/film/2017/jul/28/the-emoji-movie-review-a-big-thumb-down
(accessed 1 May 2018).

4. Do Not See The Emoji Movie, www.vox.com/summer-movies/
2017/7/27/16037862/emoji-movie-review-garbage-fire-poo-
patrick-stewart (accessed 1 May 2018).

5. The Emoji Movie, www.rogerebert.com/reviews/the-emoji-movie-
2017 (accessed 1 May 2018).

6. The Emoji Movie's Rotten Tomatoes Score Is Awful, www.indepen
dent.co.uk/arts-entertainment/films/news/the-emoji-movie-
reviews-rotten-tomatoes-release-date-trailer-patrick-stewart-poop-
a7865751.html (accessed 1 May 2018).

7. The Grand Opening of Disneyland, www.designingdisney.com/con
tent/grand-opening-disneyland (accessed 1 May 2018).

8. Disneyland's Disastrous Opening Day, www.history.com/news/dis
neylands-disastrous-opening-day-60-years-ago (accessed 1 May
2018).

9. http://worldemojiday.com (accessed 1 May 2018).

10. How Donald Trump Came up with 'Make America Great
Again', www.washingtonpost.com/politics/how-donald-trump-
came-up-with-make-america-great-again/2017/01/17/fb6acf5e-
dbf7-11e6-ad42-f3375f271c9c_story.html (accessed 1 May 2018).

11. Collectible Ornament, https://shop.donaldjtrump.com/products/
red-cap-collectible-ornament (accessed 1 May 2018).

12. Official Trump-Pence Mini Megaphones – Set of 2, https://shop
.donaldjtrump.com/products/official-trump-pence-mini-mega
phones-red-blue-set-of-2 (accessed 1 May 2018).

13. The 15 Most Ridiculous Trademark Attempts Ever, www.busines
sinsider.com/15-ridiculous-trademarking-attempts-2011–4
(accessed 1 May 2018).

14. The Original Smiley Brand, www.smiley.com (accessed 1 May
2018).

15. The Smiley Company, www.smiley.com/corporate#history
(accessed 1 May 2018).

16. The Rise and Fall of the Infamous SarcMark, www.thedailybeast
    .com/articles/2013/09/24/the-rise-and-fall-of-the-infamous-sarc
    mark (accessed 1 May 2018).

17. SarcMark: For When You're Not Smart Enough to Express Sarcasm
    Online, www.gizmodo.com.au/2010/01/sarcmark-for-when-youre-
    not-smart-enough-to-express-sarcasm-online/ (accessed 1 May
    2018).

18. OpenSarcasm: Sarcasm for the People, http://opensarcasm.org
    (accessed 1 May 2018).

19. Improving Communication at Home with IKEA Emoticons, www
    .ikea.com/nl/nl/campagne/emoticons.html (accessed 1 May 2018).

20. #EndangeredEmoji, http://endangeredemoji.com (accessed 1 May
    2018).

21. Twitter's Branded Emojis Come with a Million-Dollar Commitment,
    www.adweek.com/digital/twitters-branded-emojis-come-million-dol
    lar-commitment-169327/ (accessed 1 May 2018).

22. The English Effect, www.britishcouncil.org/sites/default/files/eng
    lish-effect-report-v2.pdf (accessed 1 May 2018).

23. Why Military Power Is No Longer Enough, www.theguardian.com/
    world/2002/mar/31/1 (accessed 1 May 2018).

24. Traganou, J. (2009) Olympic Design and National History: The
    Cases of Tokyo 1964 and Beijing 2008, *Hitotsubashi Journal of
    Arts and Sciences*, 50, pp. 65–79.

25. Neurath, O. (1973) *Empiricism and Sociology*, Springer, p. 220.

26. Tokyo's 1964 Olympic Design as a 'Realm of [Design] Memory',
    www.tandfonline.com/doi/abs/10.1080/17430437.2011.565925?
    journalCode=fcss20 (accessed 1 May 2018).

27. Kinsella, S. (1995) Cuties in Japan, in L. Skov and B. Moeran (eds.),
    Women, Media and Consumption in Japan, Curzon Press, pp. 220–254.

28. Namahage, www.namahage.co.jp/namahagekan/english/namah
    age.php (accessed 1 May 2018).

29. Samsung Puts Japan Back on the Map, http://blog.emojipedia.org/
    samsung-puts-japan-back-on-the-map/ (accessed 1 May 2018).

30. The Westernization of Emoji, www.theatlantic.com/technology/
    archive/2017/05/the-westernization-of-emoji/527616/ (accessed 1
    May 2018).

31. About Oomoto, www.oomoto.or.jp/English/enFaq/indexfaq.html
    (accessed 1 May 2018).

32. Demandoj kaj Respondoj pri instruoj de Oomoto [Questions and Answers about Oomoto's Teachings], www.oomoto.or.jp/ Esperanto/esDokt/demres.html (accessed 1 May 2018).

33. Korzhenkov, A. (2009) *Zamenhof: The Life, Works, and Ideas of the Author of Esperanto*, trans. I. M. Richmond, Esperantic Studies Foundation, www.esperantic.org/wp-content/uploads/2016/06/ LLZ-Bio-En.pdf (accessed 1 May 2018).

34. Dr. Esperanto's International Language, www.genekeyes.com/ Dr_Esperanto.html

35. About ESW and the Holocaust Museum, https://web.archive.org/ web/20101125045310/http://esperantodc.org/esw6.html (accessed 1 May 2018).

36. Emoji, the New Global Language? www.bbvaopenmind.com/en/ emoji-the-new-global-language/ (accessed 1 May 2018).

37. A Great Australian: The Inventor of Semantography, http://www .the-symbols.net/blissymbolics/biography/ (accessed 1 May 2018).

38. Bliss, C. K. (1965) *Semantography (Blissymbolics): A Logical Writing for an illogical World*, Semantography (Blissymbolic) Publications, www.the-symbols.net/semantography/ (accessed 1 May 2018).

39. 5 Billion Emojis Sent Daily on Messenger, http://blog.emojipedia .org/5-billion-emojis-sent-daily-on-messenger/ (accessed 1 May 2018).

40. FAQ: Emoji and Pictographs, http://unicode.org/faq/emoji_ding bats.html (accessed 1 May 2018).

41. Will the Future Really Look like 'Minority Report'? https://web .archive.org/web/20110514220445/http://dir.salon.com/story/ent/ movies/int/2002/07/10/underkoffler_belker/index.html (accessed 1 May 2018).

Index

Made in the USA
Monee, IL
16 June 2020